78177

' RNING RESO~~

MANAGING THE ~ENTRE

~1116

D0727651

MANAGING THE SUPPLY CHAIN

A STRATEGIC PERSPECTIVE

J. L. Gattorna

and

D. W. Walters

palgrave

First published 1996 by
PALGRAVE
Houndmills, Basingstoke, Hampshire RG21 6XS and
175 Fifth Avenue, New York, N. Y. 10010
Companies and representatives throughout the world

PALGRAVE is the new global academic imprint of
St. Martin's Press LLC Scholarly and Reference Division and
Palgrave Publishers Ltd (formerly Macmillan Press Ltd).

ISBN 0–333–64816–1 hardback
ISBN 0–333–64817–X paperback

This book is printed on paper suitable for recycling and
made from fully managed and sustained forest sources.

A catalogue record for this book is available
from the British Library.

10   9
05   04   03   02

Copy-edited and typeset by Povey-Edmondson
Tavistock and Rochdale, England

Printed and bound in Great Britain by
Antony Rowe Ltd, Chippenham, Wiltshire

Contents

List of Figures

List of Tables

▌Acknowledgements

While authors claim that writing is a difficult creative task, which by virtue of its nature cannot be undertaken in any planned or structured way, there is, at the end of the day, considerable satisfaction at seeing the realization of hours of efforts take shape.

Just as important are the efforts of those without whose help the book simply would not appear. A huge debt therefore is owed to Jackie Wingle, who has probably produced drafts of each chapter more times than she cares to remember, only because we changed our minds just as many times!

These thanks are particularly pertinent at this time. John Gattorna has merged his activities with Andersen Consulting, and, while some of the Gattorna Strategy team have joined him there, others have gone their separate ways. We acknowledge their efforts over the years. Much of what they did in the company has, in one way or another, made this text more effective. We thank them and wish them well.

J. L. GATTORNA
D. W. WALTERS

Introduction

In a very short space of time 'physical distribution management' became 'logistics management', and now, in the more forward-thinking companies, is developing into 'supply chain management'.

This text considers a number of issues that confront management as supply chain management becomes accepted on a wider basis. The concept suggests that the company's focus extends beyond its own performance to become much more of an inter-organizational focus. At the same time, managers whose tasks are primarily involved in making the supply chain cost effective are aware of the need for their activities to be effective in a corporate financial performance context. The recent attention paid to creating shareholder value implies that any and all corporate activity should be value creating. In this context we see a need for management to be aware of the implications of their decisions and activities on margin and asset management and the impact on cash flow.

We have attempted to address these issues through the way we have structured this text (see Figure I.1). We consider the financial responsibilities and interface areas between supply chain activities and financial management (Chapter 4). The main task here is to explore the components of supply chain strategy and this is achieved by considering two vital perspectives of the strategy activity – **performance drivers** and **performance facilitators**.

The primary performance driver is customer service. In Chapters 2 and 3 we consider the role of customer service in augmenting the company's product-service offer. These chapters discuss the components of customer service policy. In these chapters the methodology of customer service policy, research and service performance are explored.

Effective supply chain management requires a thorough knowledge of distribution channels, their structures (economic and social), their management and the emerging trends and issues. Chapters 12 and 20 consider distribution channel design and management.

The inter-organizational dimension of supply chain management suggests that communications and information management are essential if decision making is to be effective. Therefore, the design and management of communications and information systems are the topics of Chapters 10 and 18.

As with physical distribution and logistics managment, the roles of inventory management, selection of transportation modes and the design of facilities and the selection of suitable locations play important roles. These are considered in Chapters 7, 8 and 9.

A supply chain strategy also requires a number of back-up or support activities. Furthermore, in common with other business functions, the logistics

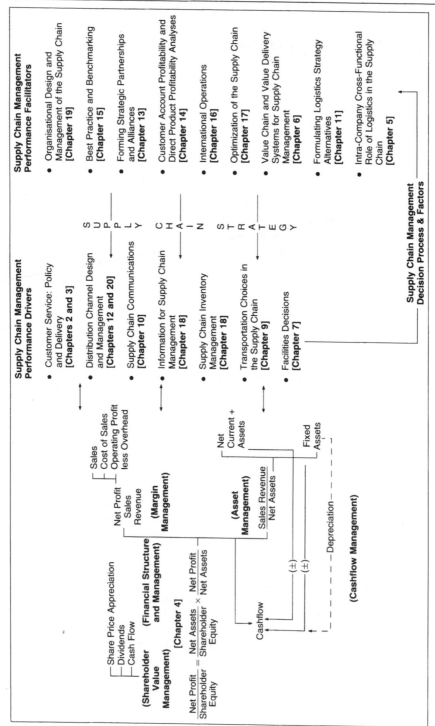

Figure I.1

element of the firm has an inter-company cross-functional role. This is discussed in detail in Chapter 5.

As the concept of the supply chain expands, a method of analysis is requires. Chapter 6 uses the established value chain concept to examine 'delivery' alternatives. The value chain approach is extended into customer account profitability and direct product profitability analyses in Chapter 14. Other performance-monitoring approaches (and indeed design methods) are considered in Chapter 15, which reviews and applies the current approaches in best practice and benchmarking. Best practice and benchmarking imply performance efficiency, and increasingly managers are applying computer-based models to the problems of identifying supply chain structures which, within given strategic and operational constraints, will optimize customer service and system operating costs. This is the topic of Chapter 17.

The changing organizational context of the supply chain, together with the moves by many companies to become 'global' or 'international' businesses, have implications for supply chain management decisions. In Chapter 13 we review the increasing importance of strategic partnerships and alliances, while Chapter 16 considers the international aspects of supply chain management.

Clearly, we need to identify organizational design and management issues within the supply chain and consider the process by which strategy alternatives are formulated and evaluated. Chapters 11 and 19 cover these topics.

In writing this text we have been conscious of the need to be aware of the dynamic changes occurring in supply chain management. To this end we have identified the current issues and methodologies. In addition, we offer the reader some new approaches and methods to apply to both existing and emerging supply chain management issues; this is the challenge we leave with the reader.

J. L. GATTORNA
D. W. WALTERS

CHAPTER 1

The Evolution of Logistics and the Supply Chain as Management Disciplines

Introduction

The somewhat distant but legendary comments of Peter Drucker when referring to distribution as 'the last dark continent' for business to conquer resulted in a flood of activity which in a relatively short time resulted in the emergence and growth of an important management function.

This chapter considers the changes that have occurred during this period of time, focusing upon the internal changes that have brought about changes in management perspectives and philosophy and upon the external environment which has influenced business activities.

We shall also consider the development of the logistics function. In particular our discussions will consider the expansion of the function from an operational (albeit important) activity where the concern of management was focused on costs, to a strategic function responsible (to a large degree) for the management of resources required to achieve specified levels of customer satisfaction.

The Era of Physical Distribution Management (PDM)

Drucker's comments raised an important issue concerning the costs of distribution to companies and a secondary issue (but in some ways more important) as to who was responsible for managing distribution activities.

It is arguable that the second issue was the more important. By identifying and locating responsibility, accountability follows. Once accountability was established, then the cost issue could be addressed. Research into responsibility and accountability is largely anecdotal. Typically distribution was considered to be two activities. The marketing (and/or sales) function was responsible for appointing distributors (intermediaries) and establishing the terms of the trade which governed the commercial activities of what became known as *transaction channels*.

However, the management of physical stocks and flows was usually the responsibility of a number of individual functions (for example, warehouse and

1

transport managers, shipping managers, etc.) and the overall responsibility (as and when it existed) was lodged at board level, varying between production (operations), finance, the managing director and occasionally marketing/sales. In the 1960s and early 1970s physical distribution directors/managers were very much an emerging breed. Figure 1.1 suggests the structure and management focus at that time.

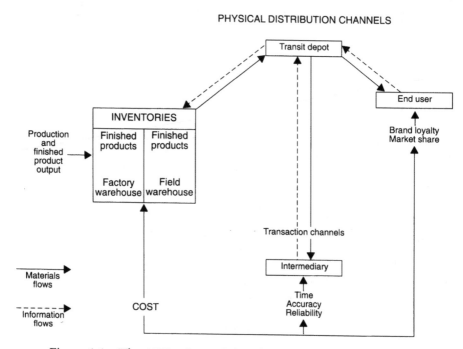

Figure 1.1   The 1970s physical distribution management concept

Management then had three concerns. It saw physical distribution management (PDM) as a key activity in creating and maintaining brand loyalty and market share in consumer markets. To do this effectively required the company to perform well across three critical service criteria: timeliness of deliveries, accurate order completion and reliability in terms of deliveries and other fulfilment. The third area concerned cost. Typically objectives would be set for intermediary and end-user (consumer) performance levels, and budgets set for their achievement and management.

Effective management of the physical distribution function became an important issue. The coordination of stockholding and deliveries was an obvious area upon which to concentrate, and five activities came to represent the PDM mix. These were:

- *Inventory*: initially finished goods in manufacturing and field locations which was responsible for meeting and satisfying customer demand.
- *Transportation*: the means by which inventory might be transferred from the vendor through the physical channel.
- *Warehousing*: the storage function that gave cost benefits from the economies of scale in manufacturing *and* facilitated the servicing of customer/consumer demand.
- *Order communications*: which, through rudimentary information systems, permitted the processing and progressing of customer orders.
- *Utilization*: an approach to managing the effectiveness of the use of cubic capacity in the entire system. The topics of interest were focused on efficiencies and economies in handling product. Thus the application of palletization and mechanical handling techniques were (and remain) important features.

A number of issues existed. It was obvious to most companies that if the overall costs of physical distribution were to be reduced *or* if service to customers was to be improved there had to be an effort made to coordinate these mix activities. It was variously estimated that in the 1970s physical distribution costs (as a percentage of sales) could vary between less than 10 per cent to in excess of 40 per cent of sales revenue. The problem invariably was exacerbated by not knowing what it should or could be!

The integration of the activities into organizational entities helped. However, vested interests and often powerful personalities operated, and the overall performance of the activity, more often than not, became sub-optimal. Customer service was often achieved at levels of cost that were unnecessarily excessive or, at the levels of cost allocated for the task, the service offered failed to meet customers' expectations.

■ The Concept of Trade-Off Analysis

During the early 1970s the notion was proposed that the problems of sub-optimal performance might be overcome if sub-optimal performance in one, or even two, of the distribution activities be accepted (even introduced) and that the economies obtained from the other activities would lower the overall costs of the distribution function. This is what happened and, once the behavioural issues and problems had been overcome, stronger and much more effective distribution functions became available.

Examples of the concept in practice were legion at this time. Inventory-holding costs and warehouse costs (storing inventory) were reduced considerably when faster transportation modes replaced slower, traditional methods. Often one trade-off situation led to another. For example, the substitution of sea freight by air freight not only lowered inventory-holding costs, but also reduced packaging costs by reducing the need for expensive protective packaging.

The number of locations in which inventory was held often revealed cost excesses (including obsolescence costs) which could be reduced by increasing the involvement (and use of) larger more frequent deliveries to the remaining facility locations and often directly to customers; here, increased terms of trade were part of the trade-off considerations.

■ Organizational Issues

The problems of responsibility and accountability, and particularly of their resolution, were surfaced by the 'trade-off' issues. Very soon clear managerial roles were identified and distribution managers (and distribution directors) were appointed within the corporate structures of a number of large companies. Initially there was a dominance of distribution management within fast-moving consumer goods companies. However, once the overall benefits of a coordinated distribution activity became widely known and understood, the structure was adopted by consumer durable and industrial product companies.

Essentially, distribution management placed the responsibility of effecting distribution service management within prescribed levels of performance (for example: delivery frequencies, product availability, order delivery accuracy *and* order cycle time management) and within agreed budgeted costs for the activity. As such, the anomalies of sub-optimal performance were eliminated because management of the distribution activity components (transport, warehousing, inventory, communications, etc.) were now coordinated by one management activity.

■ The Role of Information

Information has always been an important element of the distribution process. *Order communications* were seen as a major component of the 'distribution mix' and were important (and remain so) in the management of performance within physical distribution channels.

During the 1970s and for much of the 1980s information was seen as a necessity, very much a lubricant, without which the distribution system would not run smoothly (if at all). But towards the end of the 1980s this perspective had changed and information had become a means by which competitive advantage might be established. It should be said that information technology (as with many other elements of technology) was often applied indiscriminately. As Gattorna and Kerr (1990) suggest, any application of technology should be evaluated to ensure it provides a net positive effect. For example, an information system that effectively traces orders throughout the physical distribution channel has positive benefits only for those who 'subscribe' and organize their business activities in a specific way. Others may find that because of a number of problems (for example, the need to offer customers a range of products) the benefits are limited and, when compared with investment required, are negative.

An early development in the broadest application of information technology to PDM was EDI, electronic data interchange, which transfers files from one computer to another by telephone. It offered both advantages and disadvantages.

Among its potential advantages are:

- An ability to maintain control over the movements (inbound and outbound) of materials, thereby enhancing its ability to participate (either directly or indirectly) in *JIT (just-in-time) manufacturing* or *quick response* distribution, otherwise known as ECR (efficient consumer response).
- A reduction in labour content and corresponding costs;
- A reduction in these routine tasks that are typically the sources for error;
- A reduction in stockholding and accounts receivable;
- An increase in cash flow due to the effective management of trade creditors;
- An increase in customer service (both actual and perceived);
- A move to 'one time entry', and the elimination of superfluous administrative activities.

EDI also has some disadvantages:

- Personal contact between vendor and customer staff is reduced (often eliminated unless problems emerge).
- Problems may be created with staff who are resistant to change and may adopt a 'Luddite' response.
- The need for cooperation within transaction and physical distribution channels may be difficult to obtain.

The principles of EDI were reinforced once EPOS (electronic point-of-sale) data capture became widely adopted. The availability of EPOS data has provided a vital information link between suppliers and distributors with the information on product movements (volumes, rates of flow (and indirectly stock levels)) necessary to link the activities and close the gaps.

However, it is the increased application of EDI that has effectively created a supply chain and which makes supply chain management effective. During the 1980s TRADACOMS established an agreed standard structure and sequence for documentation essential for trading. TRADANET evolved from TRADACOMS and provides a network of information exchange. TRADANET is now becoming well established as a communications link between trading partners and offers a facility for the development of the operational planning of physical distribution activities.

Other IT applications that have benefited have been software programs for scheduling and routing delivery vehicles. Computer vehicle routing and scheduling (CVRS) has demonstrated efficiencies by reducing transport costs, increasing vehicle utilization and delivery effectiveness, improved overall customer service response, reducing investment, and offering a 'what if?' facility for operational planning activities. Clearly the addition of 'live' data makes such systems even more effective and extends the planning and control perspective into strategic dimensions.

■ The Concept of Value Added and Customer Service

Customer Service is concerned with making the product available to the customer . . . there is no value in a product or service until it is in the hands of the customer. . . 'Availability' in itself is a complex concept, impacted by many factors which might include delivery frequency and reliability, stock levels and order cycle time. Ultimately customer service is determined by the interaction of all those factors that affect the process of making products and services available to the buyer. (Christopher, 1990)

Customer service may be seen as a way in which value is added to the product–service package purchased by the customer. Value becomes the amount a customer is willing to pay for the products/services provided by a supplier. Value added is the difference between what the customer pays and the cost of providing the service. The decisions that are made are twofold. The customer must decide whether or not the 'service package' can be provided internally more cost-effectively or whether the 'inclusive price' of a supplier is preferable.

The vendor must approach the problem from the stance which simply asks: if we provide this service will the marginal cost be exceeded by the marginal revenue it earns?

Customer service and value added are clearly linked. In Figure 1.2 we identify the value added services that may be provided by a manufacturer to a fast-moving consumer goods retailer. The issue confronting the retailer is which of the services to select and which to provide internally. This is the classical 'make or buy?' decision. The issues for the purchaser concern the 'cost' of providing the service versus the margin available and the control over the specific activity the purchaser (retailer in this example) wishes to retain.

During the early 1980s customer service was seen as an opportunity to develop competitive advantage. Typically, the services offered were generic: that is, there was no major attempt at differentiation. However by the mid to late 1980s 'information' availability made it possible to differentiate customer service offers; and selective service packages began to form the basis of specific supplier/distributor relationships.

Value added services		Profitability = Realized revenue – Margin forgone Realized revenue
Merchandising/ display, etc. Inventory management and re-ordering	Customer conversion and revenue generation value	↑ Service/ Margin
Market activities: Advertising Promotions Market research, and Market testing	Customer awareness and attraction value	↑ Service/ Margin
Distribution activities: Transportation Storage Unitization & packaging Information	Time, place, assortment and market information value	↑ Service/ Margin

Figure 1.2 Value added and terms of trade

■ Operational Physical Distribution Management Issues

The foregoing paragraphs have identified some of the major issues that were of concern to management during the 1970s. Figure 1.3 illustrates these issues within the context of a decision-making structure. The emphasis of distribution decision-making was to support the marketing decisions and ensure that as and where distribution service played a major role in customer satisfaction the required service was made available as cost-effectively as possible. 'Cost-effectiveness' inferred the use of trade-off analysis and customer service differentiation.

The service emphasis for most companies implied a focus on minimizing costs around a predetermined level of service achievement. For some organizations a view emerged which suggested that customer service, if viewed as a means by which the overall package could be differentiated, should be seen as a revenue or profit centre activity.

■ Logistics Management

The logic of including raw materials, components, manufactured parts and packaging materials within an overall flow of materials expanded the responsibilities of management into a broader *logistics* concept.

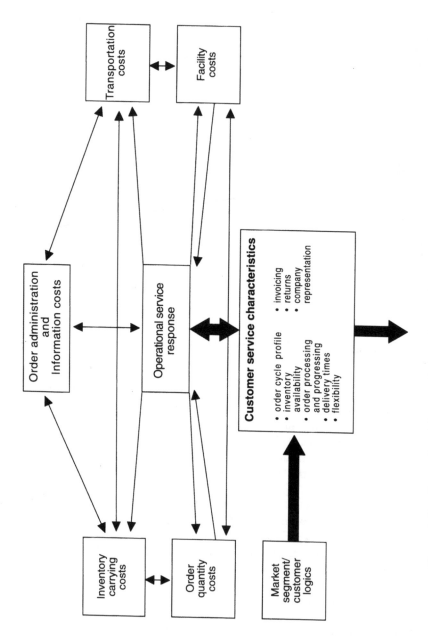

Figure 1.3 Operational issues: the emphasis of physical distribution management

This broader view of materials flows within the business corresponded with a new emphasis on strategic decision-making. A typically accepted view of logistics at the time is shown in Figure 1.4 which differs from Figure 1.1 by the addition of materials management activities and the consideration of production issues.

■ Logistics as an Influence on Strategic Decisions

In this broader context logistics can play a major role in determining the nature of the overall corporate response to market opportunities. Figure 1.5 illustrates the role logistics assumes in an increasing number of companies. The investigation of any market opportunity commences with marketing forecasts which identify the potential overall and market segment volumes available, the price/volume combinations, and the profiles of both customers and resellers. From this analysis a profile of the market can be made which will identify the location and nature of demand and the service requirements of customers and intermediaries (if they are seen as an important feature in reaching overall marketing objectives).

Such a profile will identify the infrastructure best suited to maximize the opportunities available. The inclusion of a logistics activity enables a broader view to be taken of how the opportunity might best be approached. If the economics of logistics activities across a range of throughput volumes are known, it is possible for management to review a number of production options that may include total manufacturing of all components, a predominantly assembly operation or a combination of manufacturing and assembly of components. The important characteristics of the decision usually concern the relationship between fixed and variable costs, both initially and throughout the product forecast life cycle. This does require a view of the market, its competitors and an assessment of market risk. Figure 1.6 illustrates the manufacturing/assembly options facing the business. Clearly much the same argument may be made concerning the distribution/logistics infrastructure. Increasingly companies are evaluating the efficacy of 'make or buy' in both production and distribution activities. Operational gearing (the relationship between fixed costs and total costs) is an important decision area.

A number of issues are illustrated by Figure 1.6 which influence management's decision-making. The break-even volume is important. For many markets (fashion led) it is important for the business to ensure that it can achieve sufficient sales volume to exceed the break-even point and generate profit. The implications for logistics decisions are for high levels of service in terms of availability and delivery reliability: failure to do so may result in loss of opportunity to establish a strong market position. The margin (as a percentage of sales) is also important. The larger the margins the greater is the risk of competitors entering the market and of subsequent price competition. The point at which the company should cease production and distribution (where revenues = fixed costs) is another consideration. As we can see from Figure 1.6,

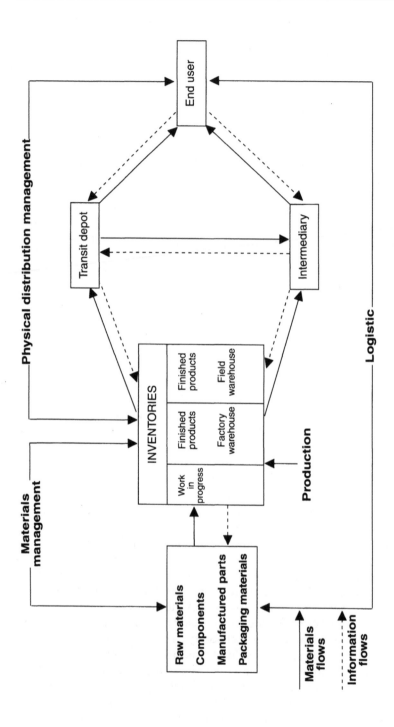

Figure 1.4   Logistics management

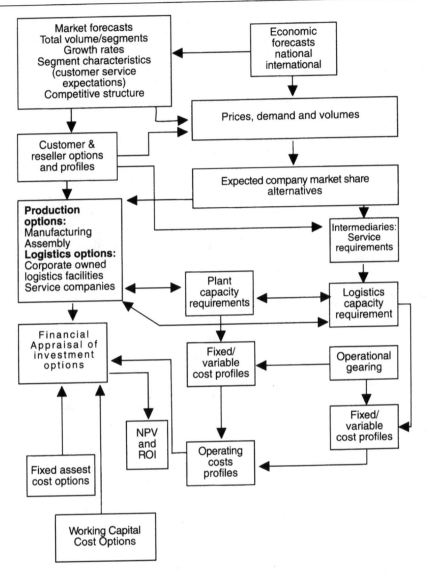

Figure 1.5   Logistics as an integral part of corporate investment decisions

organizations with low fixed costs (low operational gearing) have more flexibility in this respect. This may be important more from the perspective of time. With no (or low) commitment for fixed costs infrastructure the low operationally geared company can take steps to rationalize its offer and its activities.

The long-term perspectives of cost behaviour are also important. Again the structure of the response (operational gearing decisions) will be influenced by the expected market trend. Possible situations are illustrated by Figure 1.7. Two cost structures are shown together with two sales responses. Sales response A suggests a high growth/high volume market with low competitive/price activities, while sales response B rapidly plateaus (possibly due to competition or perhaps because it is a commodity product). The organizational structure options suggest that to meet the opportunity offered by sales response A a company would have a larger contribution rate (and more control of its activities) by opting for a structure with high fixed costs. The structure to maximize contribution from sales response B would be favoured by a structure with low operational gearing.

Returning to Figure 1.5, we can see the importance of identifying and exploring the likely development of markets. An understanding of the market *and* of the behaviour of production and logistics operations costs is of considerable competitive benefit. Not only does this knowledge facilitate strategic decision-making, but it also ensures that the structure most likely to provide long-term profitability can be identified.

■ The Concept of the Supply Chain

If logistics management is to exert a large influence on strategy, a structured or formal approach to making this contribution is necessary. This structured approach is available via the concept of the supply chain.

The concept of the supply chain is not new. Muller (1990) suggests that practitioners' views concerning supply chain management are 'much the same theory of integrated logistics that you have been reading so much about in the past few years. . . The major difference seems to be that supply chain management is the preferred name for the *actualization* of "integrated logistics" theory'. DuPont's director of logistics (Clifford Sayre) defines supply chain management as a loop: 'It starts with the customer and it ends with the customer.' Through the loop flows all materials and finished goods, all information, even all transactions. 'It requires looking at your business as one continuous process' and further, 'This process absorbs such traditionally distinct functions as forecasting, purchasing, manufacturing, distribution and sales and marketing into a continuous flow of business interaction. Gone are the functional 'stove pipes' of corporate activity; instead departments are structured as a pipeline that stretches between a company's suppliers and its customers.'

Sayre suggests that while the theory is some twenty years old, it has until recently, been difficult for companies to market a reality. 'No one then believed that communication could be handled efficiently enough to link all the aspects of the supply chain without gaps somewhere along the line.' Our previous comments on the importance of the contribution of information technology should be seen in this context.

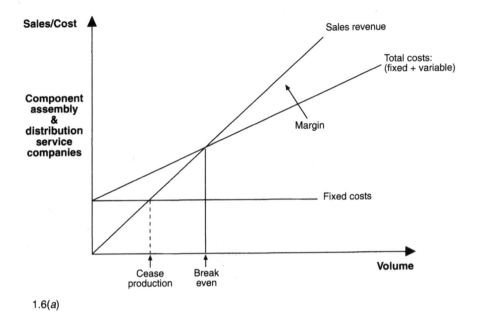

1.6(*a*)

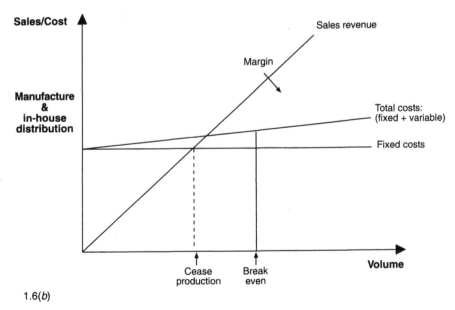

1.6(*b*)

Figure 1.6   The implications for fixed and variable costs of the 'make or buy' decision: operational gearing

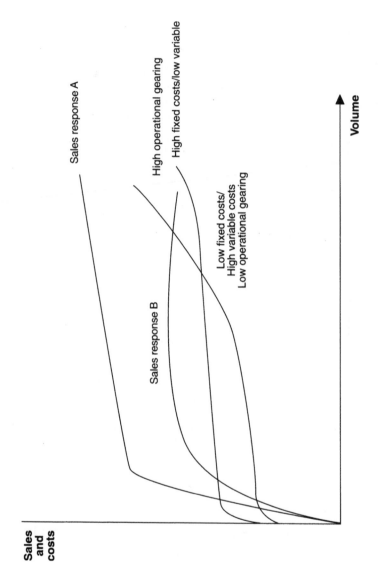

Figure 1.7 Cost profiles (high and low operational gearing) and sales responses

'The cost of making information available to more people has steadily gone down, while the physical costs of business, such as facilities and inventory, have steadily risen' (Max Stenross, Xerox). Information technology has been important to the development of the logistics activity, not only because of the fact that costs have decreased and accuracy and frequency have become accepted, but – possibly more importantly – information offers the facility to coordinate activities and to opt for 'control by information' rather than have 'control by doing'. This has enabled management to focus upon managing the core business and delegating the management of the support infrastructure to specialists who have developed the necessary expertise and can apply the benefits of economies of scale.

■ Distribution Requirements Planning (DRP)

The developments in IT have permitted much more control over production operations and the development of just-in-time and quick response systems. Quick response (and just-in-time) operations have been developed within the concept of the supply chain and because of the benefits that IT developments offer.

DRP was developed from MRP (materials requirements planning) and both seek to reduce the overall operating costs of the business, principally by eliminating unnecessary stockholding within the supply chain.

DRP relies upon forecasts of customer demand being generated, and works backwards towards establishing a realistic and economically justified supply chain system wide plan for ordering and processing the required finished goods demand. DRP is a time-phased plan for distributing product from plants, warehouses and other planned locations to points where it is required, at relevant times, to maintain specified levels of customer satisfaction.

Christopher (1985) describes logistics requirements planning (LRP) as potentially 'the biggest pay-off for total system optimisation . . . [it has] an overwhelming logic . . . but it is extremely difficult to implement in practice'. Much the same may be said concerning MRP II and DRP II systems which extend resource planning into the medium and long term. Here the intention is to re-examine existing physical facilities to match them more precisely to the streamlined materials flow planned and facilitated through requirements planning. Figure 1.8 illustrates the concept of logistics requirements planning.

The objectives of both DRP and MRP (and the conceptual LRP) are to maximize customer satisfaction at an optimum supply chain cost. This requires a strategic approach in which cooperation between supplier and distributor are required. Until recently the computer technology was not available by which investment decisions concerning fixed and current asset deployment could be reviewed with the objectives of providing overall levels of customer service at minimum costs. Optimization models will be discussed in a subsequent chapter.

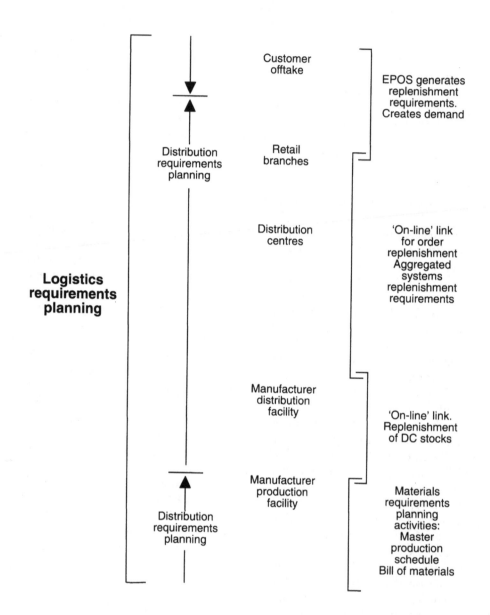

Figure 1.8   LRP (DRP/MRP) maintaining customer satisfaction through physical distribution and manufacturing systems linked by EDI

■ Channels Strategy and Alliances

For some time distribution channels were considered to be 'flows of economic goods and services', with the emphasis always on the economics of the flow.

Typically, suppliers' concerns were with cost minimization and maximizing efficiency. Important issues such as creating long-term integrated channel system-wide plans which developed upon coordinated activities on behalf of supplier and distribution organizations was ignored by most organizations. The dominant features of channel relationships were power relationships and conflict.

A comprehensive market (increasing in intensity for most markets), increasing product technological complexity, broadening product ranges and increasing economic pressures have increased the need for organizations to seek mutually acceptable objectives and strategies. Increased interdependence rather than coercion and conflict is now seen as the necessary element of long-term profitability. Interdependence implies cooperation and the establishment of mutually beneficial relationships.

The earlier discussion on 'value added' by distribution activities is tenable in a channels context. It provides a different perspective for channels decisions: one which focused on benefits to be delivered throughout the channel and which increased the eventual benefits delivered to the end user/customer. This view asked two questions:

- How much value is being added to the product as it moves down the channel from supplier to consumer? and
- How much does it cost the supplier to have such value added at each level?

Associated with this change of view was another which hitherto considered distribution inputs (transportation, storage, packaging, etc.) as commodities. However, a shift of emphasis towards *value added* by these inputs changed the view concerning their input values. Clearly when customers require a fast and dependable service they do so because it adds value to their product-service and accordingly they are prepared to pay a premium for this service improvement.

Alliances (or partnerships) between (and among) channel members improve channel relationships and the cost-effectiveness of the channel structures. Strategic alliances within distribution channels and logistics networks are discussed in detail in Chapter 14.

■ The Changing Business Environment

It has become very apparent in recent years that the elements of stability and predictability that were features of the 1960s and 1970s are unlikely to be seen again. A review of some of the characteristics of the pre-1970s business environment makes for interesting reflection:

- Protected domestic markets
- Regulated financial markets
- Stable exchange rates
- Regulated labour markets with relatively low levels of unemployment
- Relatively stable government fiscal and monetary policies
- Two major economic power bases (Europe and North America)
- Successful industrialized economies
- Complex organization structures
- 'Prosperous' bureaucratic organizations (large private companies and government).

The recessionary period of the late 1980s was long, deep and widespread in its effects. Business across an international spectrum restructured, and in doing so made many employees redundant. This, together with rapidly rising interest rates and restricted consumer spending, produced a level of consumer confidence so low that it is doubtful that it will recover to the mid-1980 levels.

Governments on an international basis began to divest themselves of public corporations. Airlines, communications, welfare activities, health, even corrective establishments became public corporations with shareholders and their expectations for share value and dividend growth. The result – was typically – more redundancies, often in middle and senior management grades, where the long-term implications were very serious. As a result of these events, the current and foreseeable business environment comprises:

- Open (deregulated) markets
- Deregulated financial markets
- Floating (often volatile) exchange rates
- Increasingly 'de-unionized' labour structures
- Previously polarized political views becoming more 'centralized'
- Fluctuating, short term, government fiscal and monetary policies
- An increase in the number of economic power bases. Expanded European Union (EU) and North American Free Trade Area (NAFTA) together with rapid (explosive) expansion of the Asian/Pacific Area.
- Focusing of manufacturing on low labour cost areas (Asia/Pacific areas)
- Sophisticated and expanding service industries
- Leaner, flatter organization structures.

Hitherto, change was predictable. It occured at a rate that permitted sufficient time to plan for change: now it occurs so rapidly that planning becomes reactive. Clearly the successful companies will be those who anticipate change. This may well require a change in the culture of many businesses and will require entrepreneurial leadership.

Drucker (1988) suggested:

The only certainty about the times ahead is that they will be turbulent times, and in turbulent times the first task of management is to make sure of the institution's capacity for survival, to make sure of its capacity to survive a blow, to adapt to sudden change, and to avail itself of new opportunities.

It should be said that change is nothing new. What is different is the rate of change. Thus far the 1990s have demonstrated an accelerating rate of change. The business environment for the 1990s is likely to comprise a combination of fix elements: complexity, ambiguity, uncertainty, paradox, discontinuity and competitive intensity; recent experience suggests that the degree of turbulence is predominantly influenced by two of these elements, uncertainty and competitive intensity. The model illustrated by Figure 1.9 describes the situation.

Competitive intensity measures the concentration of potential aggressive behaviour among competing enterprises. The *(un)certainty* dimension measures the degree of discontinuous change in an industry or market. The reality of most competitive environments is such that they may seldom be so simplistically analysed, but these classifications do provide a framework for an analysis. The model comprises four possible dominant types of business environment:

Forgiving situations are characterized by high uncertainty, slow change, good margins and non-discriminating customers.

Turbulent situations are characteriztised by high uncertainty, rapid change, novel markets, high margins and very demanding customers.

Predictable situations are characterized by low uncertainty, slow change, growing markets, low margins and demanding customers.

Stable situations are characterized by low uncertainty, little change, mature markets, ageing technology and undemanding customers.

In the following chapter we shall explore the implications of these in some detail. At this juncture it is sufficient to point towards some of the underlying features creating change. Some were suggested above (the current and foreseeable business environment) but for most businesses they may be summarized as:

Deregulation: the relaxation of government controls in several key areas such as transport, communications and finance affect decisions both domestically and internationally.

Product change: product life cycles are shortening dramatically and product ranges are proliferating as a response to consumer change and in an attempt by many companies to develop differentiation and hence competitive advantage.

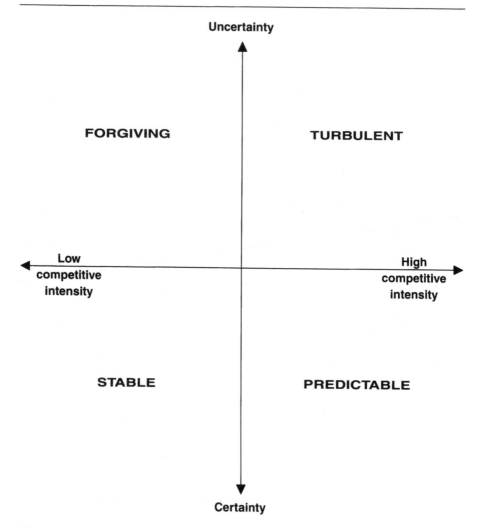

Figure 1.9   The elements of a turbulent business environment

Rising costs: inflation is becoming controlled by most industrialized economies; interest rates are varying and are typically used by governments to control the rate of growth of economies. By so doing they hope to control wage rates and influence investment.

Technology: both process and product technology are demonstrating increasing effectiveness often accompanied by decreasing costs. Information technology is providing more information, more accurate information, more frequent information, more relevant information – at lower cost!

Logistics: the ways and means of reaching and servicing customers. We have seen (the earlier discussion) how changes have occurred as philosophies and practices have changed.

We can suggest a definition of logistics, and that will act as a reference point for the remainder of this text:

Logistics is a component of strategic management. It is responsible for managing the acquisition, movement and storage of materials, parts and finished goods inventory (together with the related information flows) through an organisation and its marketing channels to meet customer expectations – thereby meeting the company's profit objectives.

An effective logistics activity functions at both *strategic* and *operational levels*. The complete process is illustrated by Figure 1.10 which adds a strategic perspective to the operational perspective already described by Figure 1.3. The processes described in Figure 1.5 are implicit in Figure 1.10, and are indicated as corporate expectations. The strategic elements of logistics decisions are concerned with the allocation of capital resources (facilities, transportation, inventory, etc.) in order to facilitate implementing the operational service response. Both strategy and operational service response are influenced by economic and market trends *and* customer expectations.

Current thinking considers the logistics activity to be an integrated managerial activity of a supply chain which extends from the extraction and processing of raw materials through a manufacturing process to the end user. Techniques which have enhanced the process, such as MRP and DRP were introduced in this chapter and will be discussed in detail in subsequent chapters.

An important element in the development of supply chain management concerns channel strategy and alliances and partnerships created within channels which enhance channel effectiveness.

Finally the impact of the changing business environment was discussed. Some of the issues were found to have widespread significance in terms of industry sectors and international operations.

■ Summary

In this chapter we have reviewed the development of supply chain management from an initial focus on physical distribution management to its current role as an activity which, through the value it is able to add to the market offer of an organisation, has become of major significance to the strategic decision-making activity of most companies.

The discussion has considered the components of physical distribution management and their role in the overall management of the supply chain

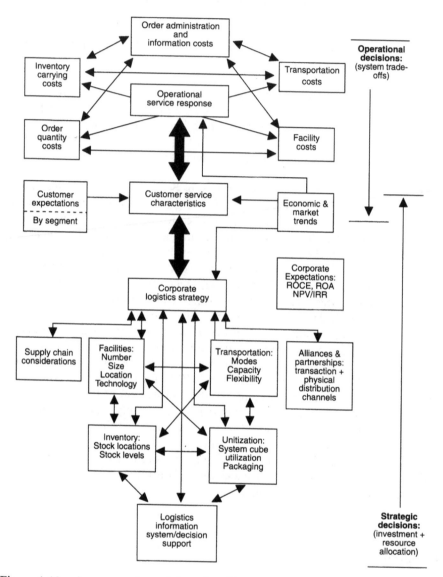

Figure 1.10   A current view of the role of logistics as an input into strategic and operational management

functions. The increasing importance of information in the supply chain and the intra- and inter-organisational role of management information is suggested to have been a major influence in the development of supply chain management through EDI, JIT and EPOS applications.

The concept of value added through customer service has been yet another significant development in the role played by logistics in the overall development of competitive advantage at a corporate level of management.

CHAPTER 2

Customer Focus in the Supply Chain

■ Introduction

The use of market segmentation techniques to identify market opportunities and customer profile targets has become widespread. Where it is particularly successful is in defining market segments for which there are two or three major criteria that remain stable over a period of time and are flexible enough to permit some movement of the criteria which does not result in disrupting the positioning of the business offer. The use of broad demographic and socio-economic criteria is sufficient for many retailing situations such as locating food superstore outlets. The successes of Tesco and Sainsbury in the UK are examples.

The introduction of 'Lifestyle' characteristics has had varied success. Often the concept has been misunderstood, or perhaps incorrectly applied. The reasons may be many. Likely as not, criteria which were assumed to be fundamental in driving purchasing behaviour were only short term and could be abandoned (and were) when consumers' personal circumstances changed. The growth of market share of food discounters in the UK is an example here; their expansion was accompanied by loss of volume by market incumbents; However, the market shows very little overall growth.

Another aspect of the problem is one addressed by the view that purchasing situations vary and that individuals demonstrate quite different behaviour sets between purchase situations. Central to this is the notion that consumer buying can be classified into shopping missions (see Walters, 1994) which reflect the buying situation of the individual. This explains the different 'behaviours' demonstrated in different shopping situations. Similar responses are evident in industrial buying.

Yet another approach (see Jung (personality types), Adizes (management styles), Chorn (organizational cultures)) argues that understanding consumer behaviour sets is in itself insufficient. They suggest that for sustained success the company strategy, its culture and its management style (or leadership) should be aligned and that the market should be researched in order that its 'logics' be understood. This approach (discussed below) uses the principle of strategic 'fit' which considers the degree of alignment that exists between competitive situation, strategy, organization and leadership style. In this sense, alignment refers to the 'appropriateness' of the various elements relevant to one another.

Ongoing research in North America, Australia and Europe reveals that superior performance (measured in a variety of ways) is associated with high degrees of alignment between these four elements. Strategic fit rests on the premise that the competitive situation, strategy, culture and leadership can be described as a combination of 'logics'. The logics combine in various and numerous ways to produce a unique competitive situation, strategy response, corporate culture and leadership style. Monitoring the market environment, understanding its changes, and being flexible in response enables the business to establish a rapport with a dynamic market and in so doing maintain a strong competitive position with continued sales growth.

■ The Alignment Theory

There are four key elements that comprise the strategic alignment model:

- The market and/or client base;
- The organization's strategy with which it responds to the market;
- The organization's culture which represents its internal capability to implement this strategy;
- The leadership/management style it uses to shape the culture and drive the strategy.

The alignment thesis is simple in essence. Any strategy is only appropriate in a given set of competitive conditions. Similarly, specific organization cultures and leadership styles are only appropriate for given strategic situations.

Essentially the principle of strategic fit considers the degree of alignment that exists between the four elements identified above (see Figure 2.1). In this context alignment refers to the 'appropriateness' of the various elements relative to one another.

■ Dimensions of Strategic Fit

The notion of strategic fit is based upon the premise that competitive situation, strategy, culture and leadership style can be described along the same dimensions. Jung suggested that an individual's behaviour is not random but has a pattern, and more recent work suggests further that behaviour may be aggregated such that groups share similar behaviour traits, such as in corporate cultures or market segments.

Essentially we are looking at four basic forces or 'logics', each of which may be characterized by its orientation to one of four main activities: 'production', 'administration', 'development' and 'integration'. These logics combine in various ways to produce a unique competitive situation, strategy, culture or leadership style. It should be emphasized that this is not a linear framework. Strategic alignment can be achieved through any of the following situations:

- Management responds to a change in the competitive environment by altering strategy and culture.
- Management pre-empts competitive changes by proactively changing the organization strategy and culture ahead of the market.
- Management creates a shift in the competitive environment by altering strategy and culture, thereby influencing the marketplace.
- A new chief executive may change the culture of the organization through his/her style.

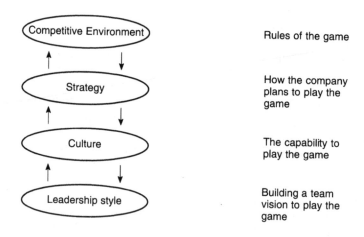

Figure 2.1   The principle of strategic alignment

There are examples for each of these responses. For example, the change in the competitive environment brought about by the increase in discount offers in food retailing in the UK during the early 1990s brought about strategic changes in the major multiples. It was the activities of Aldi, Netto and Rewe that influenced the changes in Tesco and Sainsbury which resulted in reduced prices across commodity product ranges. The implications for logistics management are clear. Availability, changes in sales volumes, and so on, require a corresponding shift of service emphasis.

A number of examples exist in which a shift in the competitive environment has occurred due to the changes in strategy and culture of one company. The strategy and culture of Next in the early 1980s was responsible for dramatic changes in customer response and expectations as well as major changes to the merchandise strategy of competitors. Marks & Spencer developed a much more positive approach to visual merchandising, and Burton responded with Principles. Both responses were accompanied by significant implications for logistics activities in the respective companies.

The influence of a change of chief executive often heralds a shift in culture such as that seen at Tesco when Ian MacLaurin assumed control, a shift from an operations and price led business towards a marketing-customer led approach; David Jones in Australia in the early 1980s, led by Brian Walsh, introduced a service orientation into the business, together with exclusivity and quality. Neither case was implemented without changes occurring in the logistics function.

■ Alignment Logics

Carl Jung's theory that behaviour is not random but demonstrates a pattern of consistency has led to the view that for each strategic alignment framework there is a corresponding set of 'logics' which describe a particular response to a competitive situation and define the 'appropriate' strategy, culture or leadership style.

The logics have common themes which are reflected throughout the alignment structure. These are described in the table.

Logic	Means	Output	Characteristics
P Production	Action	Results	Objectives, goal orientation, drive, persistence
A Administration	Control	Order	Systems, measurement, stability
D Development	Create	Change	Innovation, creativity, discontinuity
I Integration	Integrate	Cohesion	Synergy, teamwork, co-operation

The alignment theory holds that the production, administration, development and integration logics are the basis of consistency in behaviour *throughout* the structure, from competitive situation to leadership style. Figure 2.2 suggests how this may appear within a market/company situation. The levels of strategic focus should reflect the dominant logic characteristics.

An essential issue in alignment theory is the need for the 'logics' at each level to 'fit' with each other. Strategic fit occurs when the particular combination of logics, or a 'logic set', is replicated in the four elements of competitive situation, strategy, organization culture and leadership style: alignment occurs, and can only occur, when the logic sets in these four elements bear a close similarity to each other. Clearly this requires an understanding of the logic profiles at each level from which a dominant logic can be determined. This becomes more apparent if we consider each element in some detail. To do this, however, we should be clear concerning the internal and external aspects of the process. The *competitive situation* and the company's response to its *business strategy* are visible to the 'market'. By market we include customers, competitors, suppliers

Competitive situation
(Rules of the game)

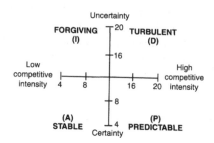

Business strategy
(How we plan to play the game)

Externally visible

- -

Internally visible

Organization culture
(Capability to play the game)

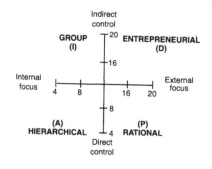

Leadership style
(Building a team vision)

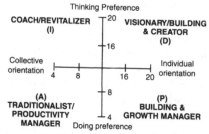

Figure 2.2   Identifying a hierarchy of 'logics'

and other stakeholder entities. However, the *organization culture* and *leadership style* are integral to the company, and visibility externally is limited and often controlled by the company by means of 'corporate communications' programmes implemented by public relations activities.

Strategic fit occurs when there is an alignment of the logics at each level. The brief profiles given for each logic thus far suggest that any conflict of a serious degree is likely to result in sub-optimal performance. This becomes clearer if we take a closer look at the logic set. In effect the logics can be seen as profiles which are either individual or may be combined. Likely combinations (and for that matter unlikely combinations) become clear once the descriptions are examined closely.

.For example, 'D' and 'A' would appear to be opposites in most respects, so too do 'I' and 'P' type logics. Thus we would hardly expect to see D and A combinations or I and P combinations. There are however balancing factors in each combination. For example, given that most innovative, creative (D) types of businesses do have some systems (albeit not particularly effective), we could expect a DA or AD combination. Similarly IP or PI combinations may exist. More likely are combinations that couple D and P characteristics (or A and P, A and I and I and D), the reason being that they are adjacent rather than opposite, but may, in many situations, be complementary. For example a DI combination could exist between a specialist R&D activity (say a university research institute) and an applications activity (a manufacturing business), as could an AP combination of a well established (in a market sense) company and a performance-oriented service company. For similar reasons DP and IA combinations are compatible.

■ The Competitive Situation

Marketplace 'logics' are described in Figure 2.3. The competitive situation confronting the company may be described in detail and this is considered in Figure 2.4 which identifies customer expectations associated with the four logic 'alternatives'. From Figure 2.4 we can see there may be quite different customer expectations for the alternative situations confronting a company. Further, the quadrants may be seen to be indicating product life cycle stage positions.

Clearly the implications for logistics management vary. In the early stages of a *product introduction* it is important that the product is available to the innovator customer group that will account for the success (or lack of success) of the product. Costs are not unimportant but are viewed less rigorously than will subsequently be the case. In the *growth stage* the channels of distribution are expanded as demand grows. It is also important to ensure that availability and delivery reliability are at high levels of performance if sustained growth is to be maintained. As the product reaches *maturity* while sales volumes are high and competition is intense, ways and means of maintaining margins must be investigated. Within the context of logistics decisions the use of third-party distribution service companies may help maintain such cost-effectiveness.

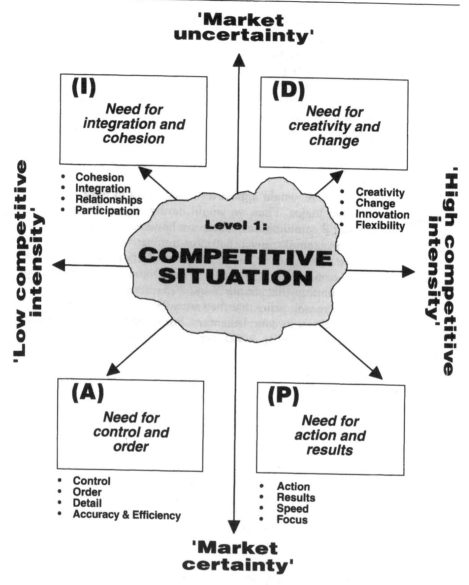

Figure 2.3   Marketplace logics

Upon reaching the *decline* stage, both product and distribution service characteristics should be rationalized. The fact that typically customers may become highly price sensitive means that margins will be seriously affected unless the logistics activity is reviewed. It may be that alternatives such as telephone sales, with service companies managing both sales and logistics activities, is among solutions considered.

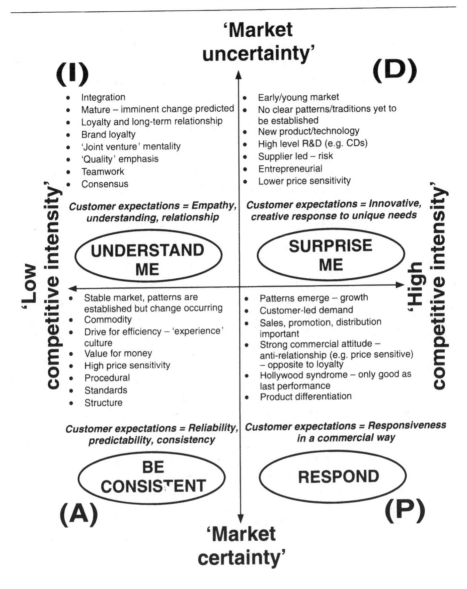

'Market uncertainty'

(I)

- Integration
- Mature – imminent change predicted
- Loyalty and long-term relationship
- Brand loyalty
- 'Joint venture' mentality
- 'Quality' emphasis
- Teamwork
- Consensus

Customer expectations = Empathy, understanding, relationship

UNDERSTAND ME

- Stable market, patterns are established but change occurring
- Commodity
- Drive for efficiency – 'experience' culture
- Value for money
- High price sensitivity
- Procedural
- Standards
- Structure

Customer expectations = Reliability, predictability, consistency

BE CONSISTENT

(A)

(D)

- Early/young market
- No clear patterns/traditions yet to be established
- New product/technology
- High level R&D (e.g. CDs)
- Supplier led – risk
- Entrepreneurial
- Lower price sensitivity

Customer expectations = Innovative, creative response to unique needs

SURPRISE ME

- Patterns emerge – growth
- Customer-led demand
- Sales, promotion, distribution important
- Strong commercial attitude – anti-relationship (e.g. price sensitive) – opposite to loyalty
- Hollywood syndrome – only good as last performance
- Product differentiation

Customer expectations = Responsiveness in a commercial way

RESPOND

(P)

'Low competitive intensity'

'High competitive intensity'

'Market certainty'

Figure 2.4 Customer expectations

It should be pointed out that different product-markets may demonstrate differing characteristics in the maturity/decline stages of the product life cycle. An obvious difference is that between consumer and industrial product-markets. Within consumer sectors differences will occur between fast-moving products and durables. An important feature concerns the level of technology in the product. Product development based on an existing technology is likely to require less after-sales service such as parts availability and often such support infrastructure as is needed may be outsourced. Conversely new technology may require an opposite approach with the service activity closely managed in-house.

Product manufacturing may differ. For example, one option is to manufacture a large proportion of the product and thereby retain as much of the benefits of value added as may be possible. Alternatively a minimum of manufacturing may occur with much of the requirement being obtained from external component manufacturers. In this situation it may be possible to extend the supplier relationship to cover after-sales service aspects.

Clearly, there are no 'ground rules' and each market situation is likely to demonstrate its own characteristics. Figure 2.5 suggests there are two transitional areas where D logic becomes P logic, and I becomes A logic. These issues can be seen in the expansive matrix approach of Figure 2.6.

■ Business Strategy

It follows that customer expectations and behaviour patterns are likely to vary and these become the basis for segmenting markets. This will be discussed in some detail below. However at this juncture we should address the issues arising from the discussion above (competitive situation).

Figure 2.2 suggests there are two dimensions in the business strategy component of the alignment. One dimension concerns the level of risk involved and the other is the extent to which the company is either proactive (suggesting D and/or I type logics) or reactive to opportunity (an A or P type).

Clearly the strategic response should reflect the company's perceptions of the competitive situation *as well as* a response based upon its innate capability. For example, a company hitherto used to monitoring competitors' activities and becoming involved in product-markets as and when they become established in their growth stage obviously has a preference for lower levels of risk than a product-market innovator. As such, the company would demonstrate A or P type characteristics as opposed to the D profile of an innovative competitor.

The characteristics of business strategy direction alternatives are described in Figure 2.7. It is immediately clear that the responses suggest there is a need to develop an appropriate strategy response to competitive situation alternatives. A 'turbulent' competitive situation requires a 'pathfinder' strategy response. It is here where the concept of strategic alignment becomes much clearer. It would be very unlikely that a company with an A type strategy profile would be able to cope with a D type market situation.

The A focus is about systemized efficient organizational strategy, where the turbulent market demands flexibility and creativity to ensure that response to unforeseen customer expectations or preferences may be effective and very quickly implemented. It is also possible to understand how, in order to achieve a prompt response, D type strategies may be modified or adapted to include some I type features. Risk may be lowered if it is shared. Thus we see joint

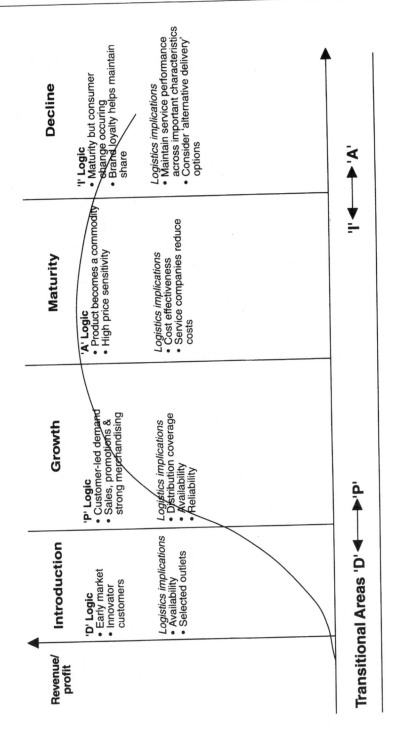

Figure 2.5 The product life cycle with market logics superimposed

MARKET RULES ⟷ CHALLENGES ⟷ ORGANIZATION LOGIC

	TURBULENT MARKET	PREDICTABLE MARKET	REPETITIVE	FORGIVING MARKET
Competitive Conditions	• High uncertainty • High rivalry • High risk • Rapid changes in industry and technology • Rapid changes in customer expectations	• Moderate uncertainty • High rivalry • High risk • Trends are evident in the industry and introduction of new technology and in developments in customer expectations	• Low uncertainty • Low rivalry • Low risk • Stability in industry and relatively mature technology • Customer preferences stabilize	• High uncertainty • Low rivalry • Low risk • Industry is negotiating the changes in structure and technology
Challenges	• Extensive R+D • First into market • Emphasis on creative and innovative solutions	• Focused and practical R+D • Second into market – get it right • Emphasis on sales management and niche management	• Ongoing product improvement • Cautious changes • Emphasis on productivity and efficiency	• Focus on service improvement • Negotiated changes with customers and other 'competitors' • Emphasis on long-term relationships
Organization response	• Individualism, creativity, flexibility • Market-based structures	• Action, objectives, results • Functional and matrix structures • Strong focus on results and agreed objectives	• Analysis, systems, control • Functional structures • Strong focus on processes and procedures	• Loyalty, teamwork, commitment • Division structures • Strong commitment to common values

Figure 2.6 Market rules and business logic

ventures (comprising combinations of, say, marketing and financial expertise) or perhaps alliances created to achieve similar objectives. Partnership arrangements between non-competing companies, perhaps with complementary product ranges, are beginning to share fixed costs in distribution and often in manufacturing. Much the same situation can be seen between 'evolutionary' and 'analytical' (A and P) strategies. Here a combination of an efficient strategy is likely to match the needs of a strategy based upon focus or segmentation in which customer service expectations would have been researched, and around which cost-effective response systems may be derived.

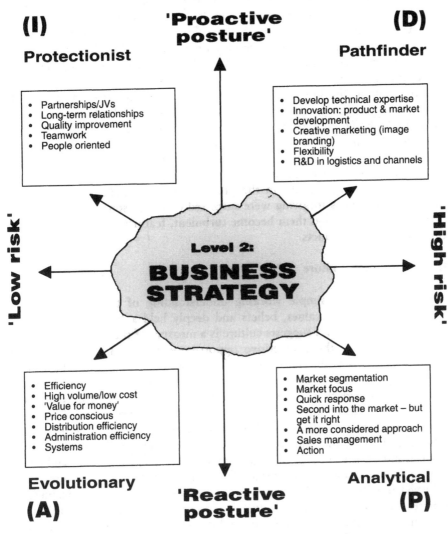

Figure 2.7   Details of strategic response options

As we mentioned earlier, the competitive situation together with the response towards highly competitive markets with unpredicatable profitability. Business strategies are *externally visible*, and changes in alignment may be observed and monitored as they occur. Often market situations change due to influences that are 'external' to the marketplace, rather than occur through evolutionary means. Transportation markets have been developing in this way. A number of governments have introduced legislation that has deregulated both transport and freight markets. Thus we have seen the markets themselves move from *forgiving* to *turbulent* profiles; from no or low competitor numbers in the market together with certainty concerning revenues and profit margins towards highly competitive markets with unpredictable profitability. In such situations *protectionist* strategy characteristics are (or were) hardly likely to enable a company to survive. Rather it is creativity and innovation that become necessary for success, services become customer led rather than product led; timetables and tariff schedules are replaced by more open-ended arrangements and terms of trade.

Often companies are slow to identify the changes around them. The information technology based market is one such example. Not only did the technology change and permit the product to become less expensive, more powerful and smaller physically, but applications and users showed dramatic changes. As a result distribution channels (both transaction and physical distribution) were 'revolutionized' to meet the new user types and their corresponding service needs. In the process, major manufacturers who once saw their markets as forgiving were surprised (if not in some instances caught totally unaware) to find them become turbulent, featuring new and numerous competitors and products.

■ Organization Culture

Put into context, a simple working understanding of organization culture comprises the shared values, beliefs and deeply held assumptions within the organization. Figure 2.8 suggests culture is a measure of the company's internal capability to meet the competitive opportunity in the marketplace. It also suggests that it is visible internally and is understood by the members of the organization. However, it is probably not true to say that an organization's culture is accepted by all members. Typically, those who have difficulty with aspects of company culture will either leave the organization or, if it is an aspect of the culture that is malleable and about which there is some concern shared by other members of the organization, then an attempt may be made to effect change. Indeed the concept of alignment suggests that culture can and should change when the logic of the marketplace shifts. But changes to culture are not achieved rapidly: often they are slow and incremental. In many instances the progress may be too slow, resulting in an organization appearing to be in a continual state of change, lagging behind its operating environment and society at large. Others attempt to make both the competitive situation and their competitive strategy 'fit' their culture, often with less than satisfactory results. It could be argued that IBM initially took such a position. Certainly the competitive situation changed quickly and IBM failed to respond for some time. Only after a considerable period did the marketplace see evidence in the IBM product-market strategy of the acceptance of the change in 'consumer' preferences and uses of computing equipment.

A look at the elements of organization culture can explain some of the reasons for a slow response by IBM. Figure 2.8 identifies the two dimensions of

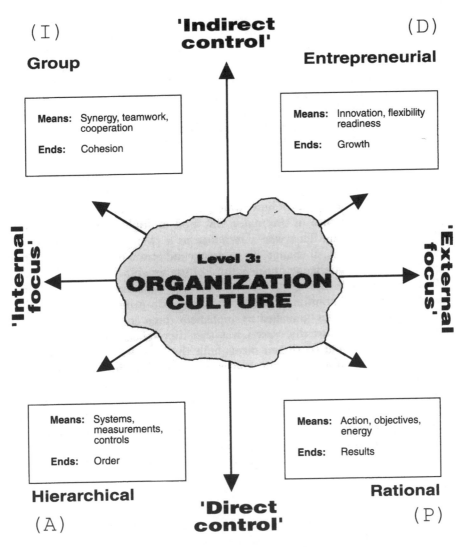

Figure 2.8   Organisation culture

organization culture which results in four sub-cultural types, i.e. the D entrepreneurial type, P rational, A hierarchical and I group type. Figure 2.8 also suggests the nature of their rationale by identifying means and ends. Returning to our example, Figure 2.8 suggests that of the four culture types, IBM's dominant logic would be an A type or *hierarchical* culture in which systems and controls and measured performance results in order (the 'company way' of doing things). Induced culture may be considered to be 'the way we do things around here'.

Again, we can see how the logics may interact. Clearly A–D and I–P are opposites and, while it should be argued that IBM has displayed innovativeness in the past, it was still overwhelmingly about 'order' and structured performance. It is not difficult to see how I and D type logics may interact, nor for that matter, A and P types. With ID mixes it is often the case that highly innovative solutions to problems do require teamwork across a range of activities. A moment's reflection would suggest that many technological-based innovations require teamwork or cooperation if growth is to be achieved. This also suggests that vertical combinations are also realistic. Growth requires action and targets (or objectives) if *results* are to be achieved.

It follows that to be effective in the marketplace and for corporate performance to be maintained, companies should accept that over time their culture may be required to shift if a more effective, more profitable response, and one more 'in line' with the marketplace is to be achieved. Earlier in this chapter we gave examples of how strategic alignment may be achieved by referring to the response of the major UK food multiples to the increase in growth of discounting. This was a *response* to a change in the competitive environment requiring a change in strategy, and probably for one or two companies significant change in the culture of the organization.

During the 1980s the term 'service culture' was very popular. Many companies saw the adoption of customer service as a primary feature of their strategies. However, few managed to implement these good intentions. Many did in fact fail: for most the reason was that they failed to recognize that a 'service culture' should be shared throughout the business and that customer service is really a cultural concept, and must spring from inside the organization. It requires acceptance by not only those elements of the business that have direct customer contact, but also the entire structure of the business, particularly the service infrastructure which is responsible for ensuring there is product to meet customer requirements or that there is capacity to respond to customer service specific needs. This usually requires strong leadership, dedicated to ensuring that service strategies are capable of being implemented.

■ Leadership Style

The final component in the alignment process is leadership style. As suggested by Figure 2.9, there are two dimensions which result in D, P, A and I types of leadership style. As with organization culture the alignment thesis suggests there to be a requirement of management to ensure that leadership style matches the alignment of the competitive situation, and there follows alignment with business strategy and organization culture.

In Figure 2.9 the two dimensions of leadership style are seen to be a 'thinking/doing' spectrum and an orientation of style varying from collective through to an individual orientation. The characteristics of each of the four types is detailed by Figure 2.9, and these suggest there is a case for arguing that specific situations will require quite different leadership skills. For example, a company whose markets are predominantly *stable* (A) types where products are (or are becoming) commodities and possibly in the decline (or maturity) stage of their life cycles. In such a situation a *productivity manager* approach is that most likely to produce the best performance, resulting in profitable outcomes rather than losses. It follows that *creators and builders* would be less than comfortable in this type of competitive situation, their skills and aptitudes being more suited to *turbulent* competitive situations.

Again the combinations of management style types are evident. For example, D and P characteristics may be required to launch a product and to take it successfully through the introduction and growth stages of its life cycle. Similarly I and A characteristics will be compatible later in the life cycle (see Figure 2.5) in the process of managing the product through the maturity stage into decline.

An important alignment issue that emerges is that between leadership style and organization culture. Figure 2.10 explores this issue in detail for each of the organizational culture types discussed earlier (and described in Figure 2.8). In each case the corresponding leadership style characteristics are described.

■ Producing Strategic Fit through Alignment

The purpose of considering strategic alignment as a strategic analytical concept for planning (and control) purposes is that if it is achieved organization performance and effectiveness will be optimized. This would occur when an organization responds to a predominantly *competitive (P)* environment with an *operational (P)* strategy, a *rational (P)* culture and a *growth management (P)* style. Clearly the same argument obtains for A, D and I alignments. The principle of strategic alignment is shown in Figure 2.11 which suggests there to be a *centre of gravity* for each level which defines the logic of specific dominance. Clearly, it is unlikely that any one PADI logic will have exclusivity in any of the four alignment categories described during these discussions. What is much more likely to occur is a combination of the logics. For example, an organization may be confronted with a competitive situation in which customer prospects may have an overriding preference for speed, results, action and performance (P logic) and a lesser need for reliability, consistency and accuracy (A logic).

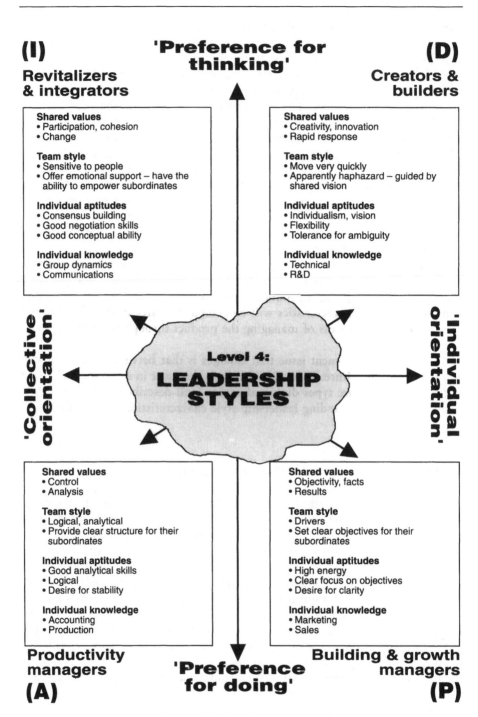

(I)
Revitalizers & integrators

'Preference for thinking'

(D)
Creators & builders

Shared values
• Participation, cohesion
• Change

Team style
• Sensitive to people
• Offer emotional support – have the ability to empower subordinates

Individual aptitudes
• Consensus building
• Good negotiation skills
• Good conceptual ability

Individual knowledge
• Group dynamics
• Communications

Shared values
• Creativity, innovation
• Rapid response

Team style
• Move very quickly
• Apparently haphazard – guided by shared vision

Individual aptitudes
• Individualism, vision
• Flexibility
• Tolerance for ambiguity

Individual knowledge
• Technical
• R&D

'Collective orientation'

Level 4: LEADERSHIP STYLES

'Individual orientation'

Shared values
• Control
• Analysis

Team style
• Logical, analytical
• Provide clear structure for their subordinates

Individual aptitudes
• Good analytical skills
• Logical
• Desire for stability

Individual knowledge
• Accounting
• Production

Shared values
• Objectivity, facts
• Results

Team style
• Drivers
• Set clear objectives for their subordinates

Individual aptitudes
• High energy
• Clear focus on objectives
• Desire for clarity

Individual knowledge
• Marketing
• Sales

Productivity managers
(A)

'Preference for doing'

Building & growth managers
(P)

Figure 2.9   Leadership styles

GROUP Revitalizers & integrators		ENTREPRENEURIAL Visionaries & creators	
Focus	I – Who?	Focus	D – Why?
Shared values	Cohesion, harmony	Shared values	Individualism, innovation
Style	Sensitive, consensus	Style	Impulsive, visionary
Support	Mutuality	Support	Inspiration
Individual aptitudes	Likes people Desire for membership	Individual aptitudes	Likes concepts Desire for change
Individual skills	Negotiation Team building	Individual skills	Creative thinking Communication
HIERARCHICAL Productivity managers		RATIONAL Building & growth managers	
Focus	A – How?	Focus	P – What?
Shared values	Tradition, control, caution	Shared values	Performance, logic competition
Style	Deliberate, directive	Style	High energy, forceful
Support	Structure	Support	Objectives
Individual aptitudes	Likes detail Desire for stability	Individual aptitudes	Likes facts Desire to achieve
Individual skills	Coordination System and method	Individual skills	Pragmatism Logical

Figure 2.10   Leadership style and organisation culture

There may also be some need for flexibility (D logic) and cohesion (I logic'). Given these requirements, the organization's market logic would be 'PA. A graphical representation is shown in Figure 2.12.

■ Customer Service and Market Logics

Strategic alliance principles can be applied to determine the *appropriate* customer service strategies to meet customer expectations and requirements. The conceptual base of strategic alliance implies that depending upon a customer's purchasing situation, the customer will have *primary logics* that determine the nature of the logistics services they require.

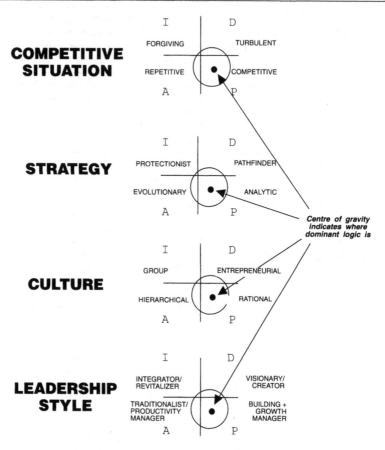

Figure 2.11   Producing strategic fit through alignment

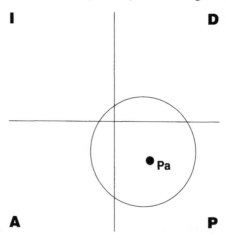

Figure 2.12   Graphical representation of logics

For example, the nature of the customer's market may require immediate response at very short lead times. To meet this may require dedicated transport and even dedicated personnel. By contrast the reseller of a commodity product will require a reliable low cost service, one which ensures high levels of availability at point of sale (or use) which guarantees a reliable service to production activities, or consumers if it is a finished product. Yet a third situation may be for a 'creative solution' to what may appear to be an 'impossible' demand.

The important point to be concluded from the alignment argument is simply that it offers a powerful albeit dynamic means by which differences may be identified and understood and service requirements then structured into relevant service packages. We can explore this in Figure 2.13.

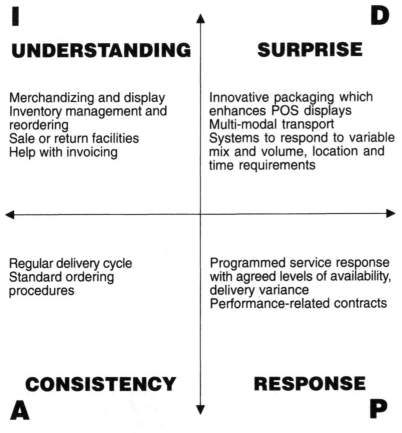

Figure 2.13   Customer service logics

The customer service items featured in Figure 2.13 are sufficient to suggest there are significant differences in the customer service requirements that a company may receive for the same product. This suggests that we should consider both product *and* the *service* augmentation surrounding the product as the overall product required by the customer. Figure 2.14 supports this argument. In Figure 2.14 the product is common across the range of outlets. Clearly what does differ is the service support package, and Figure 2.14 demonstrates how very different the package becomes when considered as product augmented with a logistics service package. This situation suggests that logistics service requirements (determined by 'buying logics') may form the basis for segmentation and subsequently a market-based organization structure.

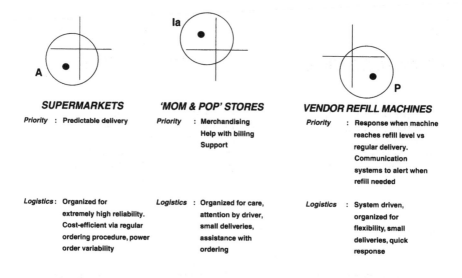

SUPERMARKETS

Priority : Predictable delivery

Logistics : Organized for
extremely high reliability.
Cost-efficient via regular
ordering procedure, power
order variability

'MOM & POP' STORES

Priority : Merchandising
Help with billing
Support

Logistics : Organized for care,
attention by driver,
small deliveries,
assistance with
ordering

VENDOR REFILL MACHINES

Priority : Response when machine
reaches refill level vs
regular delivery.
Communication
systems to alert when
refill needed

Logistics : System driven,
organized for
flexibility, small
deliveries, quick
response

Source: Adapted from *Harvard Business Review*, May–June 1993.

Figure 2.14   Logistics segments for Coca Cola Japan

This approach is suggested by Figure 2.15. The SBUs (strategic business units) are likely to be oriented towards large customers or perhaps customers who share channel categories. In this example it is suggested that 'SBU4' and 'SBU2' may have customers which share a number of service requirements (they are D and ID profiles) and these may be combined in an attempt to achieve a more cost-effective customer service function.

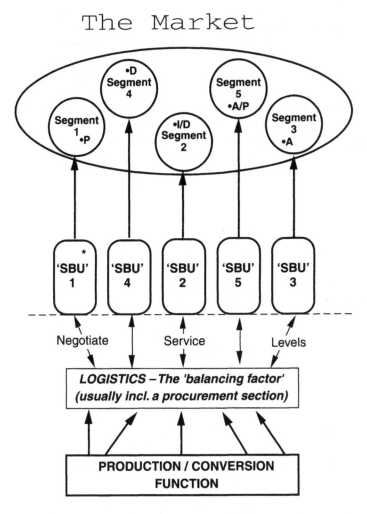

Figure 2.15   Market-based organization structure

■ Summary

The importance of understanding customers and their organisational cultures and personalities is an important consideration and should become an issue in supply chain strategy decisions.

This chapter uses an approach based on the work of Jung, Adizes and Chorn and is based on the thesis that, for sustained success, the company's strategy, its culture and its management style should be aligned and reflect the 'logics' of customer groups it deals with. The alignment theory suggests that, for strategic fit, the market, the company strategy, culture and leadership style should be congruent and described along shared vectors. The alignment theory logics, production, administration, development and integration were described in detail and examples presented of how more effective strategies were developed with the benefit of an understanding of the strategic alignment process. The application of market logics to marketing and supply chain strategy decisions were developed using the basic product life cycle model.

CHAPTER 3

Achieving Customer Satisfaction Objectives

Introduction

The previous chapter proposes that customer service may be focused more effectively if 'customer buying logics' are better understood. The 1980s demonstrated the role of customer service in developing competitive advantage, but were replete with examples of service installations that proved to be less than satisfactory. In retrospect it would seem that there were three primary problems.

First there was the approach to implementing customer service policies. Typically they were similar to those of competitors. There was little or no attempt at identifying specific needs. Thus eventually service offers became *competitive necessities* rather than a means to developing differential competitive advantage.

Very little attempt was (or is) made at measuring customer service programmes for cost-effectiveness. It follows that resources may have been wasted in providing service activities for which no benefits (in revenue and profit terms) could be identified.

The third problem follows. Without strong differentiation based upon researched customer preferences, most customer service offers became *generic*, and thus service became an additional cost which could not be justified, and often contained elements which were not adding value for the customer.

What is Customer Service?

Some of the issues were raised in Chapter 1. However, there is an extensive range of customer service items which include:

- Frequency of delivery
- Order cycle time
- Reliability of delivery
- Flexibility in replenishment
- Order fulfilment accuracy
- Accuracy of documentation

- Conformance of documentation to organizational requirements
- Continuity of supply
- Advice on supply problems
- Quality of company sales, technical and service representation.

Clearly, other topics may be added to this list. Usually these relate to specific topics that are required by one or two specialist companies. It is also important to note that the rank ordering of customer service parameters will vary not simply between industries, but quite often between companies in the same industry. The important conclusion that can be reached is that differences in preferences exist, and that these should be identified prior to determining the content of a customer service strategy. In this way appropriate contents and levels of service packages will result – at acceptable levels of cost.

It is also important to remember that even though a service offering must be relevant, *consistency* is just as important because each individual encounter is evaluated subjectively and differently by each individual customer. Central to this evaluation is the difference between expectations and perceptions of customers. Figure 3.1 illustrates the relationship between *expectations* and *perceptions*.

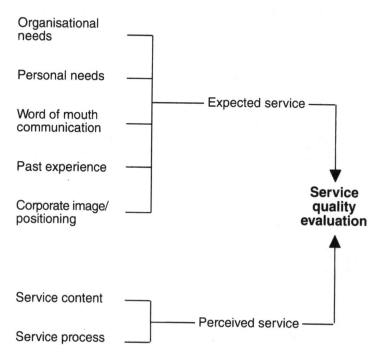

Figure 3.1   Expectations and perceptions in customer service quality evaluation

Expectations are shaped by the customer's personal needs, past experience, and the nature of the service on offer. Corporate image/positioning plays an important role in the development of these expectations. A problem that must be considered is that expectations tend to increase: what was considered to be an additional service benefit becomes 'standard service practice' as and when it is offered by competitors. Furthermore, once a reputation is established by a company for service excellence, the expectations of customers tend to increase.

Perceptions are influenced not only by what the customer receives, but how the service is delivered. Add to this both companies' objectives and strategies and changing short-term operational needs and it is not surprising that consistently high perceptions of customer service are difficult to achieve. Typically it is only when service delivery fails that customers begin to make an assessment of the level of service delivery achieved against their expectations.

Clearly economies of scale are seen to exist in service delivery. However, as the earlier discussion of strategic alignment and customer logics suggested, it is unlikely that a standard *or* generic service package will suffice. This suggests that segmenting customers on the basis of logistics service needs is more likely to offer a successful long-term relationship with the customer. Customized service often works very well when markets (and customers) are specialized with customers who are very knowledgeable about their needs and their suppliers' offers.

■ Developing a Customer Service Strategy

It follows that effective service strategies are those based upon researched customer needs which are matched against company resource capabilities. Clearly, if customers' expectations are likely to extend the capability of the resources to maintain a consistent level of service, then either resources must be increased or, alternatively, a lower level of service should be explored within the context of customers' responses. A model for determining (and improving) customer service is shown in Figure 3.2. The model's operational methodology is based upon identifying 'gaps' in the service offer; Figures 3.2 and 3.3 should be used together with Table 3.1 to gain an insight into the working method of the model.

As an example we will concentrate on interpretation (Gap One). A rigorous methodology is required if insights into customers' logics and perceptions are to be gained. Such a methodology may include the following steps:

- Identify the key parameters of customer service – in each market segment.
- Establish the relative importance of the parameters to customers in each segment.
- Identify the perceived performance on each of the parameters relevant to main competitors.
- Conduct an internal survey to ascertain if company personnel hold similar views.

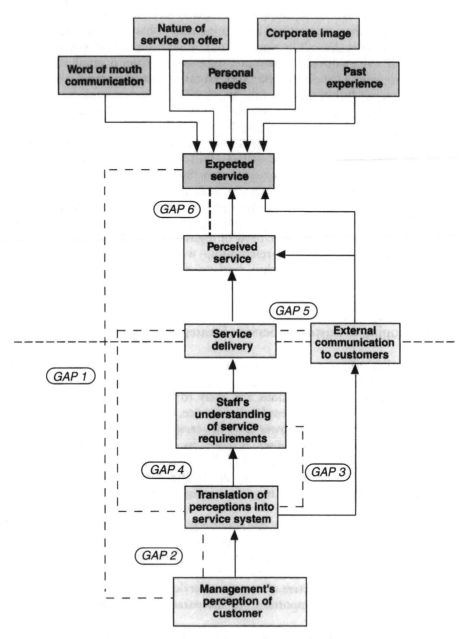

Figure 3.2   A methodology for service improvement – identifying the gaps

Table 3.1 Customer satisfaction indices as planning and monitoring documents

Customer satisfaction index	Weight	Customer group (priority) (determining service levels)			Customer group (second priority) (qualifying service levels)		
		Objectives (expectations)	*Actual performance (perceptions)*	*Gap +/−*	*Objectives (expectations)*	*Actual performance (perceptions)*	*Gap +/−*
Total weighted index: items							
Order processing performance	—	—	—	—	—	—	—
Order administration	—	—	—	—	—	—	—
Service flexibility	—	—	—	—	—	—	—
Role of staff	100	—	—	—	—	—	—
Item detail							
Order processing and performance							
Frequency of delivery	—	—	—	—	—	—	—
Order cycle time	—	—	—	—	—	—	—
Reliability of delivery	—	—	—	—	—	—	—
Order administration							
Advice on order progress	—	—	—	—	—	—	—
Invoice procedures	—	—	—	—	—	—	—
Service flexibility							
Flexibility of delivery	—	—	—	—	—	—	—
Order constraints	—	—	—	—	—	—	—
Personnel							
Representatives duties	100	—	—	—	—	—	—

Table 3.2   A methodology for service improvement: identifying and closing the service gaps

Gap	Problem	Solution
1. Interpretation	Gap between management perceptions and customer expectations will have a negative impact on customer's evaluation of *service quality*.	Understand customer's business and service needs. Get to know the market, its competitors and customers.
2. Translation	Gap between management perceptions and the methodology of the service system will impact on *service delivery*.	Integrate MIS/support. Balance the use of systems with people where personal contact is essential.
3. Communication	Gap between service system and staff understanding of what is required will impact on *service performance*.	Listen to those personnel who contact the customer. Create a shared vision of what service is and what should be delivered to the customer.
4. Reality	The gaps between intended service quality and *realized service quality*.	Develop a service culture in the business. Measure and reward service achievements.
5. Credibility	Gap between actual service delivery and organisation originated communication will impact on *customers perceptions and expectations*.	Manage service delivery to ensure that delivery equals promise not less than the service promised.
6. Perception	Service quality as perceived by customers is a function of the size and character of the gap between expected and perceived service.	The service delivered should be such that customer perceptions ≥ customer expectations.

■ Measuring Customer Service: A Customer Service Index (CSI)

There are a number of methods by which the level of customer satisfaction of products and services may be measured. However, the purpose of all effective CSI instruments is to provide a framework which allows an organization to determine customer expectations and monitor how successfully a number of prioritized factors are being met *over time*: it is able to track customer satisfaction in the areas that are *most* important to different types of customers. Typically, there are two distinct stages: design and monitor.

■ The Design Stage

The purpose of this stage is to *establish the service and product expectations held by customers*. The use of continuous customer satisfaction monitoring will only be of value if it measures those issues *regarded by customers as most important* in providing satisfaction rather than the issues *regarded as important by the organization* as 'real expectations'. Figure 3.3 illustrates the design process.

The Qualitative Phase enables the business to:

- Identify its customers;
- Generate a list of relevant service and product attributes based upon customers' experience;
- Utilize the list of 'qualitatively derived' attributes in the design of a questionnaire that will be used in the Quantitative Phases.

The Quantitative Phase is directed towards obtaining a mathematical based evaluation of customer expectations and perceptions of the customer expectations and perceptions derived during the qualitative stage.

The quantitative phase uses a simple relationship to measure customer satisfaction:

- If Performance GAP > 0 implies that the company is *overperforming*;
- If Performance GAP $= 0$ then the company is *meeting expectations*;
- If Performance GAP < 0 then the company can be said to be *underperforming*.

The output of the quantitative phase will be:

- Aggregates of customer expectations, perceptions, and performance gaps;
- Product and service attributes grouped into broader factors;
- Statistically assigned weights for these factors, indicating the level of importance of certain factors within the concept of total service or product quality;
- Behavioural requirements indicated by all factors, providing an organization with concrete guidelines for addressing the relevant delivery of the correct services and products;
- The prioritization of all service and product issues in order to allow the organization to address the most important attributes first;
- A refined customer satisfaction index questionnaire to be used for the ongoing monitoring of customer satisfaction.

■ The Monitor Stage

An ongoing measure of customer satisfaction is obtained by establishing an ongoing monitoring instrument. The frequency with which customer satisfaction is measured and reported should be directly related to the time it would take to be able to fully utilize and implement the findings. How quickly changes would be visible in customers' satisfaction after the implementation of service adjustments and developments should also be taken into consideration. Monitoring processes usually comprise five stages:

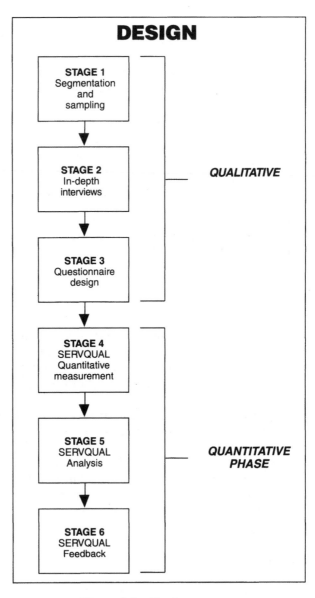

Figure 3.3   Design process

Stage 1: Segmentation and sampling;
Stage 2: Continuous monitoring of customer satisfaction;
Stage 3: Customer satisfaction index feedback;
Stage 4: Evaluation of strategies;
Stage 5: Establishing strategies.

The process of continuous monitoring allows an ongoing evaluation of existing service strategies and identifies areas in which development of strategies may be considered. It is essential that the issues identified are addressed constructively throughout the business.

When deciding upon customer service strategies it is worthwhile considering an earlier comment in more detail. We suggested that often what was initially an innovative strategy becomes, after time, regarded as part of the standard service offer within the industry. Another way of viewing this is to take the view that there are two levels of customer service offering. The first level is at a basic 'entry' point in the competitive environment and may be considered to be a *qualifying* level of service. Qualifying customer service packages contain those services that are expected to be available from all serious competitors within the market or market segment. However, to develop competitive advantage it is necessary to develop a service package beyond this service package, one which is both exclusive to the vendor *and* one which adds value for the customer. These two aspects of the service package will ensure that customers consider the service offer to be of real value and are likely to be seen as *determining* services which influence those customers whose perceptions are high to make the company a 'first choice' supplier.

Typically, the logics of such customers will be 'D' or 'I' or perhaps 'DI'. They are likely to respond to innovative ideas, be service sensitive (rather than price sensitive) and also favour 'partnership' type arrangements. Figure 3.4 illustrates this proposition. The notional increase in 'profit' is:

$$\frac{y - x}{b - a} \quad \frac{\text{(revenue)}}{\text{(costs)}}$$

It is assumed that $y - x$ is obtained without increasing fixed costs by any significant amount.

The design and monitoring stages of strategy determination clearly need objectives to work with and the expectations and perceptions which underlay the service offer are useful in this regard. To these we can add the qualifying and determining service levels which will provide service objectives *and* performance measures for the business to achieve.

Most businesses have customers who account for significant portions of their business (the 80/20 or Pareto 'Rule' is commonly used to describe the phenomena) and given this structure of accounts it is possible to derive a service offer which protects this business, and equally we may tailor service packages around those customers who may respond very positively to a specific

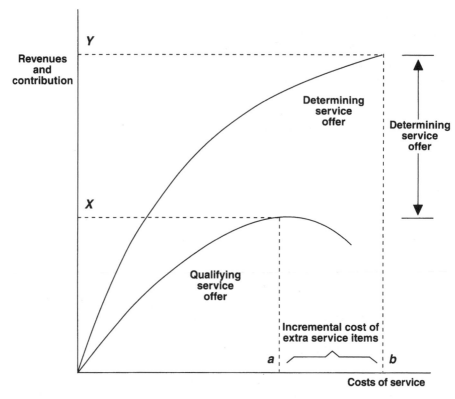

Figure 3.4   Comparison between qualifying service and determining service offers and the generation of service budgets

service offer. The notion of two levels of service offer, qualifying and determining, now has significance because we can use them to ensure that differential service offers may be made rather than the generic offer which may satisfy small and occasional customers. This would suggest that we set both service performance objectives *and* revenue objectives; see Figure 3.5 for an explanation. Note the service characteristics are not intended to be an exhaustive list.

Given the two levels of service the research findings can be used to identify the qualitative characteristics and quantitative values (performance criteria) which will become the customer service objectives the business sets by customer or by segment.

The customer satisfaction index may then be used to monitor the performance achievements of the company. By using the index to reflect expectations as objectives and perceptions as an indication of performance achievements we are in a position to respond to both under *and* over achievement situations promptly. A CSI performance monitoring document is illustrated by Table 3.1.

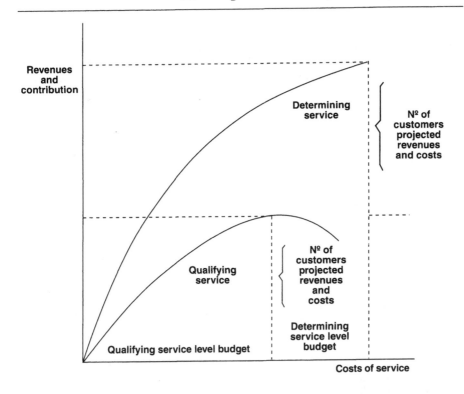

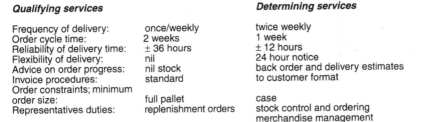

Figure 3.5 Qualifying and determining service characteristics in planning and control the customer service offer

It offers management the benefit of an ongoing method of checking its performance against customer prescribed criteria. The CSI monitor may be complemented with sales revenue and cost targets. In this way both the service performance *and* its impact on business generated may be compared.

Finally, Figure 3.6 links the process of strategic alignment with developing a customer service strategy. Figure 3.6 reinforces the arguments of both Chapter 2 and this present chapter by demonstrating that understanding the competitive situation *and* one's customer's buying behaviours allows a differentiated service strategy to be evolved, one which reflects the overall alignment of the business with its service output such that competitive advantage results rather than competitive necessity.

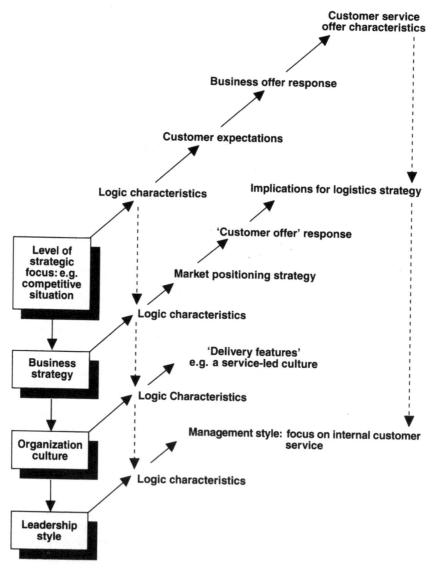

Figure 3.6   Logics lead to an alignment of strategic components and customer service strategy

■ Summary

This chapter developed a discussion on customer service based upon the application of the strategic alignment concept developed in the previous chapter.

The components of a customer service offer were identified and the discussion extended into the importance of customer expectations and perceptions of service within the supply chain.

Customer service strategy and performance measurement were discussed and the importance of a structured approach to the identification of service needs and of gaps in the service offer were explored in detail. This introduced the use of formal service performance achievement models (such as a customer service index), discussed in detail.

Corporate Profitability and the Supply Chain

■ Introduction

As with any other business activity the purpose of the logistics function is to participate in generating revenues (and profits), but in doing so it attracts costs. Logistics activities should add value to resources: typically the added-value of the logistics function is to make product/services accessible to customers at convenient times and locations. This we established in the opening chapters.

In this chapter we will explore the impact of logistics on corporate revenues and costs. Clearly the more effective the management of the logistics function, the greater the impact on revenues and profits. However, it should be recognized that there are also financial decisions that are made that can influence the ultimate level of profitability. This topic was introduced in Chapter 1, where operational gearing (the relationship between fixed and variable costs) was considered in the context of consideration of margins generated, control and risk. Financial gearing takes this issue further by considering the issues and implications of alternative methods of financing the assets required by the logistics function

One other consideration is the accounting interest: the measurement of the impact of logistics on corporate profitability, and how alternative asset structures may be evaluated in order that the most cost-effective option may be selected. It is usual to use the conventional accounting reports to consider options and to monitor the effectiveness of the selected alternative.

Logistics decisions can influence corporate profitability in three broad areas, i.e.

- Level of *operating cost* (i.e. the proportion of total operating cost that logistics absorbs);
- Influence on *sales*;
- Role in *investment*.

Any changes in the level of participation of logistics within the business should be undertaken either if overall effectiveness can be improved, or to reduce the level of input received to achieve a maintained level of output.

Operating costs may be reduced by:

- Minimizing inventory handling and the elimination of non-productive handling;
- The removal of bottlenecks within the distribution system;
- Optimizing the number of warehouses and other stock holding locations;
- Eliminating activities and intermediaries which/who do not add value to the overall activity;
- Using group leverage (purchasing power) to minimize transport and other purchased services costs;
- Regarding suppliers' transport costs as variable with the potential for cost reduction;
- Removing delays caused by documentation flows and eliminating unnecessary document transfers.;
- Considering suppliers' (and carriers') lead times as a component of overall lead time;
- Seeking to improve human and capital resource productivity increases;
- Optimizing vehicle utilization to minimize delivery costs;
- Eliminating errors and thereby reducing the 'total' costs of correction.

Sales revenues generated may be influenced by:

- Developing a customer-led approach: a customer service strategy (see Chapter 2);
- Minimizing out-of-stocks for given levels of inventory;
- Communicating stock and lead time availability information within the business and to customers;
- Minimizing lead times for 'standard item' orders;
- Maximizing selling space versus stockholding space.

Investment performance may be improved for *inventory* holding by:

- Reducing system lead times;
- Improving the accuracy of forecasting;
- Eliminating obsolete and excess inventory;
- Improving delivery reliability;
- Reducing re-order quantities.

The *investment performance* of *fixed assets* may also be improved by:

- Optimizing the number, size and location of facilities and transportation fleet and equipment;
- Evaluating the actual 'return on investment' generated and considering service alternatives.

Clearly such factors and decisions require to be analysed and evaluated. An understanding of the financial issues and decisions confronting the company, together with an understanding of the impact of logistics decisions on financial structures and performance is therefore essential. A knowledge of the information content available in financial reports is therefore helpful in this context.

■ Using Financial Reports to Make Logistics Decisions

There are three financial reports of particular interest: these are the income (profit and loss) statement, the balance sheet, and the sources and application of funds statement. From these statements a number of key performance ratios may be derived.

In any corporate context *strategic planning* is responsible for setting the *overall direction* of the business. *Marketing* is concerned with making an *effective response* to customer-based opportunities. *Operations management* concentrates on *manufacturing efficiency*, with *logistics* undertaking to '*deliver*' the product-service. *Finance* monitors the utilization and the productivity and profitability of resource allocation.

■ The Income (Profit and Loss) Statement

The income (profit and loss statement) is a measure of the organization's profitability over a specific trading period. Usually internal reporting is made monthly but a yearly report is sufficient for statutory purposes and to meet stakeholder expectations.

The format of the statement varies dependent upon the nature of the business, management's need for detailed information and their willingness to divulge that information. The income statement addresses five key elements of the company's trading performance:

1. Sales revenue
   less
2. Cost of sales
   equals
3. Gross profit (gross margin %)
   less
4. Operating expenses
   equals
5. Net profit (income) (net margin %).

Quite often the statement may be expanded to include more detail:

1. Sales revenue
   less

2. Cost of goods sold (which may detail such as raw materials and production costs)
   equals
3. Gross profit/margin
   less
   Specified direct operating expenses (which may include detail such as distribution operations and activities)
   equals
4. Operating profit/margin
   less
   Specified indirect operating expenses (which are likely to include depreciation and interest as well as 'administration')
   equals
5. Net profit before taxation
   less
6. Tax
   equals
7. Net profit after tax and before dividend payment
   less
   Dividends
   equals
8. Retained earnings transferred to Reserves

The income statement may be analysed either vertically, horizontally or clearly in both 'directions'. A *vertical* analysis relates each expense item to sales. Thus sales is taken as a base of 100 per cent and the expense items then expressed as a percentage of sales. Often this is accompanied by a *horizontal* analysis showing both actual values and percentage change factors over time.

The income statement can provide useful information to an organization concerning its own performance and that of its competitors and suppliers. Clearly the more detail that is made available the more useful the information. Details on raw materials purchases and production operating costs as a percentage of sales *and* overtime will give information to management (and competitors) on changes in productivity and possibly changes in production technology and methods. From a competitive point of view information on changes in margin performance (or their stability) will provide an indication of the vulnerability of a business to various competitive trusts.

The usefulness of information from the income statement to logistics management clearly depends upon the extent of disclosure. Indication of the amount of expense allocated to distribution, when compared with sales and possibly market share, can indicate the effectiveness of the level of expenditure. Add to this the output from customer satisfaction research, and the information (and conclusions) become very useful for the business's own purposes and for competitive analysis.

A more indirect use of income statement data concerns changes in the proportions of items such as interest payments (an increase in interest payment suggesting further investment has occurred in fixed assets (facilities and/or transport, information systems, etc.) or current assets (an increase in investment in inventory or perhaps accounts receivable as customer credit is expanded). To gain greater insight into the information offered by the income statement requires some data from other sources, i.e. the balance sheet and the sources and applications of funds. We shall consider this aspect subsequently.

■ The Balance Sheet

The balance sheet addresses six key features of a company's financial structure. Interpretations of data from each of these (and across the five elements) provides insight into the financial 'health' of the business and into its financial strategy. The topics comprising the balance sheet (together with their inter-relationships) are:

1. Fixed assets
   plus
2. Current assets
   less
3. Current liabilities
   equals
   Net assets
   equals
4. Shareholders' funds
   plus
5. Long-term debt
   equals
6. Capital employed

As with the income statement the balance sheet format and content varies. A detailed balance sheet is likely to offer data detailing the components of the key elements:

Fixed assets
  Land
  Buildings/property
  Plant and equipment
  Vehicles.
Intangible fixed assets
  Leases
  Brands
  Goodwill
  (plus)

Current assets
    Inventories (raw materials, work in progress and finished goods)
    Debtors
    (Accounts receivable) (possibly shown by age of debt outstanding)
    Cash (which may include near cash values)
    Prepaid items (tax payments, others for which incentive for prepayment exists)
    (less)
Current liabilities
    Trade creditors (payments due to suppliers)
    Overdraft (short-term loans (less than one year)
    Dividends declared and payable
    Payments due (during the next 12 months)
    (equals)
Net assets.
Long-term debt
    (plus)
Equity
    Ordinary shares issued
    Share premium account
    Retained earnings
    (equals)
Capital employed
Net assets equal Capital employed

An analysis of the balance sheet can be very helpful. It should be remembered, however, that the balance sheet reports the data it contains for *one specific day*, usually at the close of a trading year. This clearly restricts its usefulness, as often adjustments (window dressing!) may be made for reporting purposes. Nevertheless, analysis of such items as financial structure and its change over time can be very worthwhile. Much the same approach to analysing the balance sheet may be taken as that suggested for the income statement. Possibly the horizontal analysis (indicating the structure of assets and funding over time) will be more useful.

Changes in fixed assets (either acquisition, disposal or renewal) can indicate significant changes in logistics strategy. For example, an increase in facilities and/or the transportation fleet may suggest an increase in marketing activities aimed at increasing market share, or alternatively it may signal an effort to increase customer service. Any changes for these purposes would be likely to be accompanied by changes in current assets, specifically in inventory levels. An increase in accounts receivable (debtors) would suggest a broader expansion of customer service by offering extended credit facilities to customers.

Changes in current liabilities may also be revealing. For example, an increase in trade creditors may be an indication of cash flow problems (payments to suppliers are delayed to obtain longer use of sales receipts before payment is made). Similarly an increase in bank overdraft (particularly when accompanied by a decrease in cash items) will be additional evidence.

The balance sheet will also indicate term changes in the use of alternative funding methods. First of all an increase or expansion in finance indicates a change of strategy (as suggested a few paragraphs earlier for the reasons that assets may be increased); however, how the method of funding changes may be more significant. Financial gearing describes the relationship between shareholders' funds and long-term debt. Shareholder funds represent shareholders' investment in the business; long-term debt is quite different in that it is a commitment undertaken by the business to repay both the agreed interest (and the capital sum on a due date) out of the earnings generated by the business. Furthermore, the commitment to meet the interest payments continues regardless of the level of success delivered. Hence high levels of long term finance (high levels of financial gearing) can prove to be a constraint. An expansion of 'customer service assets' using debt is accompanied by relatively high levels of risk due to the vulnerability of any business that undertakes expansion on this basis, unless the growth forecast is favourable. As with the income statement, the balance sheet provides more information when considered together with other sources of information.

■ The Sources and Application of Funds Statement

Changes that occur to a company's assets and liabilities over a trading period are indicated in this report. It is useful when examining competitors' activities because any change that is made to an asset or funding component has a compensatory change elsewhere. For example an increase in stockholding will be matched by an increase in creditors or overdraft. Similarly, increases in assets (or their disposal) will be matched by changes in long-term fund totals. The sources and applications statement format varies by company but essentially shows the year on year changes for:

Sources of funds
    Pre-tax profit
    Depreciation
    Foreign exchange variances
    Loss on sale of assets
Total generated from operations
    Bank loans
    Fixed asset sale
    Divestments
    Issue of ordinary shares
    Bond/long term loan issues
Total sources of funds

Application of funds
  Acquisitions
  Purchases of tangible assets
Other investments
  Taxation
  Dividends
Increase in working capital
  Stocks
  Debtors
  Creditors
Increase in liquid funds

■ Applications of Funds

Clearly, if all three reports are analysed together with the chairman's or chief executive's report, a comprehensive picture of a company's strategy emerges. The implications for logistics are quite clear. Any changes to logistics strategy requiring a change in either fixed or current assets will be identified during the reporting process. Often the effects of such changes are logged and the investment changes usually occur ahead of their planned impact. The importance for competitive strategy should not pass unnoticed because the effect is the same for all companies. Hence an increase in fixed asset expenditure should be investigated. If it is for the development of distribution facilities, then a review of customer service performance may well suggest the changes in the service offer that may be expected.

Having discussed the main financial reports of the business and seen how they may be used to interpret changes occurring within the business, we now move on to consider the linkages between logistics activities and decisions and the individual reports.

■ The Influence of Logistics on the Income (Profit and Loss) Statement

Figure 4.1 shows the revenue and cost components of the profit and loss account together with some of the possible decisions that a company may make when considering a competitive stance. The influence that may be extended by the logistics function is shown alongside the competitive variable.

To increase *sales revenue* a company may well adjust its discount policy based upon volumes purchased. To do so effectively ideally requires a detailed knowledge of costs involved in processing and handling customers' orders (the topic of a subsequent chapter) but essentially based upon allocating as large a percentage of costs as may be identified in this process. Sales may also respond positively to 'customized' customer service packages. As we suggested in Chapter 3 it is possible to research customer expectations and the level of

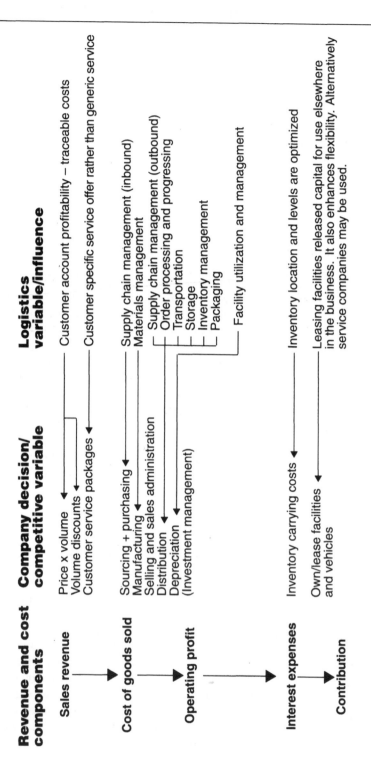

Figure 4.1 The influence of logistics on the profit and loss account

customer satisfaction achieved; thus it becomes possible to target service effectively.

Within the *cost of goods sold* items there are a number of opportunities to improve performance. Again a number of suggestions whereby logistics may exert an influence are made. Figure 4.1 proposes that effective supply chain management is the major influence on cost of goods sold and within this overall process the elements of physical distribution management are all included.

Interest expenses may be influenced by the decision to own or to lease facilities and by the inventory policy decisions of the business. Clearly the leasing costs will dilute profit contribution, but leasing (and the use of third-party distribution service companies) may ultimately prove to be less expensive. The issue involves availability of capital, control, and flexibility concerns.

■ **The Influence of Logistics on the Balance Sheet**

Logistics decisions also influence the asset and capital structure of the firm. Figure 4.2 identifies those logistics variables which may influence competitive decisions. Thus *fixed assets* may be influenced by the own-or-lease decisions, these being logistics infrastructure items. *Current assets* involve decisions on desired levels of liquidity, and here the influence of logistics management may be very significant. Figure 4.2 shows three important aspects of cost-effective logistics management. Inventory service levels will, if they are excessively high, reduce the level of liquidity through unnecessary stockholding. Accurate order processing and handling will ensure that complete orders reach customers within prescribed lead times, thereby permitting prompt invoicing and cash collection.

Logistics, as a function, competes with each of the other functions in the firm for investment funds. It is often possible to produce acceptable levels of service without owning the means by which the service is 'delivered'. Consequently, logistics management should be aware of the 'overall' issues, and evaluate leasing and distribution service company alternatives.

■ **The Influence of Logistics on the Sources and Applications of Funds (Funds Flow) Statement**

It will be recalled that earlier we described the sources and applications (funds flow) statement as a means by which a company can identify how its activities influence the structure of the assets and capital of the business over time. Figure 4.3 illustrates the logistics variables which create these changes. As can be seen, each of the variables has been mentioned in both the income statement and balance sheet discussions.

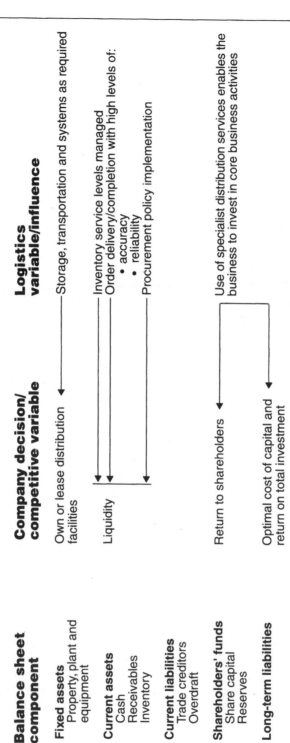

Figure 4.2 The influence of logistics on the balance sheet

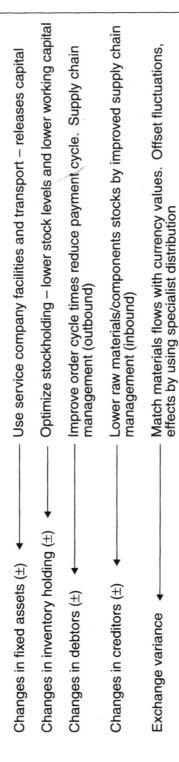

Figure 4.3 The influence of logistics on funds flow statement

The usefulness of this analysis is that it can be used to observe the effect of current activities and to evaluate alternative scenarios. Clearly an objective for any business is to restrict its use of funds to the levels of funding available. Thus a projection of alternative situations can provide management with a range of results *and* an objective view of the funding issues.

Finally in Figure 4.4 we consider the overall impact of logistics variables on the return on capital employed (or return on investment). We are in fact considering the influence of logistics on margin management and asset management which together are a measure of the return (earnings) on investment (fixed and net current assets) in the business.

Figure 4.4 outlines a concept which is important and one which we will develop in the subsequent section of this chapter. It is also a relationship central to managerial planning and control decisions.

■ Ratio Analysis

Information provided by the income statement and the balance sheet may be further evaluated using ratio analysis. The purpose of the analysis is to monitor the planned activities of the business using the relationships. The usefulness of ratio analysis was first demonstrated by the Du Pont Chemicals Company. Du Pont developed a hierarchy of ratios based upon the simple relationship between margin management and asset management:

Profit may be defined variously. At this juncture the term is used to imply excess revenue over costs.

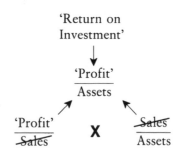

For a detailed analysis of a business a series of ratios may be constructed. There are a number of approaches available and all consider the important performance characteristics of a firm. Typically they are grouped to show specific characteristics of performance.

- Profitability ratios
- Operating (efficiency) ratios
- Financial structure ratios
- Investment ratios.

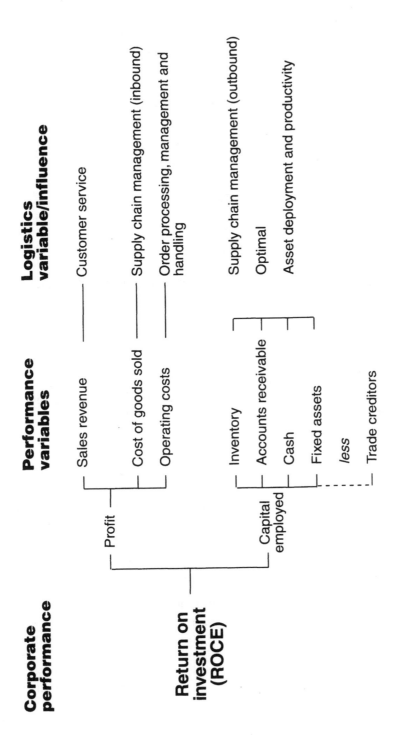

Figure 4.4   Impact of logistics on corporate financial performance

We are particularly interested in *profitability* and *efficiency* because these two groups of ratios reflect the impact of logistics on the business.

■ Profitability Ratios

There are five profitability ratios that are important:

Return on sales ROS (%) $\dfrac{\text{Profit}}{\text{Sales}}$ (carefully defined)

Asset turnover $\dfrac{\text{Sales}}{\text{Net assets}}$

Return on assets ROA (%) $\dfrac{\text{Profit}}{\text{Net assets}}$

Financial gearing $\dfrac{\text{Net assets}}{\text{Equity}}$ (alternatively: Debt/Equity)

Return on equity ROE (%) $\dfrac{\text{Profit}}{\text{Equity}}$

As explained above, the Du Pont approach linked ratios and activities as a component in its control process. The relationship between margin management and asset management may be expressed as follows:

$$\frac{\text{Profit}}{\text{Sales}} \times \frac{\text{Sales}}{\text{Assets}} = \frac{\text{Profit}}{\text{Assets}}$$

We can develop a 'profit chain' from this relationship by considering corporate funding:

$$\frac{\text{Profit}}{\text{Sales}} \times \frac{\text{Sales}}{\text{Net Assets}} = \frac{\text{Profit}}{\text{Assets}} \times \frac{\text{Net Assets}}{\text{Equity}} = \frac{\text{Profit}}{\text{Equity}}$$

Margin management	Asset management	Return on assets	Financial gearing	Return on equity
↓	↓			↓
Return on sales	Asset turnover			Return on shareholders' funds

This is a useful relationship because we can use it to evaluate current performance levels in context with each other *and* we may also pose 'what if?' questions. Consider the following example:

$$\frac{\text{'Profit'}}{\text{Sales}} \times \frac{\text{Sales}}{\text{Net Assets}} = \frac{\text{'Profit'}}{\text{Net Assets}} \times \frac{\text{Net Assets}}{\text{Equity}} = \frac{\text{'Profit'}}{\text{Equity}}$$

$$\frac{80}{800} \times \frac{800}{400} = \frac{80}{400} \times \frac{400}{200} = \frac{80}{200}$$

$$10\% \quad \times \quad 2 \quad = \quad 20\% \quad \times \quad 2 \quad = \quad 40\%$$

Supposing we dispose of our logistics infrastructure. We can evaluate the impact on the Return on equity. In disposing of the logistics infrastructure we release, say $150 million. However, we will find that our margins decrease because there is now an additional expense for the purchase of outside distribution services. However, if the capital is applied to the core business we can expect overall margins to improve. With these assumptions included the result may be:

$$\frac{\text{'Profit'}}{\text{Sales}} \times \frac{\text{Sales}}{\text{Net Assets}} = \frac{\text{'Profit'}}{\text{Net Assets}} \times \frac{\text{Net Assets}}{\text{Equity}} = \frac{\text{'Profit'}}{\text{Equity}}$$

$$\downarrow \qquad\qquad \downarrow \qquad\qquad \downarrow$$

$$\frac{90}{800} \times \frac{800}{400} = \frac{90}{400} \times \frac{400}{200} = \frac{70}{200}$$

$$11.25\% \quad \times \quad 2 \quad = \quad 22.5\% \quad \times \quad 2 \quad = \quad 45\%$$

■ Efficiency Ratios

There are three efficiency ratios that may be influenced by logistics decisions, particularly by effective supply chain management. They involve aspects of working capital (net current assets) and are a measure of how effectively an organization manages its procurement and inbound materials flows, its stocks of raw materials, work in progress and finished goods, and its physical distribution (i.e. order processing, handling and delivery) to ensure it can invoice promptly and collect its outstanding accounts:

Procurement ratios

$$\text{Purchases turnover} \quad = \quad \frac{\text{Purchase per trading period}}{\text{Trade creditors}}$$
$$\text{(Accounts payable)}$$

Days stock held $=$ $\dfrac{\text{Trading period (in days)}}{\text{Purchases turnover}}$

Inventory ratios

Inventory turnover $=$ $\dfrac{\text{Cost of good sold}}{\text{Inventory}}$

Inventory cover $=$ $\dfrac{\text{Trading period (in days)}}{\text{Inventory turnover}}$

Receivable ratios

Receivables turnover $=$ $\dfrac{\text{Credit sales}}{\text{Accounts receivable}}$

Days credit allowed $=$ $\dfrac{\text{Trading period (in days)}}{\text{Accounts receivable turnover}}$

Each set of ratios enables the organization to consider alternative targets for levels of accounts payable and receivable and inventory levels. We can demonstrate the principle of this by taking inventory holding as an example.

Consider the following ratios:

$ million

Inventory turnover $=$ $\dfrac{\text{Cost of sales}}{\text{Inventory}}$ $=$ $\dfrac{800}{80}$

$=$ 10 times

Inventory cover $=$ $\dfrac{\text{Trading period}}{\text{Inventory turnover}}$ $=$ $\dfrac{800}{10}$

$=$ 36.5 days

Assume now that due to changes in the service offered to customers and 'delivery' systems we can reduce the inventory cover and opt for a 20-day period. The target inventory holding value can then be calculated thus:

$\dfrac{\text{Actual inventory \$}}{\text{Inventory cover}}$ $\times$ Target cover $=$ Target inventory $

$\dfrac{80}{36.5}$ $\times$ 20 $=$ $43.8 million

The cost savings this represents can be calculated:

	$ million
Actual inventory	80.0
Target inventory	43.8
Reduction	36.2

If the company pays 15 per cent on overdraft we have a cost saving of:

$$\text{Reduction} \quad \times \quad \text{interest rate}$$
$$36.2 \quad \times \quad \frac{15}{100} \quad = \quad \$5.43 \text{ million}$$

The same principle may be used for accounts payable and receivable. There are other issues to be considered. One issue concerns service to customers, and here care should be taken not to affect adversely the availability levels of core products. Another issue relates to other costs (such as transportation and order communications) that may be affected by such changes. If these do not increase appreciably then clearly the option is both economically and 'politically' viable in the context of supplier/customer relations.

■ Creating Value for the Shareholder

Shareholder value is measured in a number of ways. Some proponents of the concept use a measure based upon current levels of profitability and share price, together with a measure of the return on equity spread (i.e. the return generated less the cost of the equity capital); negative measures suggest that rather than creating value the business is destroying it, and clearly positive values are adding value.

An alternative measure of shareholder value is based upon a discounted present value of the revenues likely to be generated by a strategy option. While this is financially oriented it is focused on future activities and outcomes and does present an opportunity for the firm to evaluate supply chain options, customer service alternatives and any significant influence they may have on the cash flows.

There are a number of stages in the shareholder value analysis. They are relatively simple and follow the accepted methods of investment appraisal, i.e.

- Estimating the cash flows net of fixed and variable costs, taxes and investments in fixed and working capital.
- Obtaining the discounted value of the profit stream by applying the cost of capital for the business.
- Estimating the residual value of the business unit.

The total shareholder value is then the sum of the present values of future cash flows and residual values less the market value of any debt associated with that element of the business.

It can be seen that alternative supply chain structures can have an influence on these cost elements and the differential service performance that is available may have an impact on revenues generated. Therefore we should consider the implications of decision alternatives on the value delivered to the shareholder.

■ Summary

This chapter has demonstrated how a comprehensive understanding of the impact of logistics decisions on corporate revenues and costs is essential if effective resource allocation is to be realised.

A review of the primary financial reporting instruments and their use in a supply chain context was discussed. The reports discussed in detail were the income statement, the balance sheet, and the sources and application of funds statement. For each report the influence of supply chain decisions was considered in detail. The application of standard financial ratios to measure the impact of logistics decisions was introduced. Examples using an application of the Du Pont ratio model were worked through using alternative logistics infrastructure systems. The importance of developing a thorough understanding of intra- and inter-organisational influences on overall financial performance was discussed and examples given.

CHAPTER 5

Intra-Company Cross-Functional Roles in Logistics

■ Introduction

As the role of logistics within corporations expands, it can be difficult to identify the precise role of logistics. Many managers view logistics as a coordinating or perhaps facilitating activity. It is argued that in the 1970s the distribution function comprised a smaller number of functions and activities which were seen as individual in their nature and 'owned' by departmental managers. An important aspect of the logistics management task is to coordinate the activities of the traditional distribution functions *together with* liaising with purchasing, materials planning, manufacturing, marketing and often research development (R&D). In addition, logistics managers are becoming increasingly involved in supply markets and in customers' logistics issues. Within the business, logistics management is also becoming involved in financial issues and in strategic planning. Furthermore, the role of logistics alongside marketing management to effect delivery of the customer is a major task.

This suggests an internal and external aspect to the topic, and in this chapter we shall consider the role of logistics in maximizing customer service by performing a coordinating role within the company and a similar activity across external functions.

■ The Environment of Logistics Management

The complex environment within which logistics operates is described by Figure 5.1. The focus point of any logistics activity should be the customer, and this is represented by the *customer service characteristics* which were discussed in the earlier chapters. Figure 5.1 suggests that the customer service offer or response is developed by a specific combination of the logistics variables and considers trade-off situations among them. It also suggests that to be effective logistics management should have a broader mandate, one of coordinating overall activities or functions within the organization. The assumption made is that the primary objective of the logistics system is to

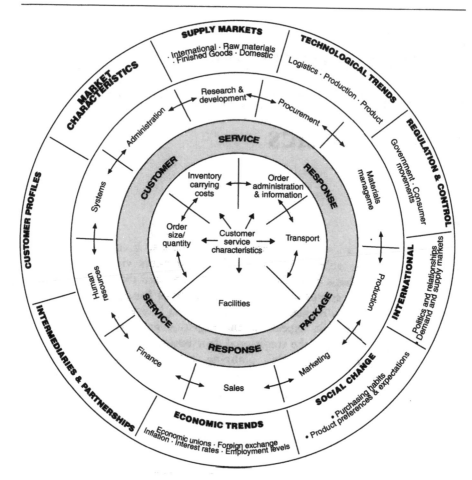

Figure 5.1   The environment of logistics management

make a cost-effective response to customers' service requirements: hence the focal point is the customer.

Increasingly the influence of the logistics function has expanded as the scope of many businesses has become global. One problem that arises because of this situation is that it is difficult to identify the exact scope of the logistics function. If we consider the concept of logistics to be that of managing a pipeline which is in effect part of the total supply chain through which product flows to the end consumer, it allows many of the basic principles of effective logistics management to be drawn together. The objective is to ensure that the flow is smooth and continuous and, at the same time, ensures that the time from supplier to end user minimized. This implies that:

- Relationships with suppliers are managed to ensure a smooth changeover *into* the organization.
- Inventory may be held by members of the supply chain pipeline to buffer variances in demand. However it is not necessary that inventory need be held by *all* parties.
- Information is used along the pipeline to facilitate the flow to the next stage and to replace inventory, e.g. point-of-sale information in sales outlets being relayed to suppliers creates replenishment and production orders.
- Trade-offs can be identified, i.e. it may be possible to trade off higher costs in one area against a lower overall cost or perhaps for improvements in service. It is possible that these trade-offs may even exist outside the firm, i.e. lower sourcing costs will give reduced material costs.
- It follows that time becomes a critical measure of how effectively the 'pipeline' operates.

See Figure 5.2 for an illustration of this concept.

■ The Internal Environment of Logistics Management

We can view the logistics internal environment from two perspectives. First there are the activities for which the function has *direct* control. These were identified in Chapter 1 (i.e. order administration and information, transport, facilities, order size/quantity and inventory costs). We shall be discussing each of these in some detail in subsequent chapters.

The other internal functions with which the logistics function is in contact and over which it exercises some *indirect* control or influence are the conventional business activities. Figure 5.1 illustrates these. The reason for such coordination to be encouraged may be explained by the logistics pipeline effect described earlier. The essence of an effective business is the management of resources conversion. This should be delivered with a minimum overall total cost but with the addition of sufficient value to meet customer satisfaction. Another way of viewing this issue is to consider the process as one which adds utility through a conversion process. Thus raw materials are 'transported' to a production process which adds form utility to the raw materials and creates a useable product. However, until the finished product reaches its ultimate owner/end user then it lacks complete utility, and it is only when the 'place' utility is added to those of 'form' and 'time' that customer satisfaction will be realized. We suggest that a logistics function is necessary if form, time and place utility are to be coordinated and done so at optimal cost.

Figure 5.1 suggests that the logistics function is well able to identify trade-off potentials between and among these functions. Furthermore it has been suggested by a number of authors that it has the ability and facility to act as

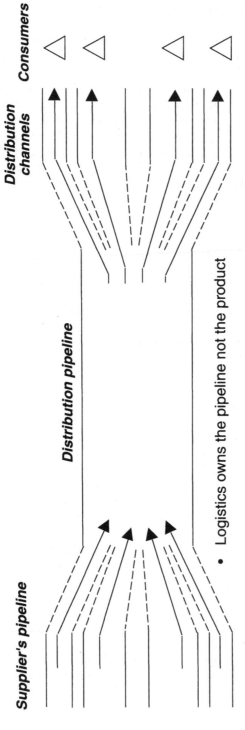

Figure 5.2   The logistics pipeline

a fulcrum for decision-making, primarily because of its involvement with time and place utilities. Some examples will amplify this suggestion.

■ The Direct Control Environment

Logistics management has direct responsibility for the coordination and control of the 'logistics mix' activities (order administration, transport, facilities, order size/quantity and inventory costs). In the not too distant past these were often separate functions or activities with *individual* managers, tasks and therefore objectives. Consequently each function sought to maximize its own objectives: for example, *order administration and information* activities might attempt to process an ever increasing number of orders and enquiries. This may occur despite accuracy, and accordingly credit checks may be overlooked or superficial and order progressing enquiries serviced ineffectively.

These and other similar 'cross inefficiencies' are avoided by the creation of an overall coordinating role in the form of the logistics function. The effectiveness of this approach can be seen by considering Table 5.1 which identifies the cross-functional concerns involved. In Table 5.1 we identify four customer service characteristics (this clearly is not an exhaustive list) and consider the issues confronting the 'logistics mix' activities.

It can be seen immediately that some aspects of customer service can impose cost penalties. For example, *frequent deliveries*, a not uncommon requirement by customers operating JIT production systems can result in a number of problem areas. Indeed, Table 5.1 suggests that for each of the activities other than *inventory carrying costs and facilities* there are disadvantages. Shorter order cycle times will lead to a similar result.

The conclusion that is reached is simple, if difficult to interpret and implement: customer service decisions require careful analysis. It follows that unless it can be demonstrated that the overall benefits of a specified level of customer service exceed the overall costs then there is obvious doubt concerning the efficacy of that particular customer service offer. The benefit of a coordinating function (such as that offered by a logistics management role) is that trade-off situations across the mix can be explored. Furthermore alternatives can be explored, as can alternative logistics systems structures.

An excellent (if not dated) example can be found in the decisions taken by a UK-based automobile manufacturer. During the early 1980s it was found that the costs of maintaining inventories of parts in Scandinavia were excessive in comparison with the returns obtained. Parts were transported by sea to Norway and Sweden. The entire range of service parts was maintained in a number of locations. Usage began to suggest seasonal trends and also identified the slow-moving items. As a result of a study to identify cost-effective alternatives, a radical solution emerged. The range cover was reduced with only fast-moving (and some medium-moving) parts being held on territory, with the remainder being serviced by air freight from the Midlands-based distribution centre in the UK. Figure 5.3 illustrates the situation as it was and as it became. The example

Table 5.1 Examples of varying cross-functional issues when determining customer service logistics mix function

Customer service characteristics	Order administration and information	Transport	Facilities	Order size/quantity	Inventory carrying costs
More frequent deliveries	*Disadvantage:* Increases processing costs	*Disadvantage:* Increased costs. Lowers utilization	*Disadvantage:* Increased labour cost + inventory movements *Advantage:* Reduces space and cube requirements	*Disadvantage:* Possibility of uneconomic unit loads	*Advantage:* Lowers inventory holding costs *Disadvantage:* Increased OOS probability
Shortened order cycle time	*Disadvantage:* Increases processing and progressing costs	*Disadvantage:* Increases delivery frequency and scheduling costs	*Disadvantage:* Increased handling costs	*Disadvantage:* Possibility of uneconomic unit loads	*Advantage:* Lowers inventory holding costs *Disadvantage:* Increased OOS probability
Increases in delivery reliability		*Disadvantage:* Increases costs *Advantage:* Increases scheduling efficiency	*Disadvantage:* Increased supervision costs		*Advantage:* Increases inventory management efficiency *Disadvantage:* Increased stockholding costs
Increased stock availability/ continuity of supply		*Disadvantage:* Back order deliveries will increase costs	*Disadvantage:* Increases space and cube requirements		*Disadvantage:* Increases stockholding costs

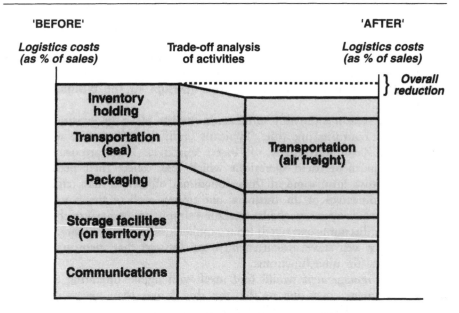

Figure 5.3   The concept of 'trade-off' in distribution and logistics: an example

is a good case study to demonstrate how an increase in one logistics element, in this case transportation (air freight replaced sea freight) can lower the overall costs of service. In addition to the reduction of logistics costs there were economies from reduced obsolescence of a number of service parts.

■ The Indirect Control Environment

Let us consider the sequence of, say, R&D, procurement, materials management, production scheduling and marketing. An unsatisfied customer need may be identified to R&D where initial activities would benefit considerably if, together with a projection of market volume potential, additional information concerning 'shelf life' expectancy or other supply chain characteristics were identified. This would help prescribe materials inputs, packaging, and so on, in the process of developing a product with 'ideal' customer expectancy characteristics.

More direct is the influence that logistics management can have on sales and marketing results. Sales volume can be directly influenced by an effectively managed level of customer service and may also be enhanced by the introduction of new technology.

At the level of strategic planning there is usually a major input from logistics management. There are a number of reasons why this should be the case. First, the logistic activity is responsible for the management of a significant amount of corporate assets (facilities, vehicles and inventories) and expenses (usages and transport operating costs) can only represent two of the more dominant cost centres. The other reason for this involvement is the broad (but detailed) understanding that the logistics function develops of the business and its functions.

This latter reason is possibly sufficient in itself to place the logistics function in a central coordinating role. Typically individual functions within the business will have, individually, self-based objectives. These are usually based on those aspects of their operations which best reflect their performance. Table 5.2 shows how some of these functional objectives may conflict with the overall objectives of the business *and* among each of the functions. For example, if *procurement* was to be measured simply on the basis of the margins generated (or discounts extracted) from suppliers, then while this single focused objective may well serve procurement it can be seen that there may well be disadvantages for other functions.

Materials management would find itself with higher operating costs (and initial investment costs due to the fact that larger than necessary storage facilities would have been built). *Marketing* could find that full prices for products were not obtainable owing either to excess stocks or perhaps 'dated' merchandise (or possibly both). *Finance*, too, would be operating less than effectively: excess stockholding implies a requirement for more working capital than is necessary.

Another example, one which is not unusual, concerns the width of the product usage offer. A *wide product range* may give *marketing* the advantage of wider appeal for customers, and may also increase the size of *sales* transactions. However, it has a number of disadvantages. A wide product range requires a larger stockholding of raw materials (a disadvantage for *procurement, materials management* and *production*). *Finance* is faced with higher working capital requirements.

It follows that an overall coordinating role by the logistics function which uses its skills in managing 'stocks and flows' through procurement, materials management, production and the physical distribution of finished products is invaluable at both the strategic and operational levels of business planning.

■ The External Environment of Logistics Management

Each of the external elements represented on the periphery of Figure 5.1 has significant meaning for logistics management. Their effects may be felt over differing time scales. Furthermore, the nature and timing of their impact may change and may well be related to changes in one or more of the other elements. A brief review of each of the topics may put their relationships to logistics in perspective.

Table 5.2 Examples of conflicting functional objectives

Functional objectives	Procurement	Materials management	R&D	Production	Marketing	Sales	Finance
						Functions	
Product excellence and quality			*Advantage:* Maximizes skills and expertise	*Disadvantage:* High costs of quality control	*Advantage:* Exclusivity competitive advantage	*Advantage:* Easier to sell	*Disadvantage:* Increases both investment and operating costs. Longer investment recovery
Bulk purchases of materials	*Advantage:* Larger discounts	*Disadvantage:* Higher storage costs		*Disadvantage:* Damage and obsolescence risks and costs	*Disadvantage:* Markdowns may result from excess and obsolete stocks		*Disadvantage:* Working capital commitment
Long production runs		*Disadvantage:* Higher storage costs		*Advantage:* Low costs	*Disadvantage:* Narrow product range	*Disadvantage:* Low average transaction values	*Disadvantage:* Working capital commitment: High finished goods inventory
Wide product range	*Disadvantage:* Lower discounts on low purchase volumes may occur	*Disadvantage:* High storage and stock obsolescence costs		*Disadvantage:* Short, high cost production methods. Higher WIP stocks	*Advantage:* Widens appeal of offer	*Advantage:* Increases average transaction values	*Disadvantage:* Working capital commitment: High finished goods inventory

■ Supply Markets

There are a number of issues here, and the main areas of interest concern the expansion of sourcing into international markets. For a number of well-organised companies there exist structured sourcing plans which have been established on the basis of using existing skills in 'emerging' countries.

For example, there are a number of Western European manufacturers and retailers who very quickly evaluated the skills bases of the Eastern European countries as they abandoned communism. Their rationale was based on the known traditional skills levels together with the knowledge of current labour rates and assumptions concerning the medium- and long-term effects of inflation. With this knowledge a procurement/sourcing plan was evolved with the help of logistics management who were able to analyse the likely logistics considerations and therefore the impact of these on costs of raw materials, components and finished goods.

■ Technological Trends

Technology has made a major impact on all aspects of industrial activity. The influence of information technology has changed the nature of business operations beyond recognition. The impact on logistics has been twofold. Not only have logistics functions been required to assimilate changes such as EPOS data capture and EDI (electronic point-of-sale and electronic data interchange) and respond in terms of organization and operating methods, but logistics as a function has been required to change to accommodate changes in other functions. For example IT has been the basis for the introduction of *just-in-time* manufacturing methods and in marketing, lower costs of equipment and increased memory capabilities have introduced *data base marketing* into manufacturing and retailing. The application of technology to production processes and to products has required logistics to consider its response to shorter lead times in production and in customer service response. In addition, the nature of many products has changed. Products have changed shape, size and value. Some have undergone complete changes of physical characteristics requiring the development of new logistics technology; the food industry is a very good example of how changes in products (such as convenience foods) have brought about entirely new logistics systems for the delivery of chilled products.

■ Regulation and Control

The previous topic is closely related to regulation and control. The accuracy and reliability of technology has enabled the legislators to introduce stringent conditions for the delivery and sale of many products. The control of food distribution would be very difficult without the knowledge that temperature control equipment and vehicle performance reliability are at very high levels.

Thus it is possible for government to impose strict requirements concerning the delivery and selling ambience of perishable products (particularly food and drugs requiring temperature control). There are other aspects to this topic. Quality control and consumer protection across a range of product sectors have increased and there are many issues for logistics managers to concern themselves with. For example, the increased 'rights' that have accompanied consumer legislation concerning product liability (and performance) have increased the number of returns of defective products.

This is particularly important in products for very small children where faults which appear in products may be dangerous and require immediate replacement or rectification. Consequently *reverse distribution* becomes important if customer goodwill is to be maintained.

■ International Politics and Relationships

In recent years there have been a number of changes in international relations which have (or may) influence the patterns of demand and supply markets. The removal of sanctions, subsequent to an international agreement, in South Africa has opened a market opportunity for many products and eased the situation for South African exporters. Both require the attention of logistics management to ensure cost-effective 'stocks and flows' systems. The general, overall reduction of tension in many parts of the globe also changes the pattern of expenditure. With less of the GDP allocated to military expenditures, more may be allocated to industrial and consumer goods (over time) thus resulting in an increase in product flows. Again these are issues of concern for logistics managers. Clearly there are situations where the reverse is occurring (the Balkans) and the logistics role may not be commercial. Rather, here is a need for the expertise (and capacity) to be applied to supporting the shipment of aid supplies.

■ Social Change

Social change begets consumer change and behaviour. Typically consumer preferences evolve and change over extended time periods and consequently the implications of change may be monitored and accommodated. An exception may be fad and fashion markets, but changes in these markets are often 'product' changes rather than large capacity changes and as such do not usually create significant problems for logistics management. Often the important consumer changes are those of 'delivery' preferences.

The potential growth of home shopping will present logistics management with opportunities (and challenges) to develop systems which can accommodate multi-deliveries at customer designated times. The problems associated with such systems are not totally new: furniture and consumer durables manufacturers and retailers have been working together to achieve this for some time. The majority of large multiple durables retailers have arrangements with suppliers whereby they maintain sales floor merchandise stocks and sell from

that of their supplier; delivery is effected from the supplier (manufacturers')
stockholding. It follows that while the problems of home delivery of fast-
moving consumer goods have some major differences, the overall problem is
not new.

■ Economic Trends

As the interests of large businesses expand and become global in their nature so
the impact of local economic trends became important. Logistics management
is one area of management where some solutions are available. The truly global
companies do have logistics systems able to respond to changes in long term
inflation and fluctuating exchange rates. Responsive logistics management is
often the only way in which increasing procurement costs may be contained,
either by utilizing more cost-effective transportation modes or methods; i.e.
using lower cost transport modes or preferably using *partnering arrangements*
with other companies whose problems are similar. The growth of economic
unions is likely to present new challenges to logistics management.

The expansion of the European Union, the North American Free Trade Area,
and the Asian grouping will see some interesting developments. One obvious
challenge will be the aggregation of the impact of economic trends. The recent
(1989/94) recession in Europe had a dampening effect on both industrial and
consumer markets, and therefore on expenditure. In these circumstances there
are considerable problems for business whose sales volume is concentrated
within that economic area. For example, UK companies have some 70–80 per
cent of their turnover within the Union.

A prolonged recession can, therefore, be damaging unless the variable costs
of operations can be minimized. Alternatively, other markets may be considered, but these are often long term and require considerable amounts of
information outlining the structure of markets and demand. However, it is
(or could be) a logistics task to identify the 'stocks and flows' characteristics
and to monitor the potential infrastructure and its costs in order that businesses
take every opportunity available to spread the increased risk that the growth of
trade blocs may bring. Logistics management should be permitted to play an
increasing role in global and international business decisions. The disciplines
that have been developed over recent years, i.e. the ability to look *across*
solutions and see trade-off opportunities and the ability to coordinate functional activities, will prove invaluable as global enterprise increases.

■ Intermediaries and Partnerships

There has been an increase in the interest in both transaction channels and
physical distribution channels. One aspect of this interest has been focused on
increasing the cooperation between supplier and distributor in conventional
channel structures. The growth in market importance of multiple retailers has
resulted in board level appointments responsible for retailer liaison at the

supplier level. This has developed out of the *trade marketing* structures that were seen as an answer to distributor expectations for specific, rather than generic, service packages in the early and mid-1980s. The other aspect of intermediaries and partnerships is perhaps more interesting.

It is concerned with identifying, as partners, companies who share mutual trade objectives, strategies and target markets (and customers) but who may have less than effective delivery systems. As markets expand and develop in locations which are increasingly distant, economies of scale become very significant.

These may extend throughout the supply chain, from procurement of materials and components to servicing end users. It is now not unusual to find both vertical (partnership) and horizontal (alliance) relationships in most industrial sectors which results in sustained cooperation. Perhaps the longest alliances are those that have been established between manufacturers and retailers with distribution companies; Marks & Spencer and BOC Transhield is one such alliance of very long standing. We shall be discussing partnerships and alliances in a subsequent chapter.

■ Customer Profiles

An important consideration for both marketing and logistics is an understanding of the customer (or customers). Chapter 2 described in some detail the rationale behind the concept of strategic alignment, and the methodology used to ensure that the prescribed strategy is one which is relevant when addressing one (or more) market segment(s). This is a concept with particular meaning for logistics management and the reader is advised to consider Figures 2.13, 2.14 and 2.15 to review the topics described there and reflect upon their relevance and importance in this discussion. It follows that within the overall context of strategy decisions a clear customer profile concerning the relative importance of elements of customer service be established alongside those developed by marketing for product purposes.

■ Market Characteristics

By market characteristics we are suggesting that specific market structures usually produce expected types of behaviour. For example, a monopolist may be in a position to determine (even dictate) levels of service to customers. Clearly they have no alternative sources of supply. However, it should be noted that such behaviour is likely to encourage the monopolist's customers to work hard at identifying alternatives (even alternative production processes) in order to be more in control of their own production and indeed marketing activities. By contrast, the situation in highly competitive markets makes for interesting situations.

There are indications that the lack of growth in markets is leading to a search for market niches by both industrial and consumer markets with the specialization that this implies, which also leads to situations in which the companies competing attempt to establish sustainable competitive advantages by using customer service creatively. In these situations it is not uncommon for them to attempt to identify elements of a customers' value chain to which considerable benefits might be added if they can develop an appropriate service characteristic. This is also a topic to which we shall return in the next section.

The discussion hitherto suggests that logistics interfaces with two particularly important activities: marketing and manufacturing. We shall complete this chapter by considering both interface situations in detail.

■ The Logistics/Marketing Interface

As we have seen earlier in this chapter, logistics operates (together with all other business functions and activities) in a dynamic environment, both internally and externally to the organization.

We can summarize the external environment faced by both marketing and logistics functions in any company as:

- Rapidly changing economic circumstances:
    Few growth markets,
    High levels of unemployment.
- Market fragmentation:
    A polarization into 'up-market' (high quality and high price) and 'down market (low quality and low price (both viable as means of differentiation)) which is putting pressure on organizations with neither of these (or other) forms of differentiation,
    The search for 'exclusive' market niches, and the growth of specialist 'delivery' systems.
- Competitive intensity:
    As market growth opportunities decline, competition becomes more intense.

■ Issues for Marketing and Logistics

As industries have become increasingly globalized, we have been faced with worldwide marketing, worldwide sourcing, and worldwide logistics support. The mechanics involved in coordinating trade activities have become immensely complicated.

The extended length of the logistics pipeline, coupled with customer demand for shorter lead times, blurs the traditional functional boundaries which continue to exist in many companies. Responsibilities overlap as organizations ensure that customers' service expectations are met. This complexity suggests a question: who owns the product as it moves?

A simple example from retailing shows that as the product moves through the supplier/retailer systems ownership is transferred at different points in the system. The organizational divisions of distribution, operations and 'delivery' are managed by different people at different times.

As the movement through the pipeline increases in speed so should its *visibility*. In other words all members of the pipeline require to know *where* the product is at any time, regardless of its ownership. This notion raises the issue of time as a resource and from this developed the concept of *strategic lead time management* (SLTM).

Strategic lead time management focuses on the resource aspect of time and attaches a value which may be measured. Companies are now recognizing the impact that reducing time spent by products in the logistics pipeline not only provides quicker response to customers' demands but also increases stock turn and reduces the need for working capital (Tully, 1994). Tully reports on a number of large businesses who have undertaken to reduce their stockholding such that they intend to operate on 'negative working capital' (in other words they will be using their suppliers' working capital because stock turnover will be such that it will be used (sold) before payment is required by supplier). It follows that a company should look *across* functions to identify lead time excesses and measure the time spent. The maxim clearly is: does the time add value to the *whole* system. SLTM involves tracking the length of time inventories of raw materials, components and finished goods spend in the pipeline until they are sold to end-users. Figure 5.4 is an example of how more sophisticated members of the marketing channel are endeavouring to 'influence' the lead time of their suppliers as well as manage their own logistics systems better. SLTM implies that it is more effective to measure the overall or cumulative effect of the use of time within the channel rather than just that of individual channel members.

A startling example is provided by Volvo who found that the total lead time from steel ingot to finished crankshaft installed in a vehicle was six months in the following proportions:

Manufacturing/processing	50 minutes
Internal/external transport	22 hours
Idle time	5 months 29 days

Market conditions also exert a strong influence. Shortening product life cycles are presenting challenges and opportunities. Frequent product changes, a response to customer demand expectations, can lead to difficulties. Philips found that for colour television production the lead time from components to 'point of sale' was six months. But the product life cycle of the model was only twelve months! A distributor of fax machines had to order from the manufacturer five months in advance – the product life cycle was eighteen months.

The foregoing discussion suggests that markets are individual and requiring specific responses. The discipline of strategic alignment and its 'logics' offers an opportunity to understand expectations better and to service these more effectively by using a structure relevant to the strategic implementation

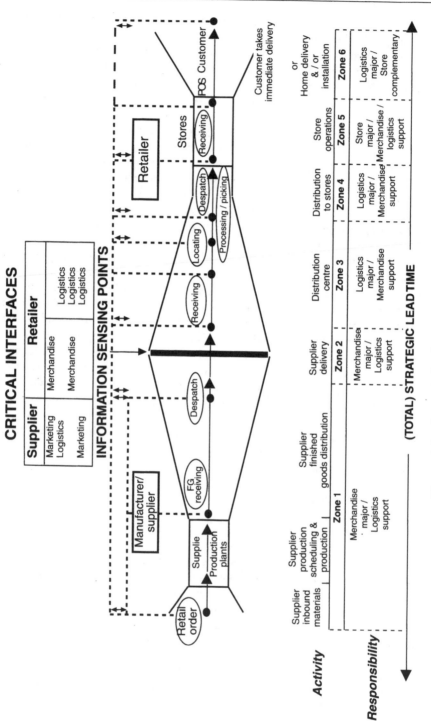

Figure 5.4 Strategic lead time management

requirements that such an overall market structure requires. The discussion surrounding Figure 2.15 responds to these issues.

■ The Logistics/Manufacturing Interface

From the previous discussion we suggest that while logistics does not own the product it does *own and manage the pipeline*. Because of this it follows that logistics management should work closely with those other activities that add value to the resources controlled by the business.

There are five issues to which logistics should relate if it is to achieve its 'traffic management' function effectively. These are:

- Forecasting methods
- Customer service levels and supporting systems
- Supplier systems and system integration
- Plant/branch network configuration
- Master production schedules.

■ Forecasting

It is interesting to observe the increase in the role of forecasting to satisfy corporate profitability demands *as well* as satisfying customer demand. This is not to suggest that forecasting customer demand is any less important, rather forecasting should be aimed at identifying which customers are likely to respond such that corporate profitability objectives *as well* as customer satisfaction will be achieved. This is important with the changes currently occurring in many customer industries. As we saw above (Tully, 1994) there is a tendency by many companies to move towards reducing inventory levels to an absolute minimum, zero if at all possible. To do this successfully the forecasting method used should fulfil a number of criteria:

- Is it comprehensive in its coverage of all of the component activities or functions on the pipeline?
- Does it provide the most timely and accurate estimates of demand available?
- Does it cover the appropriate time period?
- Does the period of time being used to record sales provide the basis for forecasting sales?
- Does it consider all of the variations required? For example, a company may operate across a range of industry sectors, some using JIT methods with others using long lead times in R&D, single-sourced companies.

New product launches pose additional problems, as often the market size/ potential is not known and many new products utilize new processes and materials making communication of requirements within the pipeline very difficult.

■ Customer Service

Logistics management is often placed in a very difficult situation. Sales/ marketing management often assumes the production process to be totally flexible or, if not, that there is infinite inventory available together with delivery capacity.

The role of logistics in these situations is to work with both manufacturing and sales/marketing to assess capability and demand and to attempt (with colleagues) to match both to achieve customer satisfaction *and* corporate profit expectations. An important aspect of this role is to identify (with both sales/ marketing and manufacturing) how the available capacity may best be used. An example of the problems that can and do occur can be found in a large biscuit and snack product manufacturer who, as well as marketing a range of successful national brands, operated a very successful 'own label' business. A salesman returned from what he considered to be a very successful sales call during which he had persuaded his customer to double his order size for the forthcoming sales period (some three months). He was, however, unaware of the fact that the plant was operating at near full capacity and that far from being welcome the news of this increased order size was an embarrassment. To complete the order, which it was decided to do because the customer was a major retail multiple, it was necessary to increase the number of shifts and doing so added considerably to the production costs; the cost increases eroded what was already a very narrow margin. At that time there was no overall logistics management function.

■ Supplier Systems Integration

As the companies within the pipeline seek to reduce operating costs and at the same time find that customers are setting similar objectives, the overall lead time reduces. This suggests that an attempt should be made to integrate suppliers into a single supply chain. This may be achieved through a combination of events: negotiations within the pipeline may result in a series of strategic partnerships (vertical combinations), while the implementation of sophisticated information systems (such as EDI) will also be necessary.

The key to success is an understanding of the role of logistics within (and between) business, particularly their materials movement management *and* information management. Subsequent chapters will expand this notion and describe techniques such as distribution resource planning and materials resource planning and how they help with integrating suppliers' systems.

■ Plant/Branch Configuration

The primary objective of the logistics system is to achieve customer satisfaction. Customer satisfaction may not necessarily be a 'quantitative' issue alone. That is to say that customers typically have prescribed levels of servicing relating to availability and delivery reliability. However, they also have 'qualitative' service issues. Often these may seem to be unrealistic. For example, some beer drinkers are prepared to pay a premium for a beer brewed and bottled in its country of origin. The logical, cost-effective, logistics answer would be to brew the beer locally but this would mean the customers' image of the product would change and the product's competitive differentiation and advantage be minimized.

This suggests that the plant/branch network should first be established on the basis of consumer/market positioning characteristics. Then the logistics network operates to ensure a cost-effective solution to the production/physical distribution issues that emerge.

Clearly there are other issues. Organizations in extractive industries (e.g. cement) usually find that the economics of production and distribution strongly influence their decision to produce at the source of raw materials (the waste materials representing well in excess of 50 per cent of the total raw material used). By contrast, motor vehicle accessory manufacturers (brakes, electrical systems, etc.) often manufacture close to the plants of their customers. Increasingly, the global business uses its sophisticated intelligence systems to evaluate the overall impact of future events and developments in order to optimize the size and shape of the logistics network.

■ Master Production Schedules

The master production schedule (MPS) is an attempt to combine the interests of all participants in the logistics pipeline and to encourage their involvement (and commitment) to a single document or plan which essentially is concerned with meeting inventory volume and location requirements within the capacity constraints of the overall pipeline. As such it is the single instrument that demonstrates an integrated plan for:

- Finished goods inventory levels
- Customer service in terms of inventory availability
- Machine utilization
- Capacity utilization
- Labour productivity
- Output levels and
- The identification of points in the system which will require reinforcement (i.e. additional labour at specific times).

As Greenhalgh (1994) comments, 'Clearly the MPS may be used as a vehicle to integrate a number of parties into the planning and decision-making process with the result being a superior plan which, when executed, results in superior customer service'.

We can summarize the short-medium and long-term significance of these issues for the logistics/manufacturing interface with the following table.

Interface issue	Short-mid term	Longer term
Forecasting	Stock availability	Capability and flexibility decisions, production planning and control systems
Customer-oriented systems	Effective production planning and sales order processing	Formalized information links
Supplier-oriented systems	Effective materials planning and control	Strategic alliance with suppliers permits integration into overall customer supply chain
Plant/branch warehouse configuration	Overall cost and service impact	Major structural input into reducing overall supply costs
Master production schedule (MPS)	Stock availability	Integrate marketing logistics manufacturing decision-making and suppliers

■ **Summary**

The role of logistics has extended beyond company boundaries and has become a link between the company, its suppliers and its customers.

The focus of this chapter has been on intra-company issues. The chapter identified and discussed the interface issues arising from the internal environment of supply chain management.

The concern of logistics management should be to understand how logistics decisions can have a major influence on not just the logistics function and its activities but also on those of the other corporate functions. This chapter has identified the interrelationships which exist and the need for decisions which offer overall corporate benefits, not simply solutions to logistics problems. Often the solutions to logistics problems result in dysfunctional results in a corporate context.

CHAPTER 6

Value Chain and Value Delivery Systems for Supply Chain Management

■ Introduction

Much of the interest in the developing areas of logistics as a discipline has been focused upon the interrrelatedness of functions, activities, companies and cultural intermediaries within developing partnerships and alliances. A useful analytical model with which to explore the tasks and roles within the overall process of delivering customer satisfaction is the value chain (see Figure 6.1).

The value chain (Porter, 1985) identifies the linkages and interdependencies between (and among) suppliers, buyers, intermediaries, and end-users. Its primary benefit is the ability to examine these linkages and identify the 'value' that is created for customers (or that which may be created), and how this in turn creates competitive advantage for a company. The 'value' may take the form of selling an undifferentiated product at below competitors' prices, or it may be that the 'value' takes the form of unique benefits that justify premium pricing. Thus Porter's argument is that the value chain may be used to identify and understand the specific sources of competitive advantage and how they relate to creating added value for customers. The value chain provides a systematic way of examining the activities of not only the company but also the activities of component companies within an overall pipeline or supply chain. It has been shown to be of practical use in determining how to achieve and maintain competitive advantage in a dynamic marketplace.

■ Value as a Concept

Business often refers to 'customer value' and 'added value' without providing corresponding definitions or understanding, of what value is to the customer. Indeed, 'value for money' is probably the most frequent question to appear on trade and consumer research questionnaires. But what is value? Clearly from a logistics strategy viewpoint a detailed understanding of value is necessary. Furthermore, there may well be a range of definitions as the customers' expectations for, or of, value vary from one market segment to another.

Thus value may be: quality, exclusivity, convenience or possibly service response (an intrinsic value); the common denominator is cost to the customer.

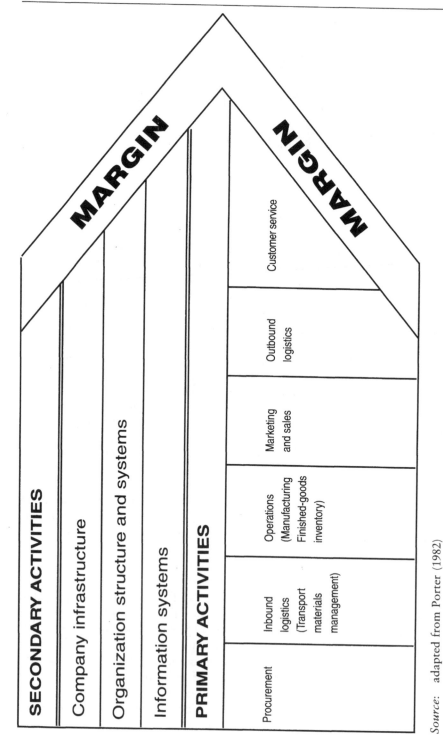

SECONDARY ACTIVITIES

Company infrastructure

Organization structure and systems

Information systems

PRIMARY ACTIVITIES

| Procurement | Inbound logistics (Transport materials management) | Operations (Manufacturing Finished-goods inventory) | Marketing and sales | Outbound logistics | Customer service |

MARGIN

MARGIN

Source: adapted from Porter (1982)

Figure 6.1 A logistics view of the value chain

In Figure 6.1 the total cost to a customer of a product or service is indicated. The *total customer cost* should consider (as a minimum) the cost of the product plus the costs incurred in acquiring the product (the logistics costs), together with the cost of lost sales (lost customer business) if the logistics service fails to deliver. However, costs on their own are not the total picture. They must be considered together with the benefits or value that are available from the total package (product and services) before the total cost to the customer can be derived. Figure 6.2 suggests that there is a value from the services provided by a supplier which increases the customers' ability to service their own customers and that the productivity and profitability of the supplier's customer will (or should) be enhanced due to the application of managerial economics of scale, experience effects, and other volume-related benefits, all of which comprise value.

This raises an interesting view concerning how the delivery of value may be effected. In Figure 6.3 we suggest a 'value delivery' system. It extends the notion of the value chain by including customer expectations for both product and service, introduces segmentation, and emphasize the role of 'value' in the value chain concept. Here we see the outputs of the primary and secondary activities.

Kotler (1994) shows how this approach may be used in the context of marketing. Our interest is more focused in that we are concerned with the functions of the logistics system *per se* and for our needs we define the *product* as:

- The *product range* (width, depth and availability) specified by the customer.
- The *order administration and delivery process* specified by the customer.
- A *customer-service process* comprising communications access and problem resolution at a level of detail and at a time period response satisfactory to meet the customer's operational requirements.

Clearly, the 'value' delivered to the customer is a function of all three items and the process is described in Figure 6.4. The primary activities of the company combine in specific product-service combinations which meet the criteria specified by individual customers or criteria which although a little flexible do meet the needs of a specific customer segment. Pricing and sourcing are important elements in the package as they reflect specific aspects of the product. Pricing reflects a negotiated overall value (value for both supplier and customer) while sourcing reflects the tasks involved in producing both the tangible product and the intangible service package that differentiates and increases the value added to the tangible element of the product package.

The application of information sciences to the logistics function has had a major impact on added value in the value chain. One particular application, EDI (electronic data interchange) has added to the *value* input with:

- More accurate and rapid information flows.
- Improved logistics system productivity.

- Closer trading relationships.
- Improved cash flows.
- A reduction in forecasting errors.

Equally it may be said that EDI would not function adequately, if at all, without the benefits of EPOS (electronic point of sale) data capture. EPOS enables real and live transactional data to be used (through the facility of EDI) to manage production operations and inventory allocations and levels. Benetton (an Italian-based knitwear manufacturer/distributor) is an excellent example of a value delivery system. Benetton is well known for its vertical integration with its

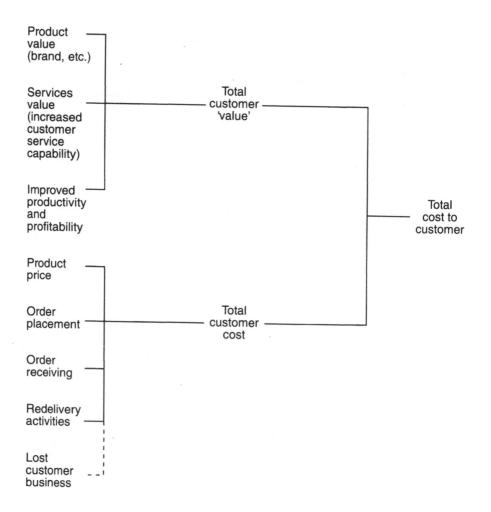

Figure 6.2   Total customer cost extends well beyond the prime cost of the product

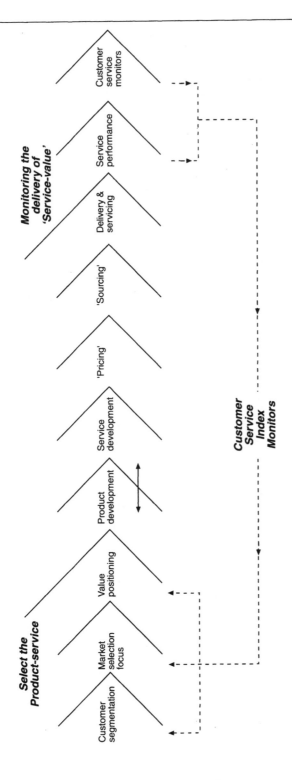

Figure 6.3 A 'value delivery system'

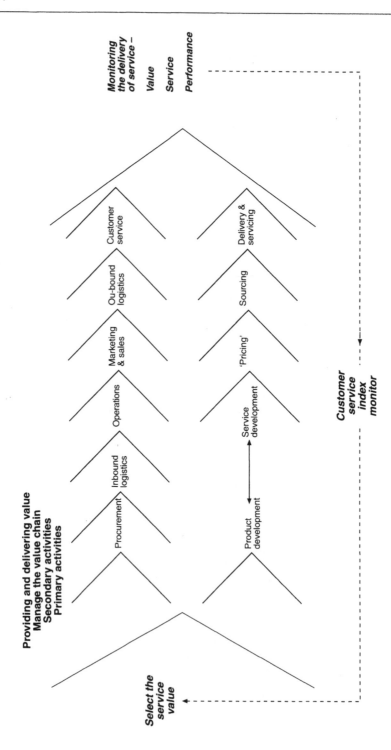

Figure 6.4 Linking the value chain with value delivery

franchised (or some Benetton-owned) outlets. By using an integrated combination of EPOS and EDI systems it has managed to delay the 'finishing' of the product until the very last moment. Garments are held in an unfinished state and 'dyed' to meet specific customer orders which are transmitted daily from outlets' transaction records. A more complex system is operated by companies such as Levi and Marks & Spencer, both of whom operate in a number of countries and both of whom manage a large number of suppliers; and in the case of Levi a wide range of customers (retail outlets). Kotler (1994) argues that marketing is an activity for which the traditional scope and responsibilities have been expanded beyond

> formulating a promotion-oriented marketing mix without much to say about product features, costs and so on. The new view of marketing is that it is responsible *for designing and managing a superior value-delivery system to reach target customer segments.* Today's marketing executive must think not only about selling today's products, but how to stimulate the development of improved company products, working actively with other departments in managing core business processes, and building stronger external partnerships.

The value chain concept is an ideal vehicle from which this notion can be developed. Figure 6.5 shows the value chain extended to include marketing channel activities as well as logistics tasks. The benefits are:

- It identifies the roles and tasks to be undertaken in the total process of customer satisfaction.
- Having identified roles and tasks they may be evaluated in cost terms and decisions made concerning trade-off potential *and* the extent to which intermediaries may be involved.
- The analysis may be used to determine more accurate costs for providing the service requirements of customers using an activity-based costing methodology.

An additional benefit that will become apparent in a subsequent chapter is the extension of the value chain activities into customer account profitability.

■ The Supply Chain

The key to the development of the supply chain concept has been the rapid progress made by information technology and the fact that cost of making information available to more decision-makers has steadily decreased, while concurrently the physical costs of business, such as facilities and inventory have steadily risen. This will be discussed in a subsequent chapter.

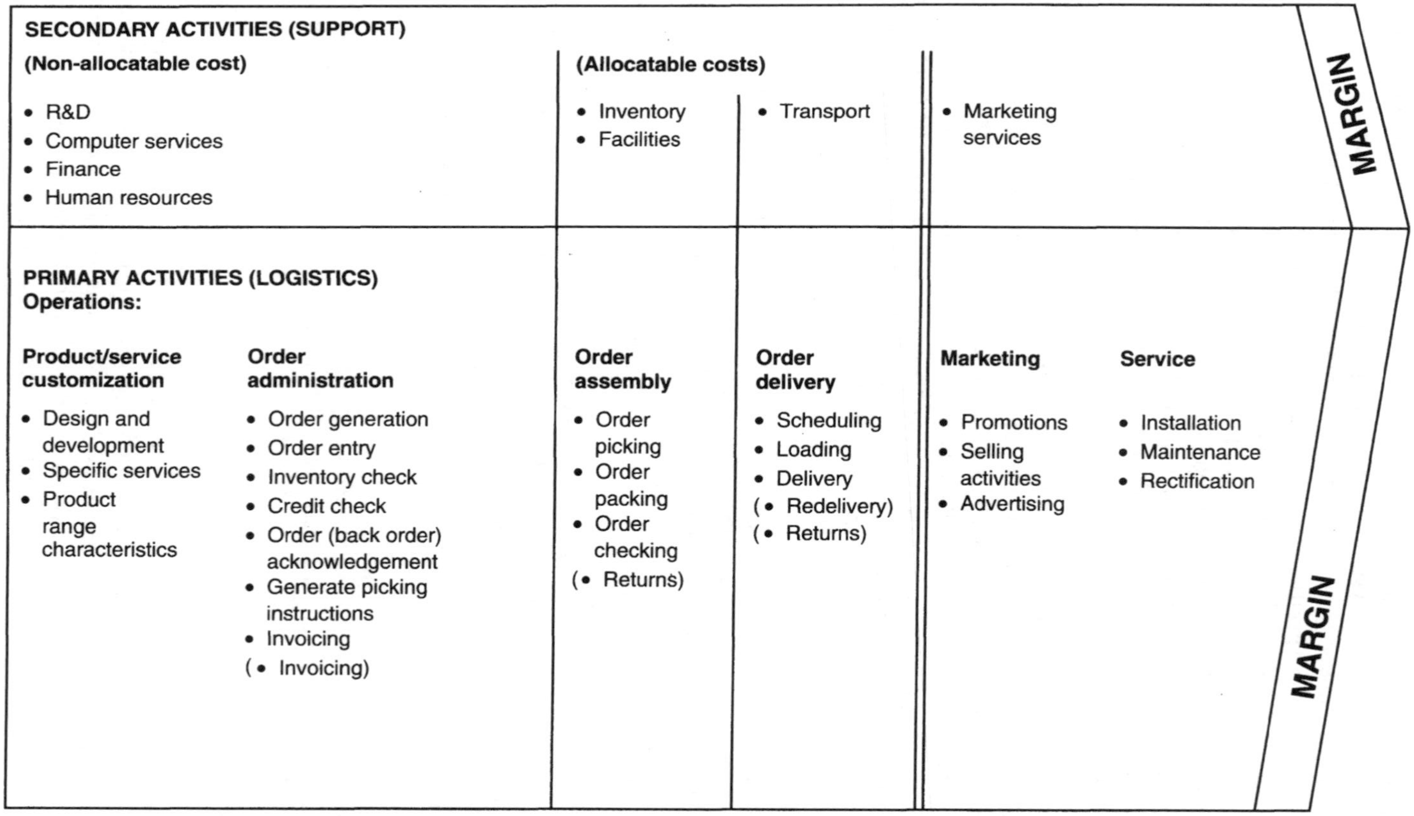

SECONDARY ACTIVITIES (SUPPORT) (Non-allocatable cost)			(Allocatable costs)		
• R&D • Computer services • Finance • Human resources			• Inventory • Facilities	• Transport	• Marketing services

PRIMARY ACTIVITIES (LOGISTICS) Operations:					
Product/service customization	**Order administration**	**Order assembly**	**Order delivery**	**Marketing**	**Service**
• Design and development • Specific services • Product range characteristics	• Order generation • Order entry • Inventory check • Credit check • Order (back order) acknowledgement • Generate picking instructions • Invoicing (• Invoicing)	• Order picking • Order packing • Order checking (• Returns)	• Scheduling • Loading • Delivery (• Redelivery) (• Returns)	• Promotions • Selling activities • Advertising	• Installation • Maintenance • Rectification

MARGIN

MARGIN

Figure 6.5 The value chain and logistics activities

Another major influence accompanied this phenomena – the developments made in JIT. The change in manufacturing philosophy brought about by the Japanese Kanban (just-in-time) concept which was specifically devised to eliminate waste (any activity or process which does not directly add value to the product service) has clear implications for logistics. For example, holding excess inventory was seen as wasteful and therefore companies should minimize (even eliminate) inventories. JIT introduced the commitment to short (but consistent) lead times, minimum levels of inventory *but*, at the same time, optimal levels of customer service.

The rationale behind the concept is that stocks of components (or finished items for resale) should be planned to arrive only at the time they are actually needed. In effect it saves money on downstream inventories by placing greater reliance on improved responsiveness and flexibility. Hence quick response (QR) systems (the distribution equivalent) are attractive.

The implications for distribution management are not difficult to identify. Forbes (1990) describes the parallels between distribution and manufacturing applications of JIT. In distribution the objectives are twofold: to keep inventory costs at a minimum, but at the same time increase customer service levels. Forbes (like Muller's interviewees) suggests that JIT is not entirely new, because for many years retailers (for example) have been concerned to maintain high levels of stockturn frequencies and the relationship between stockturn and stock investment. Clearly there is an information requirement here, and the development of EPOS and EDI have made the concept of minimal stocks/optimal service much more feasible.

The organizational issues are important; the application is much more effective when companies are integrated within a supply chain. Farmer suggests there is evidence identifying problems between wholesalers and retailers where the concept is less effective. He points to the virtual disappearance of delivered wholesaling in food distribution and the growth of third party distribution services in which the consolidation of small individual deliveries into unit loads delivered frequently is more acceptable to large multiple retailers. A large unit load (typically containing a volume-selling commodity product) may well be an exception because no major cost savings would be realized by routing through a consolidation process.

While the savings from inventory reductions can be large, there are other areas in which the savings are significant. For example, the reduction in the levels of stockholding reduces the warehousing capacity requirements. There are cost savings available from improved vehicle utilization, a possible increase in backhauling and savings from the decreases in outer packaging materials.

■ Developing a Value Based Supply Chain

The objective of the supply chain concept is to synchronize the service requirements of the customer with the flow of materials from suppliers such that the apparent contradictory situation of conflicting goals of high customer service, low inventory investment and low operating costs may be balanced (or optimized). It follows that the design and operation of an effective supply chain is of fundamental importance. Stevens (1989) proposed a model in which the balance within the supply chain involved functional trade-offs (see Figure 6.6).

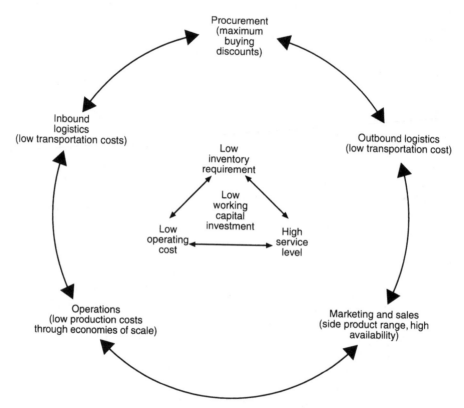

Figure 6.6   A balanced supply chain requires workable functional trade-offs within the value chain

The development of an integrated supply chain requires the management of material and information flows to be viewed from three perspectives: strategic, tactical and operational. At each level the use of facilities, people, finance, and systems must be coordinated and harmonized as a whole.

Stevens describes the *strategic perspective* as having the usual manufacturing, finance and marketing focus, but in addition the focus should also be on supply. The focus at the strategic level should develop:

- Objectives and policies for the supply chain in order to achieve competitive superiority;
- The physical components of the supply chain;
- A statement of customer service intent by product-market, customer group, or perhaps by large customer.
- An organization structure capable of bridging the functional barriers and thereby ensuring an integrated value delivery based supply chain.

The *tactical perspective* focuses on the *means* by which the strategic objectives may be realized. Objectives for each element of the supply chain provide the directions for achieving balance within the supply chain. The tactical perspective involves identifying the necessary resources with which the balance may be achieved. Thus the JIT and quick response approaches discussed earlier have their place here.

The *operational perspective* is concerned with the efficient operation of the supply chain. Its focus is on detail: detail for systems, controls and performance measures. Stevens recommends that the company should establish (and measure) performance criteria for the supply chain in terms of inventory investment, availability (service levels), throughput efficiency, supplier performance and cost performances.

If a structured approach is followed, a three-stage process emerges. The first is an *evaluation of the competitive environment*. A detailed review of customers and competitors results in a schedule of customer service characteristics by customer and product-market (or segment), against which current service offers may be compared and the implications for the company of changes that appear necessary. Those characteristics which will create competitive advantage will then emerge.

The second phase comprised a *supply chain diagnostic review*. Typically a cost model is developed and it is important to note that usually the traditional methods of management accounting do not identify the true cost of activities, and the model developed should also provide a realistic method for allocating overhead costs to products, market segments and customers. We shall discuss these issues in a subsequent chapter. However, it should be noted that Figure 6.5, the value chain and logistics activities, provides a basis for this work. In addition to costing the activities, Stevens recommends that effort be directed towards identifying in which of the activities it is necessary to *excel* on the basis that if this is planned to occur then *competitive advantage* will be enhanced.

The third phase for Stevens is *supply chain development* in which the supply chain strategy and plans for implementation are evolved. The strategy should be examined to ensure that the relevant customers (and customer service expectations) have been identified and that this is consistent with management's perception of market development trends. Implementation plans require a time-phased programme for resource allocation throughout the supply chain.

Stevens makes an interesting comment concerning supply chain development. While the impetus for the development of the strategy may be a 'top-down' approach, its success is likely to be achieved by a bottom-up approach. His experience suggests four (4) stages.

- *Stage 1* is a situation in which a company approaches supply chain tasks in discrete decisions with responsibility lodged in each of the task centres. The result is usually a lack of control *across* the supply chain function because of organizational boundaries preventing the coordinated decisions from achieving an overall customer service offer.
- *Stage 2* of development is typified by functional integration of the *inward flow* of goods through materials management, manufacturing management and distribution. The emphasis is usually on cost reduction rather than performance achievement; focused on the discrete business functions; with some attempts at achieving internal trade-offs between, for example, purchasing discounts and inventory investment and perhaps plant operating costs and batch volumes. Customer service is reactive.
- *Stage 3* accepts the necessity of managing the flow of goods to the customer by *integrating the internal activities*. At this stage integrated planning is achieved by using systems such as DRP (distribution requirements planning), JIT manufacturing techniques, etc. This level of internal integration is essential before the company can consider integrating customer demand in an overall demand management activity.
- *Stage 4* extends the integration to external activities. In doing so the company becomes customer orientated by linking customers' procurement activities with its own procurement and marketing activities. It is at this stage that the situation described by Figures 6.4 and 6.5 of an integrated value delivery chain/supply chain will emerge.

The value chain/supply chain management approach enables a company to respond to market changes. However, for the full potential to be realized the connections and interrelationships between the component parts of the supply chain must first be identified and an integrated system designed to ensure that the system which evolves can be managed such that customer product and service expectations may be met cost-effectively.

■ Summary

In this chapter we have applied the value chain concept to supply chain management analysis and decision making.

We first considered the role of customer service in the delivery of a complete value package to the customer. This approach requires an appreciation of the activities involved in constructing a value delivery system which embraces the functions involved, and the activities required, in identifying which customers are to be provided with which specific value (or service packages).

The role of information in planning and subsequently monitoring customer service delivery was also discussed. It was suggested that control be formalised through an index-based monitoring system.

The notion of identifying specific value chain activities as means by which costs may be allocated was introduced. Trade-off issues using the value chain were introduced and discussed.

CHAPTER 7

Facilities Decisions

■ Introduction

There are three fundamental questions to be addressed. How many facilities do we need? Where should they be located? And what types of facilities are required? This chapter considers the essential functions formed by facilities, i.e. to create stockholding from which to service the needs of production and customers; to act as an assurance against production failures; to absorb the benefits of economic production runs; to provide buffer stocks to meet fluctuating and uncertain sales demands; to maximize the benefits of procurement economies; and to provide support for marketing and sales activities. The type of warehouse facility required depends largely upon product characteristics, market demand volume and, of course, customer service requirements. Product characteristics determine storage and handling methods; rate of sale and sales volumes influence the methods used to process and progress orders; and customer service requirements influence lead time responses which in turn can influence the selection of materials handling equipment.

The chapter commences by reviewing some of the roles and tasks within the logistics spectrum of responsibility requiring decisions concerning facilities.

■ Some Issues Concerning Marketing Channels Functions

We shall consider the strategy and structure issues within marketing channels in a subsequent chapter. Here, however, it is relevant and necessary to consider some of the concepts.

Marketing channels exist for a number of reasons. They relate to the management of 'stocks and flows' within the transaction/physical transfer of products between supplier, distributor and consumer. It is in the context of 'stocks' that our focus is concerned.

The economic rationale for distribution is to add time, place and spatial convenience utilities to the form utility created by production. The theoretical literature on channels suggests that intermediaries exist in order that the process of exchange can be made more efficient. It is also suggested that intermediaries arise to 'adjust the discrepancy of assortments through the performance of the sorting process' (Alderson, 1954).

Alderson describes the *sorting function* as:

- *Sorting out*: breaking down heterogeneous stocks into separate, homogeneous stocks.

- *Accumulation*: bringing together similar stocks from a number of sources to create a larger, homogeneous supply.
- *Allocation*: breaking large homogeneous lots into smaller, commercial, lot sizes, i.e. breaking bulk.
- *Assorting*: building assortments of products for resale in customer convenient product groups.

Alderson's theory seeks to identify and classify the activities between production and consumption. As production shifted towards larger volumes and continuous production processes in large centralized facilities, consumption has changed very little; small purchase sizes, with either frequent or infrequent purchasing frequencies (the difference being that between fast-moving consumer goods and consumer durables) and in locations convenient to the purchaser. The role of the intermediary is quite clear and so too is that of warehousing facilities, be they manufacturer- or distributor-owned and/or operated, or perhaps used as part of a service package.

Bucklin (1966), in a discussion on channel structures and outputs, specified four service outputs:

- spatial convenience (or market decentralization)
- lot size
- waiting or delivery time, and
- product variety (assortment width and depth).

Clearly these relate to the components of Alderson's sorting function. They also relate very closely to the functions expected of a warehouse. Both are involved in a superordinate or coordinating goal: the delivery of service quality (i.e. the gap between consumer expectations and perceptions, discussed in Chapters 2 and 3).

One other channel concept that is relevant to this discussion concerns the notion of postponement and speculation. The way in which the channel is structured is largely determined by where inventories should best be held in order to deliver to customer service specifications. This requires a combination of inventory and warehouse facilities to provide appropriate availability (service levels), fulfil the sorting function processes, and remunerate channel intermediaries. Alderson (1954) and subsequently Bucklin (1966) developed the principle of *postponement and speculation* to explain the process. According to Bucklin, efficiency in marketing channels is promoted by the postponement of changes in the form and identity of a product to the latest possible point in the marketing process, and inventory location to the latest possible point in time.

Thus postponement increases efficiency by moving differentiation closer to the time of purchase, at which point demand is more certain and risk (and the associated costs) is therefore reduced. A relevant example was given in Chapter 6 of Benetton's supply chain activities in which product is maintained in an undyed state until orders are received.

Speculation is the opposite of postponement. Speculation is typified by consumer goods where relatively large inventories or products with moderate differentiation are required to provide customers with adequate variety and assortment. Whereas postponement moves risk towards the point of sale, speculation allocates risk within the channel structure. Speculation facilitates cost reductions through production economies of scale; eliminates frequent orders (which decreases the costs of order administration and of delivery); and reduces the costs of lost sales due to stock-outs. These advantages are very similar to the four basic reasons for warehouse facilities given by Ballou (1978): i.e. to reduce transportation (delivery-production) costs; to coordinate supply and demand; to assist in the production process; and to assist in the marketing process (provide customer service). Ballou continues by describing the functions of warehousing. The design of the facility usually reflects the nature of the major service performed. Those services can be classified as. (1) holding, (2) consolidation, (3) break bulk and transhipment, and (4) mixing. He describes these in more detail:

- *Holding*: stockholding in warehouses to balance the imbalances between production and demand. The size of the warehouse and its characteristics are determined by the nature of the products, the length of time stock will be held and the characteristics of demand/order patterns.
- *Consolidation*: is generally undertaken for two reasons, i.e. to consolidate lot sizes to take advantage of transportation rates, to perform sorting activities.
- *Break bulk and transshipment*: warehouses are obviously used to create assortments from large input loads. Transshipment activities occur when product is to be redistributed subsequent to a break bulk activity.
- *Mixing*: is also part of the sorting process. Homogeneous lots are converted into heterogeneous lots in response to customer orders.

Clearly within the overall logistics process facilities have a vital role. We move on to address the questions of how many? where? and what type?

■ Determining the Facilities Requirement Profile

Having identified and discussed the role and tasks of facilities, we continue to develop an approach which will enable logistics managers to determine the number, location, size and other characteristics of the facilities decision. Figure 7.1 identifies the information required to generate a facilities profile.

There are a number of factors which will influence the facilities decision. If we take a logistics view then we should consider both the materials management considerations arising out of the company's manufacturing/operations strategy, which will reflect the marketing view of the market-based opportunities available to the firm. This is an important issue because, depending upon the decision to opt for a niche market strategy with differentiated products

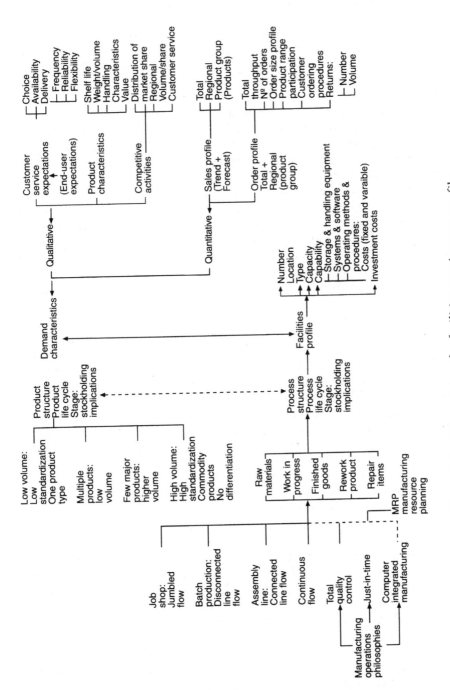

Figure 7.1 Determining the facilities requirement profile

rather than the commodity/low cost leader segment as the manufacturing/operations the response will differ. Figure 7.1 illustrates how the *process structure/process life cycle* stage of the manufacturing structure will vary depending upon the type of manufacturing system selected. This also implies quite different decisions for inventory items. Similarly, there will be differing implications for inventory storage requirements depending upon the manufacturing operations philosophies of the business.

Demand characteristics are influenced by quantitative and qualitative issues. Figure 7.1 identifies sales profile data and order profile data that will provide an indication of the throughput that can be expected. This can be an important factor because not only the volume is important here: if a pareto-type profile is found to prevail there are significant implications for the amount of inventory that is carried across each product group. Hatton (1990) suggests an interesting and novel way of determining the relative movement of items (SKUs – stock-keeping units) and suggests that it is the very fast moving items that justify the detailed analysis. The implications for the information management system are important for both investment and operating costs. If, as Hatton's example suggests, some 10–20 per cent of SKUs account for 70–90 per cent of total movement, then clearly detailed information on usage rates are important to maintain customer service availability levels.

Equally if (as the example suggests) the slowest moving 25 per cent of SKUs account for less than 1 per cent of movement it follows that less responsive (and expensive) data capturing systems will be adequate. Indeed some research is necessary because there have been situations in which the investment and operating costs of the information system have been higher than the sales revenue generated by this group of products.

Space/capacity allocation within the facility follows the same argument. In addition, the materials handling techniques may well differ. Figure 7.2 illustrates how handling technologies requirements differ when numbers of units vary per day, and the implications for storage methods. This introduces facility layout decisions as another variable. Clearly, frequently moved/fast-moving items should be held closer to the order assembly/vehicle loading area to contain handling equipment investment.

The qualitative characteristics provide data to enable management to consider additional capacity issues. For example, the customer service policy, when interpreted in quantitative terms (customer service expectations) will provide another dimension for the space consideration decisions. Product characteristics can also be important. Short shelf-life products may require cold/chilled storage; high weight/low volume items require totally different storage facilities to low weight/high volume products. Handling characteristics differ markedly. Fragile products differ from products with robust characteristics; some products have difficult physical features (termed 'uglies'). Competitors' facilities strategies are also well worth reviewing. If their market share differs (whether larger or smaller than the company share) it may be as a result

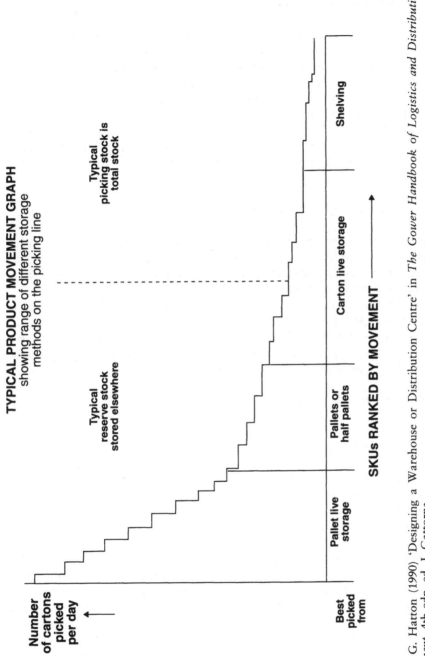

Source: G. Hatton (1990) 'Designing a Warehouse or Distribution Centre' in *The Gower Handbook of Logistics and Distribution Management*, 4th edn, ed. J. Gattorna

Figure 7.2 Typical product movement graph

of a distribution policy (perhaps facility characteristics), and this may warrant investigation.

The outcome of the analysis will be a series of data that will provide an indication of how many facilities are required, their probable locations and sizes and the throughput volumes (and by implication the equipment necessary). It is likely that no precise answer will be found, but rather that the solution will be one which will give the decision-maker a series of alternatives which will differ depending on volume breaks in production and/or sales volumes. As Figure 7.1 indicates, the production characteristics will have a strong influence on the solution, and the difference here may be quite large, the production stockholding requirements being the important factor.

■ Managing Logistics Facilities

Logistics facilities are an integral component of a total system, the purpose of which is to provide customers with a level of service which meets their expectations. Consequently the logistics facilities must be managed as an integral part of the marketing direction of the company.

Just as customer service levels are established, so too should operating service levels, costs, performance and productivity levels for activities within the facilities be determined and measured. A vital component in this process is information. Having established performance measurements, the information system should produce regular, accurate and timely performance reporting.

■ Performance Measurement

There are a number of reporting systems necessary. Campbell (1990) suggests four systems that are essential:

- Key performance factors
- Service levels
- Operating costs
- Productivity performance.

Key performance factors/critical success factors for each operation should be identified, together with a relevant unit of measurement. Often a mistake is made by assuming that *all* functions have equal importance. Clearly this is not the case, and initially sensitivity analysis should be applied to all functions to identify those for which a specific level of output is necessary and without which the overall performance of the operation will be inadequate. We shall be introducing activity-based costing in a later chapter, and the analysis required when establishing the ABC system will be helpful.

Service levels for operating activities and inventory levels should be set, based upon customer service requirements. They should be set in terms which reflect both the customers' service measurements *and* those used by the operating system to measure internal functional performance. There is also the point that accurate service-level measurement is a vital ingredient in developing labour schedules and workloads and ensuring their accuracy for forecasting purposes.

Operating costs reflect the expenses budget for a facility. Control is more efficient when costs can be broken down to reflect the activities and responsibilities within the facility. The maxim of accountability and responsibility being visible and matching is essential. Again a form of sensitivity analysis should be introduced. Costs, just as SKUs, demonstrate pareto profiles. It follows that an activity which accounts for a large proportion of an operations cost should be reported in considerably more detail than those activities which contribute little to output or cost totals. *Activity-based costing* methods are useful in this context because the breakdown of activities into cost drivers usually identifies those activities which *create* cost. Therefore measuring pallets stored, truck loads received, customer enquiries serviced, orders processed, SKUs picked, and so on, will have the benefits of:

- Being related to the work task
- Being in terms understood by employees
- Reflecting the output achieved.

Campbell makes an important point. 'Every relevant function must be costed to facilitate informed analysis and decision-making.'

Productivity measurement should reflect the relationship between inputs and outputs for every relevant operation within every relevant function. Productivity should be measured at micro-levels of activity and thus reflect:

- SKUs picked/dollar labour hour
- Invoices processed/dollar labour hour, and
- Deliveries made/dollar costs per delivery hour (vehicle and labour costs).

At a macro-level the measurements should use the same principle but report the information in terms readily understood:

- Operating unit costs/value of goods processed (%)
- Operating unit costs/value of goods received (%).

For some companies costs are reflected as a percentage of total sales. This is done to make comparisons with other operations and functions within the business.

The US-based NCPDM (now the CLM) proposals for measuring facilities performance (and the performance of other elements of the logistics system) were outlined in an extensive report prepared by A. T. Kearney, Inc. (1984). Based upon their proposals, the following is a set of comprehensive effectiveness measures for facilities:

Productivity	Utilization	Performance
1. Dollar value throughput/total warehouse cost (total square feet)	1. Actual weight throughput/maximum weight throughput	1. Actual total warehouse cost/ budgeted warehouse cost
2. Weight throughput/ total warehouse cost (total square feet)	2. Actual orders through-put/maximum orders throughput	2. Actual weight throughput per total warehouse cost
3. Orders throughput/ total warehouse cost (total square feet)	3. Actual lines throughput/maximum lines through-put	2a. Actual weight throughput per square foot/standard weight throughput per square foot
4. Lines throughput/total warehouse cost (total square feet)	4. Square feet used/ square feet available	3. Actual orders throughput per total warehouse cost/ standard orders throughput per total warehouse cost
5. Units throughput/total warehouse cost (total square feet)	5. Cubic feet used/cubic feet available	3a. Actual orders throughput per square foot/standard orders throughput per square foot
		4. Actual lines throughput per total warehouse cost/ standard lines throughput per total warehouse cost
		4a. Actual lines throughput per square foot/standard lines throughput per square foot
		5. Actual units throughput per total warehouse cost/ standard units throughput per total warehouse cost
		5a. Actual units throughput per square foot/standard units throughput per square foot
		6. Actual throughput cycle time/standard throughput cycle time
		7. Standard cost allowances earned/ actual costs incurred

Other measures suggested as useful for overall warehouse management include:

- Total labour cost/total warehouse costs.
- Total non-labour cost/total warehouse costs.
- Total warehouse costs/total logistics costs.
- Total transactions processed per day/total. transactions received for processing per day.
- Total lines (orders) throughput without error per day/total lines (orders) throughput per day.

■ Summary

Effective logistics management is required to consider how many facilities are required, where they are to be located, their size, and of course their role.

Transaction channel theory has provided a basis for the analysis of facilities requirements through its concern with postponement and speculation activities within channels. Indeed this is one area of overlap between transactions channels and physical distribution channels.

Within this context a methodology for developing a specification or profile for facilities decisions was developed. The factors considered were marketing issues such as the product life cycle and competitive advantage requirements, manufacturing operations philosophy and, importantly, the quantitative and qualitative characteristics of market demand.

Performance criteria and measurement were as discussed.

CHAPTER 8

Inventory Management in the Supply Chain

■ Introduction

Inventory management has received considerable attention in recent years; this is due to three major factors. First, a worldwide recession has had the impact of reducing sales volumes and revenues, and this has forced management to consider how best to lower the levels of inventory within logistics systems in order to maintain margins (by reducing interest and obsolescence costs). Secondly, the changes in manufacturing philosophy, specifically the growth in just-in-time applications (JIT), has reduced the need for inventory as an insurance buffer within the overall logistics activity. A third influence, one which is associated with the first topic, is the realization by many companies that a greater return-on-investment (ROI) can be obtained by developing the core business, and that investment in working capital items, such as inventory and debtors, returns far less in comparison.

This chapter considers why holding inventory is important to the business and reviews both traditional and more recent views on the purposes of inventories. We shall also discuss types of inventories and the importance to the business of identifying patterns of demand and matching these with inventory types; if done effectively the investment in inventories will be optimized.

Methods of inventory management will be discussed. However, the focus will be on managerial issues rather than a demonstration of methods of calculating inventory requirements and levels. This is done elsewhere, by other authors, very effectively.

The importance of inventory management in customer service decisions is important and is dealt with from a managerial perspective. The financial implications of inventory as an element of the company's assets are discussed, and the view expressed that management should be focusing on extracting extra financial performance from inventory investment. Finally, we shall consider appropriate performance measures for management to apply to inventory investment.

■ The Purpose of Inventory in Logistics Systems

Views as to why holding inventory is important have been expressed by a number of authors. While many of the reasons are similar, there is an interesting spectrum.

Ballou (1978) suggests six reasons, which are:

- *To improve customer service*: through a supporting role to marketing which, once having created demand, requires availability if sales are to be effected.
- *Beverages production economies*: typically unit costs are lowest when product is manufactured in long production runs at constant quantities.
- *Permits purchase and transportation economies*: the argument here being based on the notion that both product procurement and transportation costs will be reduced if lot sizes are large.
- *Hedges against price changes*: in times of high inflation (the mid to late 1970s) inflation rates were high, and this argument suggests that volume purchases will minimize the impact of suppliers' price increases. This is clearly not a tenable argument for the early 1990s: indeed, quite the opposite.
- *Protects against demand and lead-time uncertainties*: the argument made here considers the problems which confront logistics systems when both customer demand patterns and suppliers' replenishment lead times are not known with a reliable degree of certainty. It follows that if service is to be maintained at acceptable levels to customers then an investment in 'safety stock' would be necessary.
- *Hedges against contingencies*: while there are now fewer labour disputes in most economies, fires, floods and other exogenous variables can create problems. It is argued that these will be minimized if stockholding is increased.

Aschner (1990) suggests similar reasons:

- *Demand/supply fluctuations*: safety stocks, buffer stocks or just reserves are held to absorb variations in demand, and supplier performance uncertainty.
- *Anticipation*: inventory allocations made to meet seasonal demand, sales promotion and to meet customer requirements during periods in which the production facility is inoperable.
- *Transportation*: rather than focus simply on economies of scale and the benefits of fully utilized transport systems Aschner (1990) makes the point that there is a trade-off to be evaluated between the speed of transportation (and its costs) *and* the cost of inventory in a pipeline system.
- *Hedging*: again the issue of procurement economies and the cost of holding inventories versus the impact of price increases or perhaps taking advantage of price offers or some other form of speculation.
- *Lot size*: refers to the attempt to purchase in volumes which exceed immediate demand/consumption rates in order that economies may be obtained from lower transportation rates or perhaps larger buying discounts.

Lambert and Stock (1993) offer five reasons. Again there is a similarity:

- *Economies of scale*: for both production and transportation rate benefits. However, there is an additional point raised which is a disadvantage. It is suggested that long manufacturing runs do restrict response flexibility should stock-outs occur; consequently the changeover costs should be included in any costing calculations.
- *Balancing supply and demand*: this is the Aschner point. Some products demonstrate fluctuating demand patterns. While these may be predictable, the economics of the situation may be such that the cost profiles favour long production runs with stockholding occasionally at excessive levels.
- *Specialization*: manufacturing for stock does enable a business to permit specialisation within its manufacturing facilities. Finished product is then shipped to distribution centres for the assortment process. Again, it is the potential for economies of scale to operate in manufacturing and transportation that has attraction.
- *Protection from uncertainties*: the uncertainties include those raised by Ballou (1978) but in addition the authors suggest internal problems that may occur in the production process and also consider the potential problems of crop failure for food processors. They emphasize the dilemma that could occur for assembly processes reliant upon component supplies.
- *Inventory as a buffer*: here the issue of interdependencies within the procurement–manufacturing–distribution–consumption process is highlighted. They argue that because channel members are distanced geographically, philosophically and financially, often 'buffer stocks' are held at critical interfaces.

It is interesting to observe the impact of time on these issues. There have been a number of developments in both manufacturing and distribution that have had considerable influence on stockholding. For example, EPOS and EDI have considerably improved forecasting errors. Add to the impact of technology the acceptance of JIT and computer-based manufacturing methods, and stock levels have reduced considerably.

The wide acceptance of the notion of supply chain management has also had a large impact on inventory levels throughout manufacturing and logistics systems. Where there is a universal acceptance of service objectives, it is typically accompanied by a coordinated effort to maximise inventory flows through the supply chain, with inventory-holding points specifically tasked to respond to customer service requirements.

Without doubt it is the joint commitment by enlightened manufacturers and distributors to share information and to work towards optimizing supply chain stocks and flows that has reduced stock levels and eliminated some of the reasons for holding inventories.

■ Types of Inventory: Strategic Choices

Inventory may be categorized by considering its role in the overall process of customer satisfaction. Mention has been made of the supply chain (see Chapter 5) and inventory management has an important role in the effective management of the supply chain. The notion of the logistics pipeline illustrates the way in which inventory flows through the supply chain from supplier to final consumer. Activities in the pipeline should be carried out by the channel member who can add the greatest value to the task of customer satisfaction. It follows that there are specific aspects of this task:

- The requirement of the supply chain to deliver the service expectations of the customer.
- The optimization of the supply-chain costs, and the need to review the cost-effectiveness of inventory allocation in the supply chain. This further suggests trade-off analysis within the logistics pipeline to identify where the greatest added value occurs, and the corresponding organization design to reinforce this.
- An exploration of exterior trade-off potentials by considering the role of information in the logistics pipeline and the opportunity that information management systems offer to reduce the levels of inventory held at any location within the pipeline.

The strategic considerations are important here. If we refer back to Chapter Four, the implications of inventory levels on corporate performance can be significant. Excessive inventory within the logistics pipeline will increase the overall working capital requirements of the pipeline and may put a large cost burden on one or more member companies. Clearly if we can reduce the levels of inventory throughout the logistics pipeline a more effective operation will result.

This suggests that the strategic choices confronting the supply chain concerning inventory management decisions are:

- Who is the materials or component supplier to be?
- Who will hold the inventory, and where?
- How much inventory is required to be held?
- Where (or with whom) will the customer place orders; directly with the supplier or through an intermediary?
- How will orders be delivered, directly to the customer by an intermediary, or by a dedicated service company?

Effective answers to these strategic questions require intimate knowledge of cost structure and behaviour within the supply chain, and specifically those of the inventory component within the logistics pipeline.

■ Inventory Carrying Costs

Inventory carrying costs comprise a range of items over which varying degrees of control may be exercised by management. We have labelled them direct and indirect costs in Figure 8.1 to represent the accounting and management control issues.

■ Direct Costs

There are four cost characteristics that are important direct cost items. These are closely related to the levels of inventory carried in the system. The *capital costs* of inventory are influenced by customer service policy, which in turn is influenced by supply-chain (logistics pipeline) tasks and roles, and as such can contribute a large amount to the overall costs of carrying inventory. To obtain an estimate of the amount of the investment it is not unusual for companies to apply a rate of interest which best reflects their view of the role of inventory and, at the same time, may also reflect the opportunity cost of capital. An alternative measure may use the weighted cost of capital.

Storage space costs include the storage requirements for all categories of inventories. It is important to remember that the costs of company-owned facilities are primarily fixed costs, although some variable costs may occur with throughput. Given this situation it becomes important to consider the relationship between storage space costs and inventory levels; an excess of stocks requires additional storage capacity, which may be available from service company resources for seasonal variations, but if it is increased unnecessarily for a long period of time it is a penalty cost that could be avoided.

Inventory insurance may be considered in a similar manner. Such *service costs* are volume related and again can be regarded as a penalty on the business if the inventory levels are excessive. Clearly there is also an impact on facilities' insurance levels which reflect the size and value of the storage space.

Risk costs will vary with the nature of the business, and may extend beyond the value of the inventory. Obsolescence may not simply mark down the value of the stock item; it may render it worthless. For example, service parts for construction equipment are often modified and the modifications render existing components valueless (clearly, there are often reasons other than simply efficiency improvements) and furthermore, if the replaced parts were to be used, the equipment warranty would be invalid.

Damage often reduces product value. This may occur through unnecessary handling and may often be divided by reconfiguring distribution system arrangements. Furniture manufacturers and retailers have agreed joint approaches to this problem by reducing the amount of stock items for sale throughout the system. Retailers hold only display items and deliveries are despatched from manufacturers' stocks to meet individual customer purchases.

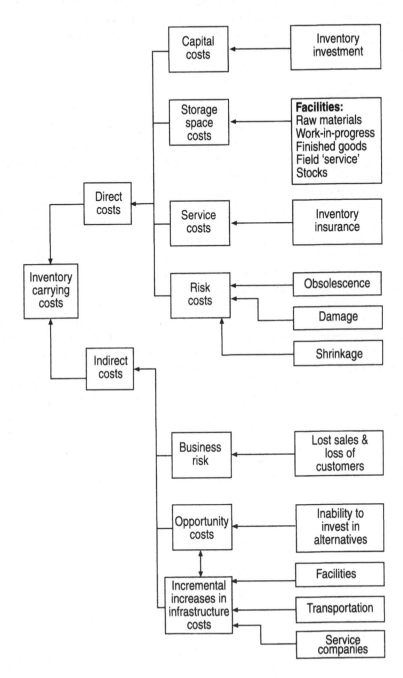

Figure 8.1   Inventory carrying costs

Shrinkage, due to *loss* or perhaps theft, can be a major problem. The extent of the problem is correlated with the attractiveness of the item and the ease with which it may be removed. Unaccountable losses are (or should be) reduced by accurate, and timely, information flows.

■ Indirect Costs

There are three important indirect cost items of concern to logistics. These are more related to the overall role of inventory within a logistics system.

Business risk concerns two issues. A company carrying insufficient inventory may be unable to meet and satisfy demand. The reverse situation is that too much inventory may satisfy demand but will increase the *direct costs* by increasing the capital costs, storage costs, service and risk costs. The reasons given earlier clearly apply. So management has to decide on the level of service or availability considered necessary to achieve their logistics objectives and, in turn, their marketing and corporate objectives. It follows that the level of inventory investment seen as necessary to minimize the level of lost sales and maintain customer loyalty can be derived.

Dynamic companies usually have a range of investment alternatives they can pursue. Clearly if the investment in inventory is accounting for too much capital investment, then the alternatives become limited in number and impose *opportunity costs* through the lack of capital available to invest in alternatives.

An important aspect of indirect costs is the *incremental increases in infrastructure costs* caused by carrying excess inventory. This point was suggested earlier but the cost penalty of excess stockholding can (and does) involve companies in an over-investment in facilities and transportation, together with incurring unnecessary charges from service companies. The cost penalties are both fixed and variable in their context, and as Figure 8.1 suggests, they are closely linked with opportunity costs, making it more difficult or expensive for the company to undertake additional investment.

■ Inventory as an Element of Customer Service

As we discussed in Chapter 3, inventory availability is a component of customer service and the preceding paragraphs have indicated the extent to which the problem may compound the costs of service. Figure 8.2 portrays a typical inventory carrying cost/customer sales response profile. For most companies the availability/service level policy is a matter of managerial judgement. For many companies the 'service' is improved by adding additional 'safety' stock to the stock levels calculated as necessary to service the on-going business. As Figure 8.2 suggests, the inventory levels increase disproportionately as the availability/service levels increase toward 100 per cent. In one (unpublished) study it was estimated that the incremental increase in stockholding was some 15 per cent of stockholding costs as the availability response increased from 95 to 97 per cent. Clearly, in this case, alternative policies should be considered. One solution is to identify those inventory items for which high levels of availability are necessary due to the nature of customer demand requirements and/or the extent of competition within the industry for which availability may be seen as a convert element of competitive advantage. Another is to use rapid transportation as a substitute. A third solution is to examine rates of sale and demand patterns of inventory items and to stock high volume, short lead-time items close to those customers most likely to require high levels of availability.

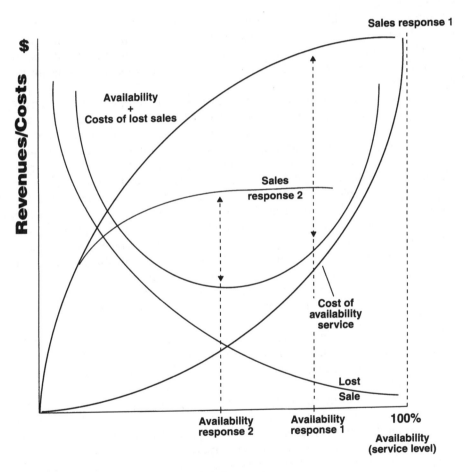

Figure 8.2 Availability and customer response

■ Types of Inventory

Conventional approaches consider inventories to be categorized into six types, each type indicating their reason for existing in a logistics system.

Cycle stock: is inventory that results from the replenishment process and typifies predictable demand and replenishment rates. In a certain world with constant demand, say at 40 units per day with a lead time for replenishment at 10 days, no inventory other than that necessary to service this regular demand (the cycle stock) would be required.

In-transit inventories: are items that are being transported from one location to another. Usually in-transit inventories are included in the inventory-carrying costs of the location from which they are despatched. Clearly, the longer the channel, and the more shipping locations, the greater the level of in-transit inventories will be.

Safety stock: is held over and above the levels of cycle stock because of uncertainties that occur in the demand pattern or lead time. Thus there is a proportion of the average inventory holding at any stockholding point which will be devoted to short-term variations in either demand and/or replenishment lead time.

Speculative stock: is held often because there have been opportunities to gain advantageous discounts (quantity discounts) if larger than average orders are placed. Alternatively prudent procurement has been undertaken ahead of forecast shortages or price increases. Production economies of scale may also dictate that production lot sizes greater than demand are manufactured and held in stock. Finally, it is not unusual to process seasonally produced items (vegetables, fruit, etc.) when they are available and to hold inventories for consumption throughout the year. This may also maintain production capacity at more even levels together with maintaining stable levels of employment.

Seasonal stock: is a form of speculative stock, which involves the accumulation of inventory prior to a season commencing. This provides continuity of merchandise and economies of production for producers.

Dead/obsolete stock: is inventory for which no demand has been registered for a specific period of time. Typically it is held in one location and written down in value.

By now it is quite clear that inventory investment is a critical factor to corporate success. Having appropriate levels of inventory positioned at suitable locations is essential if sales are to be achieved at optimal levels of profitability.

The description of inventory types in the immediately preceding paragraphs also identifies the costs of holding inventory and points to the need for inventory levels to be prescribed accurately to prevent excess cost accumulation. It should also be apparent that the descriptions are *static*. A more *dynamic* approach is one that considers a classification of inventory which reflects the type of business and nature of product flows through the business. Clearly, the inventory type mix will vary among different businesses. For example, a retailer selling commodity items will have a different inventory mix to that of a fashion (ladieswear) retailer targeting teenagers.

A dynamic view may be reached if the characteristics of the business and its demand patterns are examined more closely. To this end we suggest a series of characteristics that may be helpful:

☐ *Predictability of demand*

Constant predictable demand which is easily managed can be described as inventory with *base flow* characteristics.

Seasonal demand products, which may be relatively easy to predict but which reflect high levels of demand at specific periods, are described as *wave flow* product characteristics. Seasonal fashion wear is an example.

Surge flow products are those with highly unpredictable levels of demand. Surge flow products are 'fad' products for which there is often no repeat purchasing. However, a standard product which is suddenly required takes on surge characteristics.

The important issue which emerges here is that many businesses fail to classify their inventory in such a way that reflects patterns of customer demand in their markets. These patterns of demand are usually accompanied by differential levels of margins reflecting the risk involved in their stockholding; see Figure 8.3. Figure 8.3a portrays the types of inventory that reflect demand patterns; Figure 8.3b suggests the inventory mix of a *low risk* profile business while Figure 8.3c is that of a high risk business.

The low risk profile could well be that of a ladieswear retailing business targeted at 45–60-year-old C2 customers. The opposite is suggested by Figure 8.3c where the target market is likely to be late teens customers, possibly with B1/B2 parents.

Some comparisons may be made with the earlier classifications. Base flow inventory is likely to be the cycle stock inventory, while wave flow inventory aligns with seasonal stock, and surge flow and speculative types of stockholding are likely to have much in common. The issue for the manufacturer and/or reseller is to decide upon the demand characteristics of the target customer group and develop a merchandise/inventory mix that will obtain the desired response from the customer, *and* deliver the required level of profitability and cash flow. Both objectives can be seen to be closely related to stock turns and gross margins, topics covered in Chapter 4. Stockholding policies are suggested in Table 8.1.

■ Principal Issues in Inventory Management

There are a number of techniques designed to make inventory management effective. These are ABC analysis, forecasting methods, inventory models, and advanced order processing systems. We will give an appraisal of each although a detailed treatment of inventory management issues can be found in Lambert and Stock (1993) including worked examples.

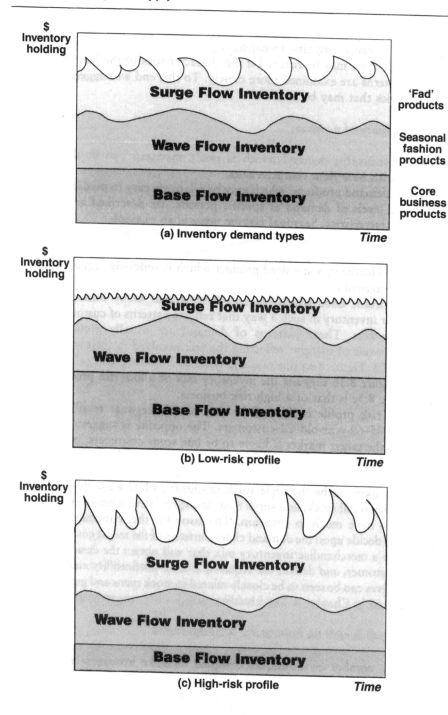

Figure 8.3 The dynamics of inventory stockholding

Table 8.1   Stockholding policy: a function of inventory characteristics

Type	Characteristics	Stockholding policy
Base flow	Predictable high flow rates	Minimum (zero) stocks. Direct deliveries from suppliers.
Wave flow	Slow moving flow rates. High criticality. Perishable. Peaks are relatively predictable.	Minimize stockholdings, building them only during peak demand period. Direct delivery from supplier where possible.
Surge flow (1)	High criticality Low value Long lead time Small physical size.	Hold high level of stock thereby allowing safety stock for delivery lead time and demand fluctuations.
Surge flow (2)	Low criticality High value Bulky physical characteristics Peaks are relatively predictable	Minimize stockholdings, building them only during peak demand period. Direct delivery from supplier where possible.

■ **ABC Analysis**

For most businesses there is a relationship between the sales produced across a range of products. Typically some 20 per cent of the product range will account for 80 per cent of the total sales. ABC analysis ranks products by sales or contribution to profitability and then checks for significant differences between the high and low volume items which may give an indication of how best each may be managed. An obvious issue to be resolved concerns the location of stockholding points. If reliable service is to be given to customers, and a complete range of products is stocked in all locations, the costs will be high and probably excessive. For each item both cycle stock and safety stock will be required, together with the direct and indirect cost items discussed earlier. It has been found that the favoured cost-effective solution is to limit the number of stockholding points for slow moving items and use transportation to effect a direct delivery service. The increase in transportation costs is not as large as the increase that would occur for stockholding should all locations carry a complete inventory range. ABC analysis permits differential availability levels and order processing methods. With the adoption of JIT manufacturing, many companies adjust their stockholding policies to reflect customer requirements; ABC analysis can be helpful in responding to customer JIT requirements.

■ **Forecasting Methods**

There are a number of forecasting methods used to estimate the amount of each product that is likely to be purchased. It is important for many obvious reasons that forecasts are accurate; without an accurate forecast, customer service may be unacceptable, and the reasons for poor levels of service may not simply be attributed to lack of inventory but to the lack of labour and transportation facilities to assemble and deliver the order. Lambert and Stock give a number of alternatives:

Survey buying intentions: using mail and telephone questionnaires or personal interviews, although the latter is an expensive method and intentions can of course change. However, it does have the advantage of maintaining customer contact, often with those smaller customers not seen regularly by sales staff.

Judgement sampling: uses the experience of the field force. It can be relatively inexpensive but does suffer from accuracy problems, particularly if sales remuneration and incentives are based upon sales achievements.

Past sales trends: are used by many companies. For many companies short-term forecasting is acceptable for inventory management. The earlier discussion concerned with inventory types (i.e. base, wave and surge flows) suggests the profile necessary for lead times and forecast accuracy.

EPOS links with customers: the rapid development of point-of-sale data capture systems has enabled accuracy to be improved by using sales data to create replenishment systems and production and stockholding forecasts. Many supplier/distributor systems are becoming capable of much longer-term forecasting.

Clearly, forecasting accuracy is crucial to maintaining high levels of customer service *and* plant utilization. For these reasons JIT and similar methods are attractive as they can shorten the total time from raw materials sourcing to the delivery of final product.

■ Inventory Models

There are a number of computer-based inventory models available, most of which are able to produce purchase orders, shipping orders, delivery notes and invoices. Most models claim to reduce inventory holding costs without loss of customer service, and accordingly afford buyers more time to evaluate alternative suppliers or to work on new requirements. Improved management control is claimed because the specified rules and objectives are consistent and can be easily revised; service is more stable; workload scheduling is an integral part of the model; data inputs are consistent and can be improved to ensure improved model accuracy; and many models now link supplier and distributor systems thereby improving accuracy and decreasing costs, *but* increasing dependencies.

■ Order Processing Systems

A number of companies find that, provided they have a reliable information data source, an automated and integrated order processing system can reduce the time required to perform standard elements of the order cycle, including order entry, order processing, and inventory replenishment. By automating these activities time may be reallocated for inventory planning. The time saved usually offers savings in carrying costs by reducing the level of safety stock required. Other benefits are the improved decisions made on raw materials replenishment, inventory and production scheduling, faster invoicing and, consequently, improved cash flows.

■ Performance Measures

There are a number of indicators that suggest to management that inventory management techniques could be improved. Some of these indications are:

- Increasing customer and distributor complaints accompanied by a high rate of customer and distributor turnover and order cancellation;
- Increasing level of stockholding and decreasing stockturn performance;
- Increasing level of backorders;
- Periodic excesses and shortages of storage space;
- Increasing level of stock obsolescence.

In order that the inventory investment be maintained at a cost-effective level, a number of measures should be introduced. These are financial, operational and marketing performance features:

☐ *Financial Performance*

- Return on inventory investment
- Inventory investment/working capital investment
- Percentage of inventory increase (decrease) versus percentage of sales increase (decrease)
- Percentage of inventory increase (decrease) versus percentage of cost of sales increase (decrease)
- Stock 'write-off' and markdowns.

☐ *Operational Performance*

- Customer service levels over time
- Inventory turnover performance; product groups, rate of sale categories, etc.
- Inventory accuracy: actual count/indicated
- Number of customers *not* supplied from stock
- Number of SKUs out of stock/number of days
- Number of trading periods in which stockouts occurred
- Number of stockouts per year (or other significant period)
- Number of SKUs out of stock at month end
- Probability of stockout/product groups, rate of sale categories, etc.
- Percentage of demand supplied from stock

The US based Council of Logistics Management (CLM) proposed an extensive array of inventory performance measures, including many of the items suggested above. Using their format introduced in Chapter 7 we have (together with some additional proposed measures):

Productivity	Utilization	Performance
1. Total dollar ($) value inventory managed/ inventory holding cost	1. Stock value/working capital Stock turns by relevant category	1. Actual dollar/($) value of inventory/planned dollar ($) value of inventory
2. Total SKUs managed/ inventory holding cost		2. Actual inventory management cost/ budgeted inventory management cost
3. Total dollar/($) value inventory managed/ costs attributable to inventory management activity		

■ Summary

Inventory carrying costs are a major component of providing effective customer service. As we have seen in this chapter, the cost considerations extend well beyond the cost of inventory alone and include storage facility costs, service costs and risk from obsolescence, damage and shrinkage. In addition there are indirect costs, largely overlooked by many companies.

Cost relationships and the behaviour of cost entities resulting from responding to customer expectations of service aspects of inventory were identified and discussed together with examples.

Inventory costs, being a large proportion of logistics costs for the majority of organisations, require sophisticated methods of control. One effective method of control is to classify the inventory by the type of 'flow' that results from market demand characteristics; this in effect is a classification of inventory holding by product characteristics.

Performance criteria and measurement were also discussed.

CHAPTER 9

Transportation Choices in the Supply Chain

Introduction

Transportation is the linkage process in logistics and often consumes much of the resources provided to the logistics function. It once dominated the distribution activity (and indeed for many companies it was the distribution function) but for most companies it is now integrated into an overall activity. There are three factors that need to be considered. *Operational* factors include: customer, environmental, product and company characteristics. The choice of *transport mode* is influenced by: load size, density, value, competitive necessity and cost structures. *Channel strategy* considerations include the identification of available channels and the interfaces within each channel.

In this chapter we consider the essential steps necessary to make an appropriate transport selection decision. In doing so, the issues concerning the interface areas with other elements of the logistics system are discussed.

Transportation (with facilities) creates time utility value in the supply chain. The extent of this will be part of the decision-making process. Clearly, there are a number of options available: the decision on which one to use will be based upon a number of factors. Transportation also creates place utility value by delivering product to locations that are convenient for customers.

The Transportation/Logistics/Marketing Interface

The time and place utilities created by transportation are an important aspect of customer satisfaction and, therefore, are important aspects of the overall marketing offer. Through the process of trade-off analysis, the appropriate or relevant involvement of transportation can be decided. However, to do so requires an understanding of the scope of the transportation/logistics/marketing interface.

Transportation possibly accounts for the largest resource commitment in the logistics activity; therefore its relative cost/benefit profile must be established within the context of the level of customer satisfaction that is being set as an objective.

There are a number of interface areas, and therefore decisions shared by transportation. These should be explored by first identifying the areas of flexibility and inflexibility of the decisions and, most importantly, that of the customer service objectives. Before discussing the interface areas an example may amplify the issue. Given two customer situations, one in which the customer determines delivery schedules down to 15-minute windows and one in which the customer is flexible, it can be seen that, in the first situation, if the delivery is attempted either side of the 15-minute window it is unlikely that it will be accepted and redelivery costs will be incurred. But in the other customer situation, if the product is not one of the customers 'critical items' there may be some flexibility in the delivery schedule. It follows that the supplier may be able to use an alternative transport method for effecting delivery. Similarly, there is a need for accurate deliveries in situations where time delays may prove to be extremely serious. Medical supplies are obvious examples, but increasingly the expansion of JIT production methods is putting pressure on delivery systems and decreasing the flexibility that existed in many supplier/customer relationships.

The decisions influenced by transportation considerations include:

Customer communications: for suppliers and distributors who share an integrated ordering communications system it follows that a minimum of delay is likely in the order cycle time period. It is possible for order cycle times to be reduced, using electronic transfer, and this may enable the use of alternative transportation modes or perhaps the increased utilization of existing methods. Increasingly, as IT becomes more sophisticated and as suppliers and distributors see more benefits from closer cooperation, we may expect to find increased efficiencies in transportation.

Market coverage: transportation costs have a large influence in the size of markets covered. But cost is but one influence; other characteristics include flexibility, reliability and of course frequency of availability. The characteristics of the product will influence the economics of the decision. Clearly, a low volume/weight high value product will be able to support higher costs, and therefore extended delivery distances and, perhaps, increased delivery frequencies.

Sourcing decisions: the geographical dimensions of source markets can be influenced by the availability of low cost, relevant transportation. For example, reliable bulk freight services can extend source markets. Many large companies are beginning to consider 'trade-off' configurations between resources (price and quality) and the costs involved in delivering to the processing point (volume and costs of transportation).

Processing/manufacturing: the economic aspects of processing/manufacturing location have been mentioned earlier. Clearly, transportation costs have a large influence on the location of the manufacturing/market centre decision. Typically extraction-based industries will process close to their source of raw materials, while those products for which the value added occurs closer to the point of customer satisfaction are likely to be located near the customer.

Pricing decisions: for many businesses transportation is a large component of total product costs. Accordingly, the selection of the transportation mode will have an impact on transportation and consequently product pricing. This relationship may be more predominant in export pricing.

Customer service decisions: transportation decisions are a factor to be considered when customer service policy is being considered. Again, it may be expected that decisions will vary considerably by market type. A large distributor of industrial gases selling to a wider range of sectors is particularly conscious of the need to meet the requirements of medical customers and uses speed rather than cost when selecting transport mode.

■ Factors Affecting the Choice of Transport Selection

Slater (1990) suggests a very thorough approach to transport mode selection. His approach will influence that taken in this chapter. We shall start by considering some of the issues of strategic significance for the business which can have an influence on overall logistics decisions as well as those for transportation mode options.

■ Strategic Issues Influencing Logistics and Transportation Selection

There are five factors which should be considered in the choice of transportation:

- Company characteristics and philosophy
- Market structure
- Product characteristics (current and future)
- Customer characteristics
- Environmental issues

Company characteristics: these are important and concern the company's marketing, financial, and operations strategies. The company's *marketing strategy* is important because this will determine the parameters for the *customer service offer* (both what *aspects* of service are to be offered and the *performance levels* to be achieved); this may be customized to meet different customer needs or, in the case of markets that are not service sensitive, a standard qualifying level of service may be satisfactory. Financial strategies are equally important. The view of *how* profit objectives are to be met will be reflected in financial structure decisions. As we have seen earlier in Chapter 4 an increasing number of companies are questioning the ownership of non-essential assets; even those assets involved in the core business are being questioned. This suggests that investment in non-core activities is likely to be minimal unless there is a clear requirement to control the function, i.e. to ensure service delivery perhaps. There are obvious implications for logistics: both fixed and current assets. Performances will be expected to reflect these strategies. Clearly, transport decisions are important in this respect.

The structure of the firm's *operating* function will have an important influence. Continuous production processes with high levels of throughput usually service volume markets with a competitive need for economical but effective delivery. Increasingly, such companies are centralizing manufacturing, thereby increasing the service responsibility of the transport function within logistics systems.

Market structures are important considerations. There are two factors: competitive structure and the geographical structure or territorial considerations. In fiercely competitive markets delivery may be one of the key factors influencing customers' selection of suppliers. Add to this a national or 'pancontinental' market operation and clearly transport decisions are of a major influence in achieving customer satisfaction.

The important *product characteristics* to be considered are weight, size and shape, robustness, 'shelf-life', potential danger, value and special characteristics which may require expensive handling services and/or equipment. Often one or perhaps two of these characteristics are important and as such dominate the transport decision. For example, very heavy machinery items usually require 'heavy load' specialists who are expert at route planning and liaising with police and other authorities. 'Value' is another characteristic requiring specialist skills. The transfer and collection of cash is another expert field. Short shelf-life products require chilled or refrigerated vehicles which are expensive to acquire and to operate. The long association that has existed between Marks & Spencer and Trans-shield is another example of how Marks & Spencer view the need to utilize specialist skills.

Customer characteristics have an impact on profitability. Often it is those characteristics which influence delivery costs that are important as to whether or not a customer is profitable to the business. The characteristics of particular interest concern the value and profile of customer orders; delivery specifications (i.e. whether deliveries are made to customers' distribution facilities or direct to their outlets or subsidiary plants if manufacturers. The delivery specification should also include (and record) any time constraints that are imposed by the customer; order cycle and customer availability expectations; customer capabilities and capacities for mechanical handling; and customer after-sales service requirements.

Environmental issues: can influence a transport mode decision in a number of ways. In its broadest scope environment can be taken to include government and its influence on transport policy. There are examples of government subsidizing specific modes in an attempt either to make its selection viable or to switch use from one mode to another. Clearly, effective transport selection benefits from a current and detailed knowledge and understanding of government infrastructure policy. Transport technology changes continually and again, current knowledge of the benefits offered by technological developments in both the short and long run can assist in planning decisions. It is becoming important to be aware of international environmental issues that can affect transport decisions. An example is the control over transportation infrastructure that continues to exist in those ex-Eastern European communist countries where controls still exist and administration at both strategic and operational levels is bureaucratic and consequently difficult to deal with.

Unlike inventory investment, the transportation decision does offer an alternative. Whereas to offer service the firm has to make an investment in inventory and seeks to optimize the level of inventory held, transport decisions do vary: the company can choose to operate its own transport function, lease the vehicles and manage the service function, or it may opt to use a specialist service company.

Figure 9.1 identifies the costs to be considered. It also suggests that two other influences must be considered; the characteristics of alternative transport modes and the characteristics of the customer service policy. These two aspects are important to the overall decision. In this chapter, we shall consider the characteristics of the transport mode alternatives in some detail; customer service issues were considered in Chapters 2 and 3. Consequently, we shall deal with them in less detail here.

■ Characteristics of Alternative Transport Modes

The concept of trade-off possibilities and potential for overall costs is important within the transport decision. There are three that should be considered:

Horizontal trade-offs: occur within and between the different transport modes which could be selected to perform the same task, such as air versus sea, or road versus rail.

Vertical trade-offs: occur where a change takes place in a transport activity and offers a *greater benefit* in another area of the logistics function or the organization, such as markedly improved productivity due to an infrastructure development, for example a new motorway.

Lateral trade-offs: occur where transport costs can be weighted against *lower costs* in other areas. Using express air freight services may increase the freight cost but reduce the need for distribution centres or high inventory holding.

The effect of express freight service is particularly notable. We are now seeing market-led express freight companies, positioning themselves as 'total service' companies with the objective of reducing the customers' costs and increasing their cash flow. This has resulted in user companies closing portions of their own network in preference for that operated by the service company. Higher transport costs are incurred but are 'traded-off' against lower operating costs and fixed costs. See Exhibit 1 for an example.

The characteristics of each transport mode may make that mode more or less attractive depending upon the relevant product and customer service characteristics. We have considered some of the important *product characteristics* earlier, and we shall now consider them together with others to make comparisons of alternative transport choices:

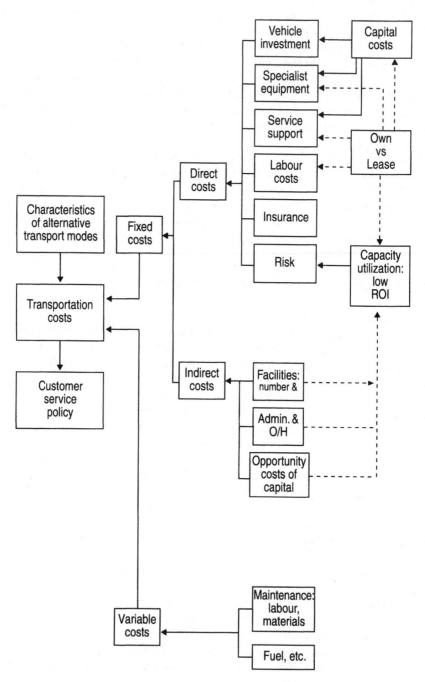

Figure 9.1   Cost factors affecting transportation decisions

Exhibit 1
Example of the express freight trade-off

BENETTON
(Extract from an article in *Distribution*, October, 1993)

■ **Air Power is Sales Power**

More than any other apparel company, Benetton understands airfreight. Half of Benetton's $2 billion in sales are shipped to 7,000 stores in 100 countries by air with an eight-day order cycle time.

'The cost of airfreight is not nearly as important as the savings in inventory and the increased sales from having the products in the stores when customers want them,' says Giancarlo Chiodini, Benetton's top logistics executive.

According to Roberto Bordo, executive vice president of WIDE, Benetton's exclusive forwarder in the United States, his company receives 14 air consolidations per week, mostly on Alitalia, the only carrier with freighter and widebody flights from Milan to New York and Los Angeles. WIDE uses motor carriers to distribute the 6,000 individual cartons in the 14 weekly air consolidations and 11 weekly ocean containers to Benetton's 250 US stores.

'We have built the transit time into the schedule,' says Chiodini. 'We want the lower landed cost allowed by ocean freight because the duty includes transportation costs.' Regular replenishment, which occurs every week or two depending on the store, is sent by regular air consolidations.

Emergency shipments all go by air. Most stores receive shipments every 12 days.

Half of all shipments go by ocean, and the other half go airfreight. Chiodini says air shipments take seven to eight days door-to-door to almost any point in the world.

'We want goods to arrive in our Sicily stores at the same time they arrive in New York,' says Chiodini. 'It is very important that goods be in stock when our advertising runs.'

Benetton expects to double its $2 billion in sales by the end of the decade, primarily with rapid sales growth in developing countries. Chiodini says this will bring different logistics challenges in the future. Instead of manufacturing more than three-quarters of the products in north-eastern Italy, more production will be done as part of joint ventures in China, Turkey, Egypt, India and Mexico.

□ *Size and Weight Restrictions*

Air:　Little or no flexibility
Sea:　Virtually unlimited
Rail:　Some dimensions restrictions (height) none for weight
Road:　Height and weight restrictions.

□ *Safety*

Air:　Highly regulated
Sea:　Less regulated than air
Rail:　Few restrictions
Road:　Less regulated than air.

□ *Fragility*

Air:　Reliable product handling
Sea:　Variable reliability
Rail:　Transport vehicles cash have vibration and shunting problems
Road:　Handling problems can occur often.

□ *Temperature*

Air:　Temperature controlled containers are available
Sea:　Controlled
Rail:　Controlled
Road:　Controlled.

□ *Cost per unit*

Air:　High
Sea:　Low
Rail:　Low
Road:　Moderate (can vary with service requirement).

■ **Characteristics of Customer Service Policy**

Customer service is, as we have found, influenced by market characteristics and competitive offers. Within the scope of transport decisions, order cycle length (delivery time) and reliability are important factors. Comparisons of transport choices in this context are:

☐ *Transit Time and Reliability*

Air: Fast and reliable
Sea: Slow; reliability varies by port: full container loads (FCL) are more
          reliable
Rail: Dedicated services reliable: part shipments have difficulties
Road: Versatile and usually offer good transit times; loading and unloading
          can slow progress. Reliability varies with the service policy of each
          company.

■ **Cost Characteristics**

Figure 9.1 makes the point of identifying the choice open to management: the
'make or buy' option. Virtually all of the cost items identified in Figure 9.1 will
vary depending upon this decision. The decision to lease transport will
eliminate or decrease many of the direct cost items, but in so doing will
increase operating or variable costs. Leasing will result in a much lower level of
investment in vehicles, specialist equipment, service support, and so on, and will
lower the risk of poor capacity utilization. However, the variable costs would
be increased by a charge based on weight/distance carried and perhaps trips
(where many costs are incurred by frequent loading and unloading).

The choice ultimately depends upon such factors as financial policy,
customer service policy, the control the company requires, and the intensity
of the competition within the market.

■ **Service Company Selection: Some Considerations**

Should carriers feature in the logistics activity some criteria should be
established for their selection. The carrier selection process is complex and
should begin with identifying carrier attributes required to implement the
company's customer service policy. They should be rank ordered to reflect
importance. Potential service companies should then be evaluated against these
criteria to determine those most suitable.

Among the many attributes used, the following represent a typical spread
from which an effective evaluation may be determined.

● *Current performance*: delivery accuracy and reliability.
● *Acceptance of responsibility*: a willingness to guarantee the service product
  offered.
● *Flexibility*: an ability to respond to emergency situations.
● *Comprehensive services offer*: the range of services offered, their capacity
  and the company's capabilities.

- *Information systems*: information availability is essential for control purposes.
- *Financial stability*: is necessary to ensure continuity of service *and* for the upgrade of the equipment within the business.
- *Compatibility*: the service company's management should share the same, or similar, views on objectives and strategy for their business. They should be capable of integrating into the customer business, sharing its confidences and its problems.

■ Performance Measures

Regardless of whether the transport function is owned or *leased*, its performance should be monitored. The NCPDM (now CLM) proposals for measuring transport management performance adopt the same format as those used for facilities and inventory management. For *overall management measures* they suggest:

Productivity	*Utilization*	*Performance*
1. Weight/distance transported/Total actual transportation cost	1. Total transportation capacity used/Total transportation capacity owned (or paid for)	1. Actual transportation cost/Budgeted transportation cost
2. Stops served/Total actual transportation cost		2. Standard transportation cost/Actual transportation cost
3. Volume of goods transported to destinations/Total actual transportation cost		3. Actual transit times/ Standard transit times
4. Shipments transported to destinations/Total actual transportation cost		
5. Standard weight distance/Total actual transportation cost.		

■ Summary

Transportation decisions are important in supply chain management because they impact upon customer service and on other areas of cost. Transportation decisions are prominent within company logistics decisions due to the trade-off potential existing between alternative transportation modes and the other logistics functions within the firm. It follows that an understanding of the costs and benefits of alternative transport modes, together with a rigorous evaluation of overall corporate implications, is essential. As with inventory management, the direct and indirect costs of transportation were found to be wide-ranging and significant.

Performance criteria were proposed and discussed.

CHAPTER 10

Supply Chain Communications

▌Introduction

The speed and efficiency with which customers' orders are processed and progressed have impact upon both profitability and marketing success. Time lags within the company in handling orders increase overall distribution costs because they necessitate larger inventory holding, and possibly faster transportation, if customer service levels are to be maintained. Larger inventories (and faster transportation) give rise to greater working capital requirements and operating costs. It follows that effective communications can eliminate some of these costs. This chapter considers the activities involved in order processing and handling, such as order acquisition and entry, document and materials processing, delivery and invoicing. An important part of the chapter is consideration of the means by which the process can be managed through the application of information technology. Information transfer through EDI, EPOS and EFTPOS (electronic funds transfer at point of sale) systems will be reviewed from a cost/benefit approach. The chapter will commence with a discussion on the role of information for decision-making and consider how the information flows within the communications activity enhances decision-making.

▌Information for Planning and Control

There are a number of roles fulfilled by the communications activities of the business, both internally and externally. Communications systems typically act as linkages within the supply chain *identifying* product needs and locations and *directing* product flows to ensure customer satisfaction. This process requires the *management* of 'stocks and flows' within the business (and from suppliers and to customers); consequently there needs to be a relevant flow of information from the activities that are responsible for the effective planning and control functions of the logistics system and, in a broader context, the supply chain.

Effective communications systems do, of necessity, imply effective planning and control. Information required to ensure efficient management of inventory stocks and flows to meet customer requirements also provides an input into the overall management of the business. A review of the stages of the customer order cycle suggests how this occurs. In Figure 10.1 we describe the path of an order from the point at which the customer places an order through to the delivery of the order. At each stage there are a number of data created which, if captured and created into structured input, can form the basis of an information management system.

We can be more structured in this context by identifying the information requirements of the three levels of management involved in logistics decisions. In Table 10.1 we identify by level of management their information requirements if the business is to be managed effectively.

At board level, responsibility is for the management of the business with respect to generating a satisfactory return for the shareholders. As we suggest, the information requirements for this level of management concern the effectiveness of the investment in the logistics function in achieving the levels of performance appropriate to this end. In addition, the board requires information indicating future development trends in markets and by customers to provide input for future investment decisions. Given information (albeit in broad detail) on company performance output, on customer service achievements and supplier delivery performance, the board retains control over the logistics performance of the business and is sufficiently well informed concerning whether to maintain its investment in the logistics assets or perhaps to reconsider ownership in favour of leasing or service arrangements with specialist service companies.

A more detailed information set is required by functional directors and senior operating managers. Here the need is for more 'hands on' data in order that effective implementation is achieved. Thus we see their requirements for performance details with respect to predetermined targets for customer service and logistics system outputs. Their specific interests are in ensuring that the logistics system operates at (or near) maximum capacity, within budgeted costs. In so doing, it will ensure that overall volume and market share targets are met.

At the supervisory level, short term, detailed performance data are required. The information frequency will be determined by the nature of the business and the demand cycles of customers. For example, fast-moving consumer goods have much shorter order cycle time periods than do industrial products. Similarly, seasonal products will have yet again quite different cycles and corresponding information cycles.

An overall view of information requirements for supply chain management is presented in Figure 10.2. The supply chain activities are represented and the information requirements of the manufacturer/distributor company (coordinating supply chain management, both inbound and outbound) are also indicated. The role of effective communications in this context is to ensure that relevant data is collected, assembled and published to the appropriate users.

■ Investment Decisions

A point we have made earlier concerning the monetary value of information is worthy of repeat. Reliable, fast and accurate information is capable of reducing the overall capital and operating logistics costs. If we return to the order cycle

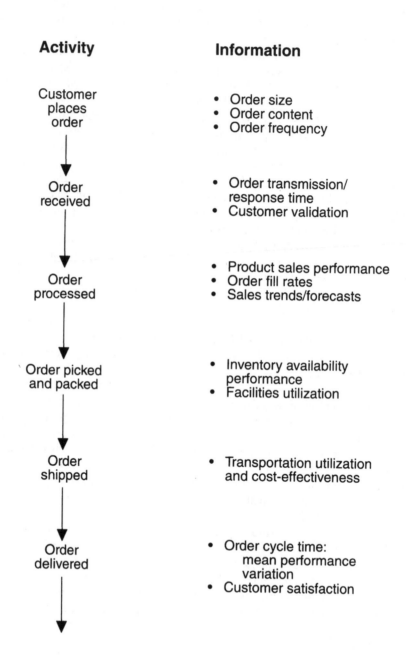

Activity	Information
Customer places order	• Order size • Order content • Order frequency
Order received	• Order transmission/ response time • Customer validation
Order processed	• Product sales performance • Order fill rates • Sales trends/forecasts
Order picked and packed	• Inventory availability performance • Facilities utilization
Order shipped	• Transportation utilization and cost-effectiveness
Order delivered	• Order cycle time: mean performance variation • Customer satisfaction

Figure 10.1   Customer order processing generates information for planning and control

Table 10.1 Strategic and operational information requirements

Level of management	Information requirements

Board level management (planning and control)	• Market development forecasts:
	 Capacity requirements:
	  number of facilities
	  location of facilities
	  transportation capacities
	  inventory holding levels
	• Customer service requirements:
	 Capability requirements:
	  customer service response
	  supplier service delivery
	• Investment return profiles:
	 Core business
	 Support activities
	• * Current system capability profile:
	 Customer service achievement
	 Supplier delivery performance
	• Customer performance profile:
	 Volume and market share
	 Margins
	 ROCE; ROE
	Note: Item marked * is for broad/macro performance indicators

Functional directors and senior operations management (managing implementation) (information may be disaggregated at the operating management level to reflect product group, territory or customer responsibility)	• Current system capacity and capability profile: – Customer service achievement; – Supplier delivery performance; – System capacity achievement; facility volume and area utilization, transport utilization, availability/inventory holding, – Customer and supplier relationships • Current performance profile (detailed): – Volume and market share (by territory and large customer segments, etc.) – Margins (gross, operating and net (Performance against budget)
Supervisory level (managing the operational business) (data frequency cycles will vary by product type)	• Customer service achievements: – Orders satisfied; response time – Order cycle time; length of order cycle reliability performance – Availability; performance achieved, backorders/follow up deliveries • Sales volume performance achievements: – Territory; – Segment; – Customer (performance against budget)

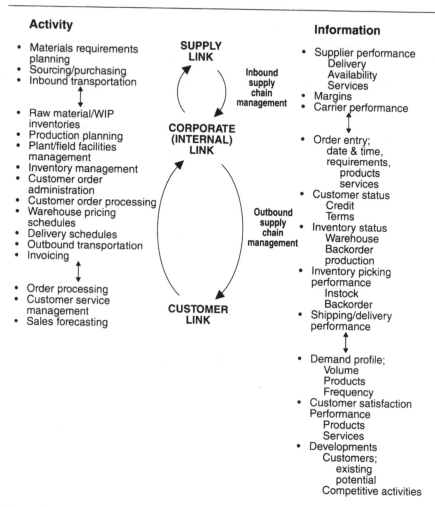

Activity

- Materials requirements planning
- Sourcing/purchasing
- Inbound transportation

- Raw material/WIP inventories
- Production planning
- Plant/field facilities management
- Inventory management
- Customer order administration
- Customer order processing
- Warehouse pricing schedules
- Delivery schedules
- Outbound transportation
- Invoicing

- Order processing
- Customer service management
- Sales forecasting

SUPPLY LINK

Inbound supply chain management

CORPORATE (INTERNAL) LINK

Outbound supply chain management

CUSTOMER LINK

Information

- Supplier performance
  Delivery
  Availability
  Services
- Margins
- Carrier performance

- Order entry;
  date & time,
  requirements,
  products
  services
- Customer status
  Credit
  Terms
- Inventory status
  Warehouse
  Backorder
  production
- Inventory picking performance
  Instock
  Backorder
- Shipping/delivery performance

- Demand profile;
  Volume
  Products
  Frequency
- Customer satisfaction
  Performance
  Products
  Services
- Developments
  Customers;
    existing
    potential
  Competitive activities

Figure 10.2   Activity and information processes: a role for communications effectiveness in the supply chain

described in Figure 10.1 we can demonstrate how this can occur. In Table 10.2 we have added invoicing and payment time as part of the overall customer ordering process. The example demonstrates how effective in reducing order-processing time the application of IT systems may be. Clearly the issue to be resolved is the comparison between the capital costs (or interest charges) and associated 'one-off' change-over costs with the long-term cost savings.

There will also be qualitative issues to be identified and evaluated. Included in this category are issues of control, confidentiality of sensitive information, improved communications effectiveness, improvements in trading relationships, and so on.

Table 10.2   Hypothetical situation involving the evaluation of an IT-based customer ordering process

Activity	Existing system time (days)	Proposed system time (days)
Customer prepares and mails order	4	1
Order received and entered into system	1	1
Order processing	2	
Order picking and packing	1	1
Order shipped	3	4
(transit time)	(11)	(6)
Invoicing	1	1
	(12)	(7)
Payment (average)	60	45
Total	(72)	(52)

Note:
1. If we assume a stockholding value of $20 million finished goods funded on overdraft, the cost of inventory holding at 15 per cent interest is $3 million. The average daily cost is $3 million/365 or $11 500.
2. If the accuracy of the proposed system is superior the payment time may be reduced due to the reduction of errors, stock-out situations, and improved invoicing accuracy.

The suggested process by which the overall impact of such a change may be evaluated is proposed in Figure 10.3. The basis of Figure 10.3 is a cost/benefit appraisal process. As is usual with such analyses there are difficulties to be overcome in assessing the financial effects of what are essentially non-accounting or accountable items. It has been found by those companies which have undertaken such appraisals that the analysis may be considerably assisted by approaching the problem in the way in which it was evaluated in Table 10.2. That is to identify each activity within the overall process of order management and to determine the time taken for each activity (and sub-activity), and *estimate* the accuracy of the output. It is quite possible for two systems to offer the same overall time period for processing, but for one to do so with more accuracy. It is only by undertaking such an analytical approach that comparisons may be made with any degree of confidence.

■ Information Transfer

Thus far we have considered information within the context of types of information to meet specific decision purposes and situations. The discussion requires expansion to consider how information utility may be enhanced by sharing data with other members of the supply chain. The remainder of this chapter details with this topic.

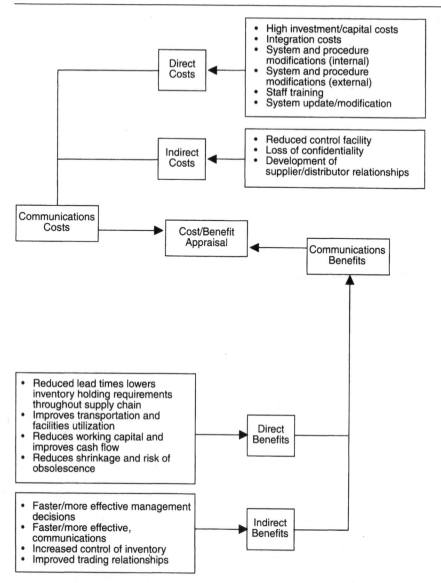

Figure 10.3   Cost/benefit appraisal of information/communications systems

The objectives of operational support systems are to assist in managing and controlling the day-to-day logistics operation which is described by de Leeuw (1990) as:

- *The physical operation*, such as transport, receiving stock and picking and despatching customer orders;

- *The paperwork operation* required to initiate and control the physical operation, such as purchase order processing, inventory control and customer order processing;
- *The accounting operation* for processing the financial transactions resulting from the physical operation, such as accounts payable and accounts receivable.

The operations may be seen as containing specific processes or activities:

- The *physical operation* comprising:
  receiving
  order picking and despatch
  control of stock by warehouse location
  physical stock-takes
  replenishment of stockholding points.
- The *paperwork operation* comprising:
  order processing
  purchasing
  stock control
  materials scheduling
- And the *accounting operation*:
  accounts receivable
  accounts payable
  general ledger.

De Leeuw sees these three operations as fundamental to operational control of the business, and also suggests them to be more effective if they are integrated. Recent software technology developments have made this possible and as a consequence the functions have become integrated into a decision support system in a number of companies.

EPOS and EFTPOS systems (electronic point-of-sale data capture and electronic funds transfer at point-of-sale) extend this integrated decision support system on two fronts. The *intra*-organization expansion enabled other functions within the business to use the data generated for planning and control purposes. For example, EPOS data which provides product movement information has been used to plan labour requirements and staffing schedules as well as plan replenishment schedules from retailer-operated warehouse facilities. The *inter*-organization feature of EPOS data was the extension of the data backwards into the supply chain in order that suppliers might more effectively plan production and raw materials acquisition. EFTPOS extended the external use of the data generated at the point of sale by linking transactions data with customers' sources of funds, thus effecting a more rapid payment cycle and thereby improving cash flows.

The increased data transfer between organizations required some structure and general acceptance by users (e.g. of the need for confidentiality, etc.). The use of EDI (electronic data interchange) in logistics applications mainly concerns the electronic interchange of trading documentation, such as purchase orders, acknowledgments and invoices, but the expansion of EPOS/EFTPOS applications has extended the list of uses. In addition to trading data, such items as technical data, credit enquiries, order status and product availability, together with price information, are becoming commonplace exchange items. EDI warrants detailed discussion.

■ 'EDI' Defined

EDI is most simply defined as:

The electronic *intercompany* transfer of *business documents* in a *standard format*.

where

• *Intercompany implies*	Interchange of documents between separate commercial entities, using unique computer operating systems.
• *Business documents implies*	Not simply electronic mail messages, it carries formal business documents and transactions of commercial and legal significance.
• *Standard format implies*	Universally agreed electronic format.

EDI is much more than simply a set of computer programs linking two or more locations and allowing computers to communicate with one another; it is a business concept of improving transactions between and among organizations. EDI is a tool which will permit organizations to exploit the availability of accurate *inter-organizational* information, facilitating the achievement of corporate objectives.

EDI is an example of trading partnership equations and, as organizations attempt to get close to their customers and their suppliers, they should *proactively* use EDI to allow the trading relationship to progress in an effective and coordinated fashion.

■ Applications of EDI

EDI takes its form in four areas of business:

- Electronic funds transfer – EFTPOS, banking clearing
- Trade data interchange – purchase orders, delivery advices, invoices
- Technical data interchange – technical drawings, scientific data
- Interactive query/response – travel bookings, customers' access

Using a simple example, let us look at trade data interchange. Traditionally, a computer application or person generates a paper document on a multipart form (e.g. a purchase order). This is sent internally for approval signatures. Copies are forwarded to various internal departments for filing, while one or more copies are sent through the postal service to a trading partner.

When the document reaches the trading partner, it is re-keyed into a computer application system. The re-keying often introduces discrepancies between the data sent and the data captured. The trading partner's system then generates a paper document for action and filing, and an acknowledgment is sent back. This cycle takes many days to complete.

Obviously, this method is neither efficient nor preferred. EDI automates data transfer between computers without human intervention – no matter if those computers are of different manufacture, or in different locations, or even on different continents.

However, the data formats must agree. Data is structured and assembled in a way that makes it recognizable to both sending and receiving computers. This enterprise-to-enterprise computing uses nationally and internationally recognized message standards – the ones used are agreed upon by the trading partners and usually are the same for a particular industry (e.g. EDIFACT = EDI for Administration, Commerce and Transport, which is slowly being adopted as the International Standard).

As a potential business tool, EDI should be treated with the same objective evaluation procedures we would use for any new idea/concept, such that the goals of the EDI project are aligned to the overall objectives of the organization. The evaluation and implementation of EDI should be viewed in four broad stages:

- Opportunity analysis
- Business case
- Requirements specification
- Implementation.

An integral part of this review is a cost/benefit analysis. Both the costs and benefits can be either direct or indirect and a list, which is by no means exhaustive, is found in Figure 10.4.

In order to determine the benefits that are likely to be derived from EDI, we must first understand the problems which exist currently. In general terms, the problems can be summarized as follows:

- Untimely/inaccurate information
- Long material lead times
- Slow manufacturing cycles
- Lengthy transportation lead times
- 'Just-in-case' philosophy

DIRECT BENEFITS	INDIRECT BENEFITS

• Highly efficient use of computers
• Reduced cost of intercompany information delivery
• Improved accuracy of information
• Reduced time of information delivery
• Improved efficiency in the areas of:
  – order processing
  – order placement
  – accounts payable/receivable
• Reduced inventory levels
	• Availability of staff for other assignments
	• Faster, better informed management decisions
	• Improved project management
	• Easier communication
	• Increased span of control
	• Improved trading relationship

DIRECT COSTS	**INDIRECT COSTS**
• Potentially high costs to fully integrate *application* systems • Need to modify/establish procedures • Need to modify existing systems • Requires effort/resource to work with trading partners • Coordinating internal efforts is time consuming • Potential loss of transaction security	• Disorganization and lower productivity • Need to build/maintain redundant systems • Few managers/staff able to understand the technology • Task forces relatively unproductive • Need new security procedures and products

Figure 10.4   EDI cost/benefit review

- What appear to be conflicting trading partner agendas. For example, in the retailer/manufacturer scenario, the retailer is looking for:
  - increased market share
  - minimal working capital
  - 100 per cent service performance from suppliers
  - improved warehouse utilization
  - no reordering
  The manufacturer is looking for:
  - increased market share
  - increased cash flow
  - zero out-of-stocks
  - establishment of partnerships.

Based on these problems, the key benefits of EDI potentially are going to include:

- More accurate and timely information flows
- Administrative savings/improved efficiency
- Closer trading relationships (a new spirit of working together)
- Improved cash flows
- A move closer to the final consumer and therefore a reduction in 'forecasting' errors.

The realization of these benefits will, however, depend on two critical factors: (1) the number of EDI documents exchanged; and (2) the number of EDI trading partners (*both up and down the supply chain*).

The more complete the document cycle, the greater the benefits to both trading partners. This means both parties will be required to share information and respect each others' need for security.

A complete *basic* transactional cycle is show in Figure 10.5.

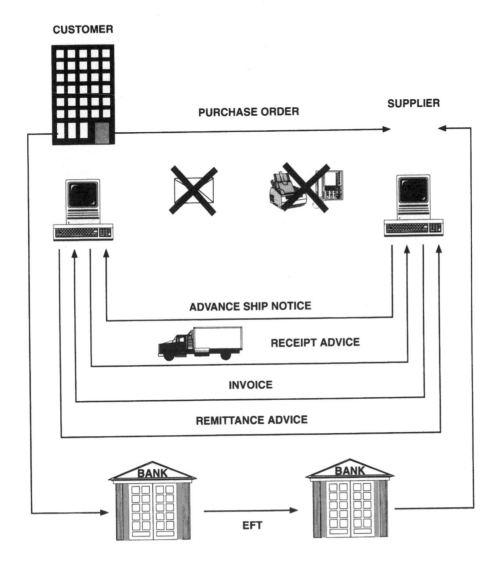

Figure 10.5 The EDI transactional flow

There are other documents, however, that are necessary if we are to succeed in shortening the supply chain. For example, inventory advice and product transfer and resale documents will ensure trading partners are aware of the quantity of stock in the supply chain and can work together to reduce it. Sales peaks, automatically highlighted by the exchange of electronic point-of-sale (EPOS) data can be taken into account in production planning and therefore material acquisition. A constant monitor of inventory levels will allow sales patterns to be more easily understood and an automatic stock replenishment policy agreed and implemented.

If EDI is to be effective its application must be broadcast with EDI links between *all* customers, otherwise the benefits of more timely and accurate information flows, and reduced paper/increased productivity will not be fully realized. Linking with suppliers is also crucial to the effective management of the total chain. The objective is obviously to create links between *each level* of the supply chain, including third-party logistics service suppliers.

Organizations that are likely to strongly benefit from EDI have the following features:

- multiple locations
- high turnover of inventory
- many recurring transactions
- need for accurate reporting and tracking
- a great deal of paperwork
- a need for timely processing.

■ EDI as a Value Added-Application: Future Issues

De Leeuw suggests that while EDI is well established in the packaged grocery business internationally and in the US motor industry, there remains some distance to be travelled.

Typical applications are between two companies with significant cost reductions in clerical activities, reductions in processing errors, tighter inventory control and time savings. Further efficiencies will be available once EDI and JIT techniques are combined. Clearly, JIT is dependent upon effective, reliable and rapid data transfer if it is to deliver the benefits it offers. Similarly quick response logistics systems will benefit from improved data flows.

The involvement of third-party service companies is seen as likely to advance the usefulness of EDI. The role of a third party will be to store and deliver data to participants. The use of direct connections is only practical when the number of participants is relatively small and stable (de Leeuw, 1990). The VAN (value added network) solution is likely to become widespread as the number of software packages available increases, which will make the technical implementation and use of EDI relatively simply.

A fully developed EDI application is described by de Leeuw, hypothetically:

The operational support system of company A generates suggested re-order quantities for a number of products which are supplied by company B. After the recommendations are approved by the Purchase Manager, the system generates a purchase order which is sent electronically to company B. Based on this purchase order, the operational support system of company B will automatically generate a sales order and perform a credit and stock availability check. If these checks are passed, company B system will electronically send an acknowledgment and will further process the order for order picking and despatch. An electronic advice will be sent to the transport company so that transport will be available on time. At the time of despatch, an invoice will be sent electronically to company A and, after the goods have been received, the accounts receivable module will check the invoice against the prices and quantities on the purchase order and against the prices and quantities actually received. If these tests are passed, an electronic message will be sent to the bank in order to trigger an electronic funds transfer or EFT, after which the amounts payable module for company B will be updated.

He suggests that human intervention is only required when actions have to be authorized or when certain checks (quantities despatched and then invoiced) are not met. Documents generated by the computer might only consist of exception reports and summarized overviews of transactions.

■ Measuring Communications Performance

The work done by the CLM on the development of productivity performance measures has been referred to in earlier chapters. We return to this work to complete this chapter. The general measures that the CLM consider suitable for order entry and related activities include:

- Actual order entry cycle time/standard order entry cycle time (by type of order);
- Order entry labour cost/total order-processing cost;
- Order entry non-labour cost/total order-processing cost;
- Total order entry cost/total distribution administrative cost;
- Actual monetary value of orders entered per period/total monetary value of orders received per period;
- Actual number of orders entered per period/total number of orders received per period;
- Actual number of SKUs entered per period/total number of SKUs received per period;
- Invoicing cost/total order-processing cost.

To monitor delays in invoicing:

- Actual value of invoices processed per period/actual value of orders available for invoicing per period;
- Actual number of invoices processed per period/actual number of orders available for invoicing per period;
- Actual number of SKUs invoiced per period/actual number of SKUs available for invoicing per period.

The following measures may be useful in evaluating the complete order processing activity:

- Actual total order cycle time per order/standard cycle time;
- Total order processing labour cost/total order-processing cost;
- Total order-processing non-labour cost/total order processing cost.

For quality control purposes the following are suggested:

- Number of transaction (order, invoice, etc.) errors/total number of transactions processed;
- Number of (company caused) emergency orders/total number of orders processed;
- Number of back orders generated/total number of orders processed;
- Number of times the phone must be allowed to ring (minimum) per customer call before it is answered;
- Number of incoming calls (minimum) going unanswered per period;
- Number of engaged signals (minimum) registered per period/total number of incoming calls.

For evaluating investment in accounts receivable:

- Total accounts receivable/total net sales;
- Total accounts receivable/net daily sales;
- Total sales on extended credit facilities/total accounts receivable on extended credit facilities;
- Average age (in days) of accounts receivable;
- Past due accounts receivable categorized by time period, e.g. 31–60 days, 61–90 days, over 90 days.

Specific measures for order entry scheduling, shipping and invoicing are suggested as:

Productivity	Utilization	Performance
1. Total orders entered/ total order entry costs	1. Total volume of orders entered/total order entry capacity	1. Actual order entry costs/budgeted order entry costs
2. Total SKUs entered/ total order entry costs	2. Total orders received/ total order entry capacity	2. Standard order entry cost allowances earned/total order entry costs incurred
3. Total monetary value of orders entered/total order entry costs	3. Total actual transaction throughput/maximum transaction capacity	3. Actual order set preparation costs/ budgeted order set preparation costs
4. Total number order sets prepared/total order set preparation costs	4. Total volume of order sets prepared/total order set preparation capacity	4. Actual 'other document' preparation costs/ budgeted 'other document' preparation costs
5. Total number other transaction documents prepared/ total cost of preparing other documents	5. Total volume of other transactions prepared/ total capacity for preparing other transactions	5. Standard order set preparation allowances earned/ total order set preparation costs incurred
6. Total number invoices prepared/total invoice preparation costs	6. Total volume of orders received for preparation/total order set preparation capacity	6. Standard 'other document' preparation allowances earned/ total 'other document' preparation costs
7. Total monetary value invoiced/total invoice preparation costs	7. Total volume of invoices processed/ total invoice processing capacity	7. Actual invoice processing costs/ budgeted invoice processing costs
8. Total number customer inquiries handled/total customer communication costs	8. Total volume of enquiries handled/ total inquiry handling capacity	8. Standard invoice processing cost allowances earned/ total invoice processing costs incurred
		9. Actual customer communication cost/ budgeted communication cost
		10. Standard customer communication cost allowances earned/ total actual costs incurred

■ Summary

Information determines the speed and efficiency with which customers' orders are processed and progressed and therefore has an important role in the overall success of the supply chain.

This chapter discusses the role of information for logistics planning and control. As such it is a communications system linking supply chain functions by identifying product needs (at specific locations and volumes) and coordinating product flows to ensure customer satisfaction. Thus information has a dominant role in the management of stocks and flows in the supply chain.

Effective information management requires effective investment decisions. These can only be made provided a thorough review of the information needs of the business are determined. It is also necessary to ensure that the cost-effectiveness of information technology is fully understood to ensure that appropriate technology is applied to the management task.

Performance criteria and measurement were also discussed.

CHAPTER 11

Formulating a Supply Chain Strategy

■ Introduction

The concept of strategy has been widely used but remains essentially a 'formula or a plan to compete effectively in a marketplace'. To be of use a strategy requires direction (vision and objectives) and resources. However, if we are to be sure of successful implementation, the organization's strategy should 'fit' the profile of the marketplace, otherwise inappropriate responses will follow. Specifically, the logistics strategy should integrate with both the corporate and marketing strategies. It follows that its success will be measured within the context of the performance of both of these. Changes made to either will require matching changes to the logistics strategy. This chapter considers the process involved in developing a logistics strategy. It assumes an understanding of the overall process of determining corporate strategy, and accordingly concentrates upon the more important issue of developing an integrated logistics strategy. The chapter also considers the impact of changes in corporate strategy on logistics strategy.

■ Formulating Strategies: Identifying the Criteria for Evaluating Strategic 'Fit'

The selection of an appropriate transaction channel strategy will be influenced by a number of considerations. The issues of strategic fit and of organizational structure are major issues, but there are others. Rumelt (1988) proposes four criteria that should be applied to a business strategy:

- *Consistency*: the strategy should not present mutually inconsistent goals and policies.
- *Consonance*: the strategy should represent an adaptive response to the external environment and to the critical changes occurring within it.
- *Advantage*: the strategy should also provide for the creation and/or maintenance of competitive advantage in the selected area.
- *Feasibility*: the strategy must neither overtax available resources nor create unsolvable sub-problems.

He suggests that a strategy which fails to meet one or more of these criteria is strongly suspect. He suggests further that 'experience within a particular industry or other setting will permit the analyst to sharpen these criteria and add others that are appropriate to the situation at hand'.

It is possible to modify Rumelt's criteria and to apply them as evaluation criteria during the formation and implementation of a logistics strategy. Clearly, the influence of each criterion will vary according to the strategic issue. The criteria we suggest as important in the context of logistics strategy selection are:

■ Consistency

The strategy should be consistent throughout the range of components (or intermediaries) within the strategy and within the planning process. The consistency should be both longitudinal and temporal. *Longitudinal consistency* is concerned with decisions taken throughout the channel structure, i.e. intermediaries' roles and tasks should be consistent with the overall objectives of the channel structure. *Temporal consistency* concerns the life cycle span of the channel structure. In this context the concern is that the overall channel structure will be durable over time and that components undertaking specific roles and tasks may be expected to have temporal durability and will be able to fulfil their specific functions during the *expected* lifespan of the strategy.

■ Consonance

This was established as an adaptive response to the environment and to the critical changes occurring within it. There are three elements of change to which the business must adapt. The first is the environment itself. The second concerns the competitive environment: not only are existing competitors attempting to change and 'fit' into the new environment but new competitors appear as new opportunities are identified, or perhaps as technology offers more cost-effective delivery methods in existing product-markets. The third element of change concerns the business itself. As we have seen in earlier chapters, culture and leadership styles can and do change; indeed, the need for senior executives to be empathetic with and aligned to their operating environment is now seen as obligatory. If culture and leadership style changes do not reflect the changes in the market environment (or are not *consonant* with them) then effective management of strategic response becomes much more difficult

There are competitive issues of consonance that are important. Rumelt describes these as the difference across firms at a given time. He describes *generic* strategies as a basic pattern of economic relationships that characterize the business and determine whether or not sufficient value is being created to sustain the corporate direction. This assumes the corporate direction to be a valid response to the current business environment. The competitive response is essentially a switch of emphasis. The analysis is comparative and external, for example the competitive view of return to the firm is concerned with the return on investment, and the measure of success is market share rather than sales growth. The issue of consonance in this context is to ensure that the view of competition and competitive comparative measures are similar to those of competitors; if they are not, the result may be that the company distances itself from the marketplace.

■ Continuity

If strategy is to be successful, then as a long-run initiative, it should be developed with continuity in mind. Gilbert and Strebel (1988) consider the importance of the industry life cycle. During the emergence stage, innovation and development are important issues. Standardization marks the first important transition whereby the product or the manufacturing/distribution process becomes an industry and rapid growth takes place. The few (but usually large) industry competitors seek to rejuvenate the product/offer (see Figure 11.1).

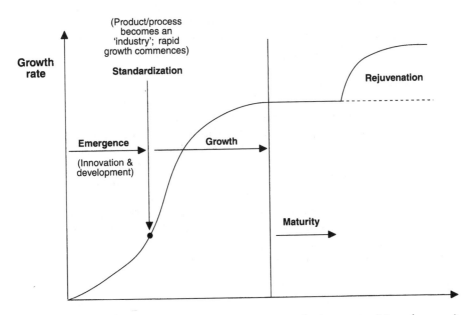

Source: adapted from X. Gilbert and P. Strebel, 'Developing competitive advantage', in J.B. Quinn *et al.*, *The Strategy Process*, New Jersey: Prentice-Hall, 1988

Figure 11.1   The industry life cycle

The issue of continuity concerns the impact of the industry life cycle on the management system structure. There will undoubtedly be significant impact on some elements such as systems, style, staff and skills, with considerable impact on structure and values. Clearly it is not always possible to forecast the development of specific life cycles. However, often it is possible to reach conclusions on how the industry may develop given similar situations in other industry activity chains. An example of similar, even parallel development has been that of the large-scale DIY format which is (like food retailing) dominated by few competitors operating large off-centre retail units. Forecasting such patterns of development enables the participants to develop the necessary *continuity* characteristics for competitive advantage.

■ Creativity

The extent to which a strategy is creative will vary. It could be assumed that there is more scope for creative thinking when the corporate direction proposes a strategy which is quite different to that currently pursued. However, perhaps a more useful way to view creativity considers the way in which the company's strategy proposes to deal with its environment.

Creativity is a way of looking at strategic problems rather than offering new and different approaches to the corporate direction – simply to be different. It is a reflection of the ability of the management system to respond to quite different external business environment situations. It is rooted in the culture of the company and is reflected in the company's leadership style as it responds to both internal and external pressures.

■ Competitive Advantage

In recent years competitive advantage has moved away from a position in which differentiation has become a competitive necessity towards a position where it is the scope and size of the value added for the customer that determines competitive advantage. Throughout the business structure, staff at all levels should be encouraged to think in terms of how value can be added to the customer offer. Rumelt suggests that competitive advantage can normally be traced to one of three roots: superior resources, superior skills, or superior positioning. Superior resources and skills can create 'real' value added; superior positioning can reinforce the perception of value added. Either way, these roots have the potential to become sustainable distinctive competences.

■ Capacity Utilization

The productive (and profitable) utilization of fixed and current assets enhances the successful strategy. In this context, the decision to be made concerns the extent to which a strategy may be more successful, dependent upon who owns the assets and the level of utilization that can be achieved. This follows because it can be shown that return on investment is a function of the role of asset circulation (the DuPont relationship described earlier); it also follows not only that return on investment will be higher if asset circulation is high, but that specialist functions may also decrease operating costs (and increase profit margins) and raise the ROI to a higher level of performance on a sustained basis.

☐ *Capacity Aspects of Culture*

Capacity has qualitative considerations. These are the facilitating characteristics available within the corporate culture to:

- Solve the problems and develop the competences required to implement strategy;
- Develop the coordinating and integrating skills necessary to implement strategy: uppermost here is *flexibility*; the ability to adapt to change – rapidly.

Clearly in an age of dynamic change within the business environment, management systems and structures must be capable of accepting changes in *roles*, both internally and externally. The rapid growth in strategic partnerships demonstrates such need. Indeed, the most successful companies are those which commence strategic development on the premise that their role may result in being a less dominant partner.

■ Credibility

Every business has the need to build relationships with suppliers and customers. To do this, the business must be seen as credible with these trading partners. Credibility also has internal characteristics. Both external and internal credibility are stakeholder issues. Customers, suppliers, employees, shareholders and the community all have concerns over the industries and companies within which they work or with whom they negotiate.

The credibility of any company strategy should be evaluated within this reference frame. Each party will have specific interests and these should be identified, and strategy 'matches' with each interest proposed to ensure that an optimal fit is achieved.

■ Corporate Performance

There is one overwhelming issue relevant for strategy decision-making: can the proposed strategy produce the performance necessary to meet satisfactory levels of return on existing and proposed investment over the proposed lifespan without demanding performances from the existing management structure and the available resources? The proposed strategy should be evaluated against a set of marketing, financial and operating objectives. The evaluation should consider each of the viable options available to the firm. Thus the question: 'can we leverage our performance by involving "intermediaries" ?' is essential if the management are seniors in their role in maximizing the shareholders' wealth and the value of the business.

■ Strategic Development Criteria: Logistics Implications

Given the factors to be considered during strategy formulation, the logistics strategy can begin to be formulated. Clearly, any channel strategy should be an integral part of a company's corporate and marketing strategy. The marketing objectives should clearly specify target markets, the positioning response, and thus the implications of customers' requirements for the logistics strategy. Just as the other components of the marketing strategy seek to achieve to deliver customers' expectations of value, so too should the logistics strategy.

The earlier paragraphs have provided a framework within which it is possible to consider logistics strategy.

The first issue, *consistency*, suggests that strategy components should align with each other throughout the planning process. This is consistent with the proposal made in the introduction to the chapter, namely that corporate, marketing and logistics strategies should be totally integrated.

Furthermore, consistency also suggests that there is internal consistency with respect to the overall objectives that the logistics activity is expected to achieve. Thus the resources requirements necessary to achieve a specified level of customer service – for example, inventory levels to maintain a 95 per cent available to volume customers – should be clearly specified in the logistics strategy.

Consonance requires that strategy at all levels is capable of responding to changes in all aspects of the company's environment. The interpretation of consonance at the level of the logistics strategy is more operational than strategic and suggests a measure of flexibility at the logistics level which will enable activity to be increased to meet increased system throughput or, alternatively, to respond to reductions in activity with no major impact on costs.

The implications of the industry life cycle are just as important for logistics strategy decisions as they are at the corporate and marketing level. Clearly, the longevity of the business, and particularly its development pattern, have similar implications for planning resource requirements as they have for manufacturing and marketing. Consequently *continuity* is an important issue to be considered in the strategy integration process.

Creativity is an essential feature for strategic planning at any level. It could be argued that the greater the constraint on resource availability (not an unusual problem within logistics) the more creative management must be to meet the objectives required by both the corporate and marketing strategies. Creative logistics solutions may require decisions that select external companies and services for sensitive tasks within the overall logistics strategy. For example, the use of third-party service companies to undertake physical distribution of product to low-volume, distant, or low-frequency-ordering customers may release company resources for use in increasing the service to high-volume customers, thereby reinforcing an already strong position with favoured customers.

Many companies are seeking to develop *competitive advantage* from a superior logistics function. Selective services which appear to target customer groups as customized service packages often do not require significant resources to achieve visible differentiation. For companies with product ranges which do not lend themselves to becoming specialist product offers, differentiated customer service is often one of the few areas within which competitive advantage may be achieved.

The productive use of logistics resources is becoming a vital component of the corporate profit plan. The planning of adequate capacity within facilities and transportation systems such that excess capacity can be avoided is an important decision for logistics managers. Productive *capacity utilization* ensures that the return on logistics assets is satisfactory in the context of the overall corporate requirement for return on capital employed.

Capacity aspects of culture are also significant within logistics strategy decisions. An example of the need for such empathy was demonstrated by the problems created within a multiple food retailer's distribution centre network when it was realized that the customer service philosophy did not extend beyond the retail stores. What occurred was that the company had neglected to extend their training programme into their distribution centres (DCs). Consequently, the DC staff continued to work as they always had and failed to respond to the service 'drive' simply because senior management had overlooked the importance of including them in this culture shift process. It follows that these issues should be extended throughout the company in order to ensure the coordinating and integrating activities and skills are developed.

An important aspect of strategy is its role in building relationships with both suppliers and customers. This was expressed earlier. The logistics strategy is one aspect of the overall strategy which will play a major role in this respect. As such the *credibility* of the business may well be enhanced considerably by an effective customer service function which is clearly the role of logistics.

Unless the logistics strategy makes an effective contribution to the overall results of the business, the corporate and marketing objectives will fail to materialize. It follows that the logistics activity must be tasked with a specific contribution to *corporate performance*. This does not necessarily require the function to 'own' and manage assets, but rather manage its financial contribution such that the desired performance results. This may be achieved by leasing the necessary assets or utilizing service companies.

■ The Logistics Strategy

■ Component Parts

The discussion so far has demonstrated the need to consider a number of issues during the strategy formulation process which will provide a check on the 'fit' of the logistics strategy with the corporate and marketing strategies.

We now move on to consider the components of logistics strategy. In Figure 11.2 we outline the major items comprising a logistics strategy as being the corporate and marketing objectives and strategies of the business and the transactions channels and physical distribution channels. The objectives and strategies of both the transaction and physical distribution channels should identify the objectives and strategies necessary as a support function for the overall strategic direction of the business. (The transactions channels component will be dealt with in more detail in Chapter 12.)

Given the principles described earlier it is clear that the resulting logistics strategy will be most effective if it is integrated with those for intended corporate and marketing performance. The process of integration will be facilitated by close attention to the criteria discussed at the beginning of the chapter. In this respect we would argue for the overall logistics strategy to be a support strategy; in this role it can be used to enhance those criteria for which it appears necessary to add emphasis. Some examples may help:

Consistency across *all* strategic activities and intentions is clearly necessary. The long-term implications of a corporate market development strategy should be reflected in the facilities and inventory intentions, and in the logistics strategy by the planned expansion of facilities coverage and the increase in inventory in the budget statement.

Consonance should be reflected in two dimensions. One concerns the intentions given to build flexibility into the logistics activity which will enable there to be changes made to both corporate and marketing intentions. The other dimension concerns an awareness to environmental changes such as technology (which may improve customer service at relatively low investment) and competitive changes (which the company should monitor and appraise the competitive implications of any changes occurring). In this respect consonance is reflecting awareness to the competitive and customer-led marketing situations.

Creativity, as we suggested earlier, is often seen as the logistics management's response to resource availability constraints. Other expressions of creativity may be found in the design of customized service packages which focus on specialist needs of customers. This approach may be important in determining *competitive advantage*.

Clearly, an overall, comprehensive, approach to strategy is likely to result in a more effective strategic response. It follows that the *process* may be improved by first identifying the *components* involved in the process (Figure 11.2) and then moving on to developing the strategy document.

■ The Logistics Strategy Process

In Figure 11.3 we are suggesting the structure or process required in developing a logistics strategy. We have resisted the temptation to offer a strategy format;

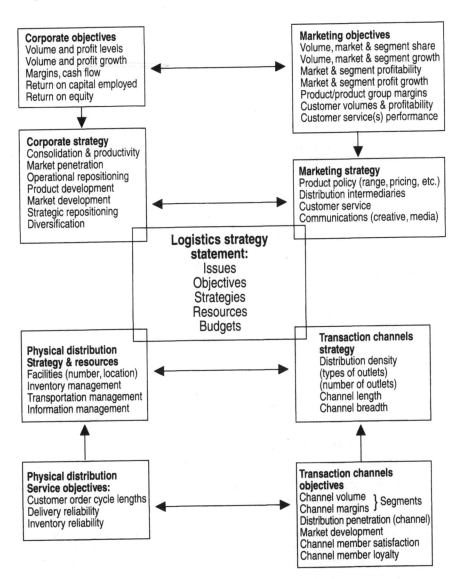

Figure 11.2 Components of the logistics strategy statement

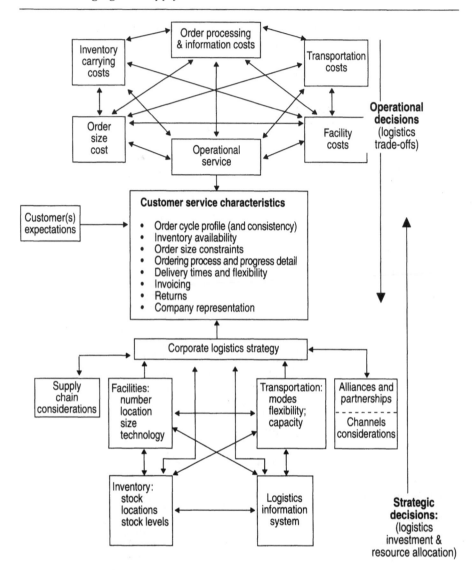

Figure 11.3 The logistics strategy process

we suggest that strategy is an individual corporate process for which (apart from topic headings), the appropriate approach is one which suits the needs of the company and its particular situation.

The structure represented in Figure 11.3 proposes customer service characteristics as being central to the strategy development process. The topics suggested as service characteristics are those typically associated with customer service offers. The strategic and operational decisions overlap at this point. It is the overlap which is the implementation process. The operational decisions are taken once the strategic direction has been established.

In reaching the *corporate logistics strategy*, management will have decided how the logistics function can best be utilized in the pursuit of overall corporate (and marketing) objectives. Having identified the components of strategy (as described in Figure 11.2), the strategy process describes *how* they will be combined in support of the stated corporate strategic direction.

Thus the logistics strategy will specify how selected aspects of customer service will be used to support the corporate/marketing initiatives and how, in turn, resources will be deployed. Figure 11.3 also suggests that the logistics strategy will describe the involvement of the business within the supply chain *and* will specify the involvement of external activities and companies within the context of alliances and partnerships. The key elements in prescribing the logistics strategy are facilities, transportation, inventory and the information technology. The strategy will describe in broad detail how these activities, and the resources contained within each, will support the corporate strategic direction: the implementation of the strategy is undertaken by the operational decision-makers who will develop detailed plans which specify quantitative performance levels of customer service performance (by segment, customer, etc.) together with detailed volume forecasts of product movement and corresponding budgets for resource acquisition and management.

■ Summary

Formulating a supply chain strategy requires an understanding of both corporate and marketing objectives and strategies and their implications for customer service characteristics and delivery. Given a full understanding of these interrelationships it is then possible to consider the strategic decisions of logistics investment and resource allocation together with the operational, implementations, decisions.

We were also reminded that, for strategy to be effective, it should have consistency, consonance, continuity, creativity, competitive advantage, capacity utilisation, credibility, and result in corporate performance.

CHAPTER 12

Distribution Channel Design and Management

■ Introduction

Logistics has two dimensions. One involves the management of the physical infrastructure involved in moving raw materials into the production process and finished goods from the end of the production line through to the end user. But there is also another vital dimension which should be designed before any physical activity takes place, i.e. the development of the commercial/transactional arrangements involved in accessing target markets. Distribution channels usually involve several parties – intermediaries in a vertical sequence of transactions, all of which are required to 'add value' if they are to survive. In essence, the 'transactions channel' decision is a 'make or buy' decision: if the channel tasks can be performed cost-effectively by the producer then the role of an intermediary becomes irrelevant and the intermediary is omitted from the channel structure. Channel design and management follows a structured approach, using criteria which evaluates optional channel structures during which alignment (compatibility), trade-offs and channel relationships are considered. Increasingly, the role of logistics service companies is included in the decision process, particularly when they are a dominant element within the supply chain.

■ Creating Customer Value

Given that the purpose of any business is to increase the value of the business for the shareholders, it follows that this is only likely to occur if the business can create some level of sustainable competitive advantage by developing a 'preferred supplier' status with customers. Added value may be created in a number of ways. Figure 12.1 illustrates the process by which value is added to a product.

The illustration makes the assumption that generally we may assume them to be used interchangeably; thus added value and utility both have a similar effect on customer satisfaction, i.e. if we increase either added value or utility we increase customer satisfaction. Customer satisfaction will increase as manufacturing combines labour and raw material to create the product and thereby adds *form utility*.

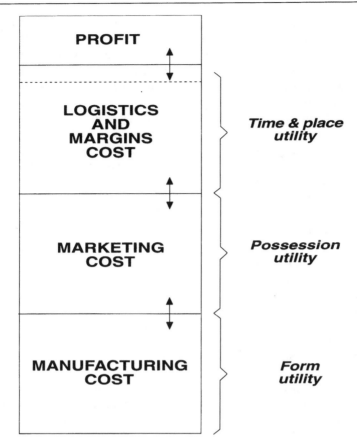

Figure 12.1   Adding value to improve customer satisfaction

Marketing activities create awareness of the product and of its character-istics. Marketing also facilitates transactions and in so doing adds *possession utility*. As information technology applications expand, the two (awareness and transactions) converge. For example, in the process of television/home sales, the customer is able to make immediate purchases. However, this occurs for only a few products and typically both involve an intermediary and take time to process.

Finally *time and place* utilities are added by the logistics process. The product is either made available at a specific location (an intermediary's showroom) or may go directly to the customer. Thus the product is available where and when it is required.

Figure 12.1 also suggests that costs are involved in creating the various utilities. It also infers that the residual profit is a function of the efficiency of the entire process. The extent of the profit residual is a function of the overall volume handled and the effectiveness of intermediaries (and the 'supplier'). Essentially we are considering a 'make or buy' situation: the 'supplier' is confronted with decisions concerning whether or not to undertake some or all of the tasks and avoid 'paying' the intermediary companies involved in creating the utility. The decision to be made concerns cost, effectiveness, and therefore profitability.

It follows from Figure 12.1 that the profit decision concerns optimization rather than maximization. By carefully selecting intermediaries and agreeing, with them, the precise nature of the tasks, these can then be allocated to best effect in the overall process. Clearly, the intermediary will not undertake to cooperate unless the remuneration is adequate. Provided it is, and is so throughout the structure, sales will be maximized and profit will be optimized.

■ Channel Tasks

The reasons for the presence of intermediaries in markets have been questioned for some time. Their existence has a long history: trading intermediaries have existed for thousands of years. The more recent reasons have been important since 'mass production' methods emerged from the industrial revolution, when it became clear that production advances brought with them new tasks for the market, as 'gaps' occurred between production and consumption Alderson (1954). Alderson described the five gaps as:

- *Time gaps*: occurring because consumers typically purchase items at discrete intervals (most food products weekly; consumer durables every three/five years); manufacturing produces on a continuous basis thereby ensuring it takes advantage of economies of scale.
- *Space gaps*: consumers are usually located throughout a market; manufacturing is centralized.
- *Quantity gaps*: manufacturing activities result in large quantities; consumption occurs in small quantities.
- *Variety gaps*: typically manufacturers' production ranges are narrower than that preferred by consumers.

Subsequently Guirdham (1972) added an additional gap:

- *Communication/information gaps*: often the consumer is unaware of exactly what it is they require, from where it can be obtained and its availability and price. In recent years the communications/information gap has been influential in closing many of the other gaps.

Alderson (1957) developed the concept of 'sorting' into four basic channel tasks:

- *Sorting out*: creating homogeneous groups or ranges from a range of heterogeneous suppliers.

- *Accumulation*: the assembly of homogeneous products into unique assortments.
- *Allocation*: the selection of an assortment of goods related to a specific demand. Homogeneous suppliers (carpet suppliers, furniture suppliers, etc.) are 'allocated' into a specific product range to meet the needs of a reseller.
- *Assorting*: is the process (usually that of a retailer) which combines a number of product groups into a specific offer to meet the needs of a target consumer group.

Since Alderson's discussion (1957), distribution has developed and evolved. It is not unusual for the allocation and assortment tasks to be merged and be managed by specialist and/or niche retailers.

Another conceptual view of marketing channel activities and of particular relevance to logistics was proposed by Vaile *et al.* (1952), who discussed specific marketing flows within channels. These comprise: physical possession, ownership, promotion, negotiation, financing, risking, ordering and payment. The authors suggest that each activity takes place at various levels of a channel (see Figure 12.2) and that subsequently they are assumed by 'specialist intermediaries' (see Figure 12.3).

More recently the specialisms have either become dominant or have been merged. For example, information and payment flows have been combined and managed by larger retailers who have developed sophisticated data bases from which promotion and transaction activities are managed as well as the monitoring of consumer behaviour.

■ Developing an Integrated Logistics Strategy: The Role of Transaction Channels

Given the background of the development of marketing/transaction channels, it is not difficult to understand their role within the overall logistics strategy. The process of developing a logistics strategy was discussed in the preceding chapter: here our focus is on the detail of transaction channels.

Figure 12.4 identifies the importance of transaction channels in the overall process of developing an integrated logistics strategy. The previous chapter (see Figure 11.2) identified issues that need to be considered in the development of objectives and strategy, while Figure 12.4 considers these within the context of market coverage and product characteristics, both of which are important for transaction channels and for physical distribution channels.

■ Market Coverage

Market coverage is clearly an important consideration for any supplier. The nature of the channel intermediaries selected will match the product type with

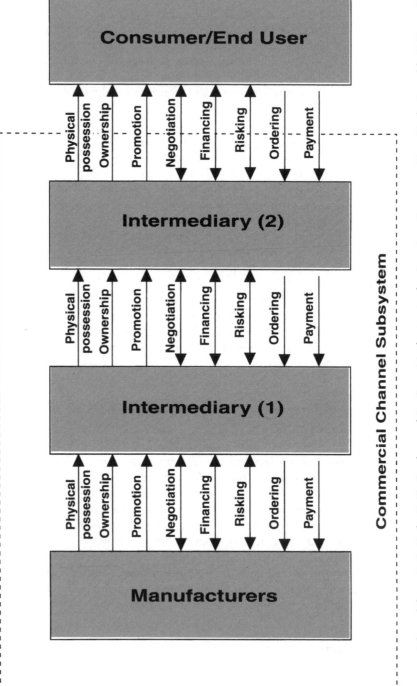

Source: Adapted from R. S. Vaile, E. T. Grether and R. Cox, *Marketing in the American Economy*, New York: Ronald, 1952, p. 113

Figure 12.2   Marketing flows in channels

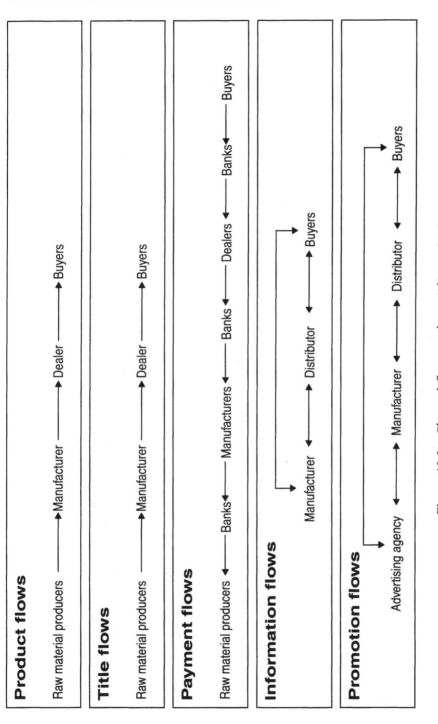

Figure 12.3　Channel flows and specialist activities

end user/customer expectations. For everyday use products (food, newspapers, basic stationery items, etc.) it is usual to use *intensive* distribution. This obtains for consumable industrial products (abrasives, lubricants, drill bits, etc.). The vendors' objectives are to offer convenient (local and easily obtainable) availability because the pattern of purchasing is typically short-term with end user maintaining low (or nil) inventories.

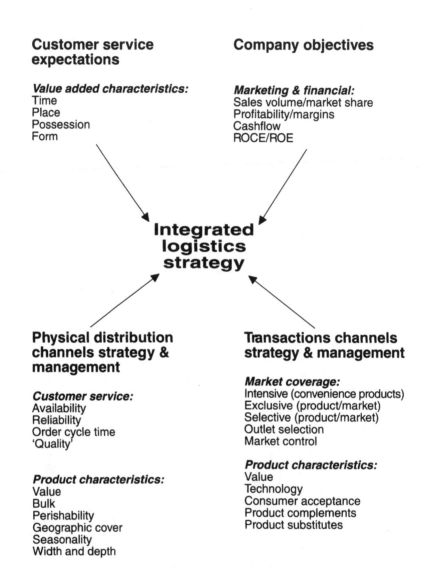

Customer service expectations

Value added characteristics:
Time
Place
Possession
Form

Company objectives

Marketing & financial:
Sales volume/market share
Profitability/margins
Cashflow
ROCE/ROE

Integrated logistics strategy

Physical distribution channels strategy & management

Customer service:
Availability
Reliability
Order cycle time
'Quality'

Product characteristics:
Value
Bulk
Perishability
Geographic cover
Seasonality
Width and depth

Transactions channels strategy & management

Market coverage:
Intensive (convenience products)
Exclusive (product/market)
Selective (product/market)
Outlet selection
Market control

Product characteristics:
Value
Technology
Consumer acceptance
Product complements
Product substitutes

Figure 12.4   The role of distribution channels design in an integrated logistics strategy

Exclusive distribution is often a partnership in which an intermediary operates a franchised territory. The partnership requires mutual support in developing sales and supporting end users with planned maintenance and ·emergency servicing requirements. Exclusive distribution is found for consumer product groups for which large inventories are required to offer consumers a wide selection. *Selective* distribution usually involves a restricted number of intermediaries within a limited market area. Usually the market is sufficiently large to support a number of resellers *and* the decision is influenced by the need to provide after sales service and service to maintain good customer relationships.

Outlet selection varies in complexity. For convenience-type products, where the investment in inventories is minimal and fixed capital investment is not a consideration, the criteria for selecting outlets are minimal. Furthermore, because the primary requirement is to obtain 'broadcast distribution', the emphasis is on density rather than on being selective. By contrast the criteria for selecting distributor networks for very expensive consumer products or high-technology industrial items can be extensive. Usually the investment requirements for both supplier and distributor are quite large and the need to be responsive to customer expectations for advice, installation and service is a major criterion. Table 12.1 suggests an extensive list of criteria for selecting channel partners. Table 12.1 also provides the basis for developing *market control* activities. The usual approach to control within channels is for suppliers to identify critical success factors without which the channel partnership structure is unlikely to operate. From these, a control device may be developed.

The distributor's view of the channel strategy issue is presented in Table 12.2. Many large distributors and multiple retailers have quite stringent expectations of suppliers. The basis of criteria they use is cost. Any activity that could or should be done by suppliers that has an impact on retailers' cost profiles is used as a selection criterion. Clearly, where there may be other factors which compensate (for example, very strong brand/consumer franchise) then they may be prepared to offset the benefits of having the brand leader for the small improvement in margins they may obtain through hard negotiation for extended credit or the facility to return merchandise.

■ Product Characteristics

There are a number of reasons why product characteristics may influence channel selection decisions.

The *value* of a product is important. The higher the value of the product, the larger the investment in working capital in the supply chain. Value and rate of sale usually correlate, and therefore the stockholding and cash flow implications of maintaining inventory levels which will meet customers' service expectations often determine the need for intermediaries. It also influences the type and number of distributors, and a further review of Figure 12.5 will identify the criteria necessary to support a supplier of a high-value product range.

Table 12.1   Criteria for selecting channel partners

Financial strength
Revenue, P + L
Balance sheet
Cash flow

Sales activities and performance
Number of selling staff
Competence/new accounts
Sales trends

Reputation
Leadership
Customers' views
Response to customers' problems

Market coverage
Geographic
Applications
Call frequency

Management strength
Planning and control
Employee relations (T/O)
Marketing orientation
Strategic direction

Advertising and promotions
Budgets
Media
Creative
Exhibitions/demonstrations

Training and development
Management & staff
Product
Selling
Cooperative programmes

Sales compensation
Programme type
Effectiveness

Facilities and equipment
Transportation
Warehousing/storage
Inventory
Order processing

After sales servicing facilities
Customer returns
Warranty

Supplier commitment
Development
Joint programmes

Willingness to share information
Customers
Sales force activities
Inventory levers/availability
Delivery frequencies

Willingness to carry inventory
New product support
Slow moving/service items

The *technology* of a product may influence distributor selection. Complex products require an investment in support equipment and a service parts inventory. Those considerations are in addition to the cost of inventory of sale products. Recently there has been a trend in specialization for service and parts by the 'popular brands' of durables. Service intermediaries undertake to maintain new (warranty service) and older products in return for territorial agreements. Others maintain direct channels.

Consumer acceptance or brand awareness/loyalty determine the extent of sales effort required to sell the product. Range additions to a well-known brand require less effort, and typically the intermediary will be enthusiastic to handle the brand. By contrast, new brands or new products within lesser-known brands may have difficulty in making volume sales. Often the solutions are either to 'bonus' the distributors, or for the supplier to undertake trade promotions and 'missionary selling' with distributors' sales people in order to move the product through the channels.

Table 12.2 The distributor's view: important criteria when selecting suppliers

Accepts damaged merchandise returns
Has effective, reliable, prompt ordering systems
Accepts unsold merchandise returns
Availability
Handles complaints effectively and promptly
Good 'trade relations' reputation
Good range of products
Provides small order deliveries/No minimum order size
Offers promotional allowances
Makes new products available
Representation is helpful and knowledgeable
Adequate margins on competitive prices
Offers quantity discounts
Credit is flexible
Offers cooperative advertising and promotions
Offers merchandizing help

It is usual for distributors to specialize in product ranges or applications. For such products it is mutually beneficial for supplier and distributor if the *product complements* the distributor's existing range. Not only does this facilitate the selling task but it offers the distributor a means by which average customer transactions may be increased and whereby costs may be amortized over all increased sales volume.

Many products are *substitutes* for competitive products. This is particularly so for convenience products with low brand loyalty and low purchase prices. This places a premium on shelf space and other point-of-sale displays in high customer traffic areas. There may be other implications. One concerns the trade margins offered; low brand loyalty products may require higher margins as an incentive, and the intermediaries may be less enthusiastic at stocking in either width or depth (or availability) and accordingly may require additional assurances concerning distribution service. Often the use of specialist distributors facilitates the task and makes it easier for the supplier to provide support.

■ Total Cost Integration: A Dual-Channel Issue

Our discussion has inferred that two distinct channel structures exist: the transaction channel and the physical distribution channel. This is not necessarily the case. Often, because of volume orders, or perhaps because of the size of the business (volume throughput) and the implications this has for economies of scale (and other managerial economies), many distributors and retailers find undertaking their own distribution (i.e. assuming some of the roles and tasks in the physical distribution channel) to be cost-effective. Figure 12.5 illustrates how the two channels may interact when this occurs.

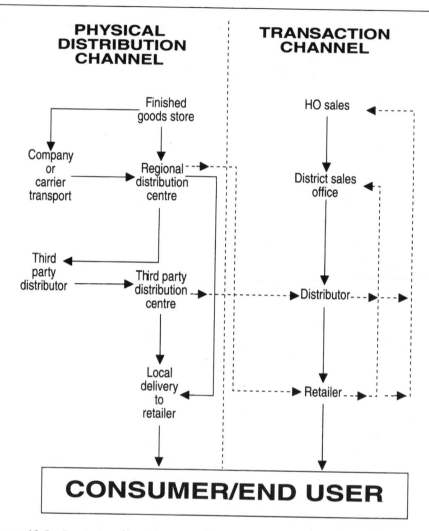

Figure 12.5   Logistics channel: an amalgamation of physical distribution and transaction channels

The rationale behind this situation is that an integrated approach to logistics management requires that consumer/end-user satisfaction expectations be met while costs are optimized. We have already discussed the topics which comprise customer service: here we consider the issues that concern both transactions channels and physical distribution channels decisions. The process described by Figure 12.6 proposes that, if the most effective cost profile is to be achieved, not only should the principles of trade-off analysis be implemented, but the optimal solution should be sort by exploring channel combinations. An understanding of the costs may help to explain.

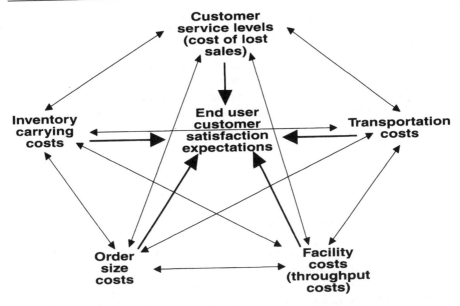

Source: Adapted from D. Lambert, *The Development of an Inventory Costing Method: A Study of the Costs Associated with Holding Inventory*, NCPDM, 1976
Figure 12.6   Cost trade-offs required within the logistics system

Customer service costs are the sales and profit lost when the opportunity to meet an order is missed due to lack of product availability. While the costs of lost sales are difficult to measure, there have been successful approaches; see Christopher and Schary (1979). If the objective is one of optimizing the total system costs at a predetermined level of service it follows that the optimal solution may be found by combining the two channels. In so doing there will undoubtedly be situations in which service companies may be able to service 'small order' companies while the larger customers are handled on a direct basis by the manufacturer/supplier.

A similar approach is possible for both *inventory holding costs* and *transportation costs*. Inventory costs, as we have seen in Chapter 8, can be complex. They include capital costs, storage space costs, servicing (insurance), risk (the costs of obsolescence, damage and shrinkage), opportunity costs and the costs of incremental increases in infrastructure. Clearly with a wide range of cost issues it is more likely that the optimal solution will be found by combining the roles and tasks of both channels. *Transportation costs* are equally complex (Chapter 9). Again, we have investment costs to consider, service support (maintenance), labour costs, insurance and risk (the impact of capacity utilisation variance on ROI). In addition, there are a number of indirect costs which influence the overall transportation costs, the significance here being the number, size and geographical dispersion of facilities.

Warehousing costs are essentially throughput costs (not the costs associated with storage). Throughput costs will change with the number of facilities. An optimal solution requires that a sufficient number are commissioned in order that service be met. There are two other considerations, apart from number; these are location and size. The solution sought may lie in using fewer but larger facilities where both economies of scale and experience benefits are available. Again, the solution may necessitate a combination of channel resources.

Order size costs are the costs that are involved in the processing, handling and progressing activities required to service customer orders. Typically, they remain much the same regardless of size, and include the cost of customer communications, issuing the orders, credit checks, picking documentation and shipping preparation. It may require some production activities such as set-up, manufacture, inspection and delivery to a finished goods store prior to shipment. Often there will be lost capacity costs involved in the production changeover. In most cases an element of materials handling is necessary and, possibly, order progressing.

It follows that effective system design will evaluate the potential impact of the integration of transaction and physical distribution channels. As the preceding paragraphs suggest, the cost of performing many physical distribution activities may be more effective if they are performed by transaction channel intermediaries. Furthermore, there may be additional benefits: intermediaries who have an investment commitment are more likely to become more involved in the sales activity, particularly if margins incentives are set to compensate for the dual role.

■ Summary

Distribution channel design is an integral part of the logistics process. Channels activities add possession, time and place utilities to the form utility created by manufacturing.

Distribution channels decisions are based upon an understanding of the relevant marketing flows within the supply chain. Without effective management of the marketing flows, cost-effective channel management and, therefore, supply chain management are unlikely. It follows that channel decisions are required to reflect company and marketing decisions and thereby integrate with an overall logistics strategy.

The nature of distribution channels and the tasks to be undertaken are such that it is unlikely that all tasks can be undertaken effectively by just one channel member. Hence the selection of channel partners is an important element of the overall process.

CHAPTER 13

Forming Strategic Partnerships and Alliances

■ Introduction

Decisions concerning the selection of channel intermediaries, and then subsequently working with them, is effectively forming a strategic partnership. The essence of successful partnerships is the extent of interdependence between the partners. The purposes of entering into a strategic partnership are to achieve objectives that otherwise could not be realized and to reduce the overall risk of a project while increasing the return on investment; at the same time the partnership will aim to maximize the utilization of scarce resources. Parties in partnership/alliance relationships should understand the implications for management that such business arrangements require. They both should expect to share difficulties as well as current and future benefits. Management of partnerships/alliances is essentially a matter of collaboration if the venture is to succeed. This chapter identifies the alternative approaches to constructing partnerships and alliances, reviews their application to channels and supply chain management tasks and considers how they may be implemented. Before discussing their application, this chapter commences by defining both types of combination and considers the alternatives.

In strategic partnerships or alliances the emphasis is on cooperation and partnership between the parties, not competition and conflict, as the basis upon which a joint competitive advantage is developed. This approach stresses the development of trust, the sharing of information and the common interest between channel members (Dowling and Robinson, 1990).

Although the terms have begun to be used interchangeably, the relationships can be either vertical or horizontal (see Figure 13.1). However, vertical relationships between supplier and customer/buyer are known as *partnerships* and horizontal relationships, such as those between two suppliers are known as *alliances*. Figure 13.2 identifies four different types of strategic relationships which have been developed to date, and identifies the objectives of each.

Whether the discussion concerns partnerships or alliances, the intent of the relationship is to provide differentiated intermediate or long-term benefits to both parties involved. Typically, organizations enter into a partnership/alliance in order to:

- Achieve strategic objectives;
- Develop joint strategies;

- Reduced risk while increasing reward;
- Improve returns on scarce resources.

■ Collaborative Advantage: The Art of Strategic Relationships

Alliances between companies, whether they are from different parts of the world or different ends of the supply chain, are a fact of life in business today. Whatever the duration and objectives of business alliances, being a good partner has become a key corporate asset. I call it a company's a *collaborative advantage*. In the global economy, a well developed ability to create and sustain fruitful collaborations gives companies a significant leg up. (Kanter, 1994)

Kanter reports on a research project based on 37 companies and their partners from 11 countries; large and small companies from both manufacturing and service industries and involved in many types of alliances were involved. The research included a number of established alliances (over 20 years) and some only recently formed. Over 500 interviews were conducted. The research uncovered three fundamental aspects of business relationships:

- They must yield immediate, short-term benefits for the partners, but also they should extend into the future, identifying for the parties new and unforeseen opportunities.
- Successful arrangements involve *collaboration* (creating new value together), rather than just exchange (a return for what is input to the arrangement). They value the skills each brings to the relationship.
- The relationship cannot be 'controlled' by formal systems but require an elaborate arrangement of interpersonal connections and internal infrastructures that enhance learning.

An interesting finding was the cultural differences that were soon to exist. North American companies 'take a very narrow, opportunistic view of relationships, evaluating them strictly in financial terms or seeing them as barely tolerable alternatives to outright acquisition . . . [they] frequently neglect the political, cultural, organizational and human aspects of the partnership'. By contrast, Asian companies 'are the most comfortable with relationships, and therefore they are the most adept at using and exploiting them. European companies fall somewhere in the middle'.

Kanter's research identified a continuum of relationships from weak and distant to strong and close. The weakest, *mutual service consortia*, comprise similar companies in similar industries pooling resources to gain benefits that alone they could not afford. In the middle, *joint ventures* pursue opportunities requiring a capability input from each of them which may be technology based, production based or distribution based. The joint venture might operate independently, or interdependently, linking the partners' operations. *Value chain partnerships* (supplier-customer/buyer relationships) involve companies in different industries, with different but complementary skills, which links their capabilities to create value for ultimate users. Here the research suggests, commitments tend to be high, the partners tend to develop joint activities in a number of functions, operations overlap, and the relationship creates substantial change within each organization.

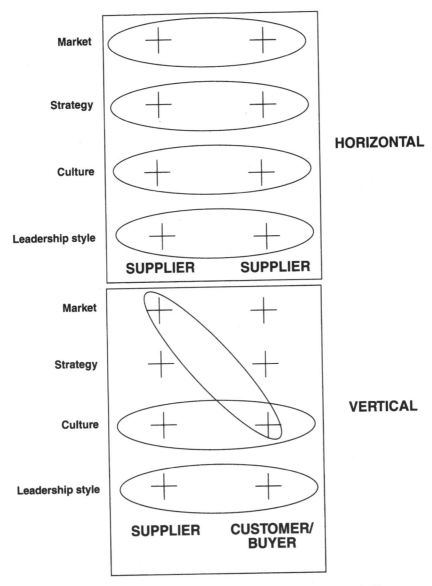

Figure 13.1 Critical interfaces: horizontal versus vertical alliances

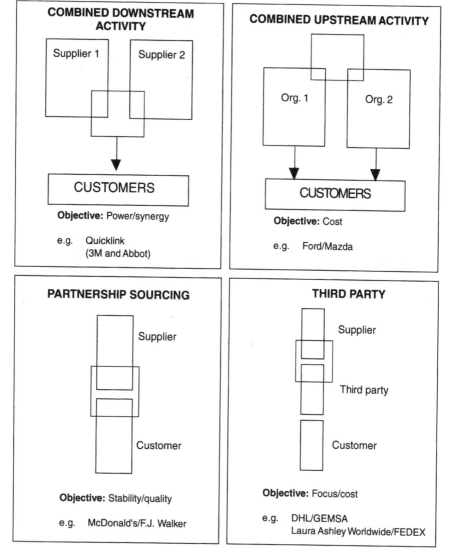

Figure 13.2   Some alliance types and corresponding objectives

Kanter suggests there are eight criteria which are necessary for organizational relationships to meet if they are to be successful:

- *Individual excellence*: both partners require to be strong and can contribute something of value to the relationship. Both have positive motives for entering the relationship.

- *Importance*: the relationship should be congruent with the strategic objectives of both partners.
- *Interdependence*: there should be mutual need of each partner; they ideally have complementary assets and skills.
- *Investment*: if each invests in the other, this signifies their respective stake in the relationship and commitment to the long term prosperity of the venture.
- *Information*: shared information is an essential feature of the success of partnerships. Information concerns their specific, individual, objectives and goals as well as technical data, performance data and information concerning changed circumstances.
- *Integration*: in which partners develop linkages and shared ways of operating to facilitate their working together easily. Connections are formed between the organizations at various (but important) levels.
- *Institutionalization*: whereby the relationship is formalized, with clear responsibilities and decision processes. It thereby extends beyond the originators.
- *Integrity*: exists and the partners behave towards each other in ways which justify, and enhance, mutual trust; they do not abuse the confidences they are privy to, nor do they undermine each other.

■ The Global Aspect

Kenichi Ohmae (1989) suggests that a problem which exists for many managers when contemplating (or when involved in) strategic relationships is that of relinquishing, or sharing control. Without one the other cannot occur. He comments that this presents no major problem in stable competitive environments, where the 'allergy to loss of control exacts little penalty . . . however, in a changeable world of rapidly globalising markets and industries – a world of converging consumer tastes, rapidly spreading technology, escalating fixed costs and growing protectionism . . . globalisation mandates alliances, makes them absolutely essential to strategy'.

The issue is emphasized by Ohmae by focusing upon the demonstrable convergence of consumer needs and preferences: consumers increasingly 'receive the same information, seek the same kind of lifestyles, and desire the same kinds of products. They all want the best products available, at the lowest prices possible'. Value is the important issue, and country of origin, or country of residence, are of little concern at the point of purchase; it is the quality, price design and service that appeal to the customer.

Technology and technological life cycles are shortening. Technology is becoming generally available and is not proprietary for long. As no one company can expect to be an overall expert in technology and global operations, strategic relationships are becoming increasingly necessary. Furthermore, Ohmae suggests, the convergence of customer need with 'this relentless dispersion of technology, has changed the logic by which managers have to steer. In the past you tried to build sustainable competitive advantage by establishing dominance in all of your business system's critical areas'. This involved building barriers to entry, market share, proprietary expertise and exclusive assets; all to 'support the defensive wall you were building against competitors'.

Ohmae argues that 'the forces of globalisation turn this logic on its head'. To meet the value-based needs of customers now requires the superior skills and technology that are possible only through strategic relationships. Global competitiveness incurs 'immense fixed costs' and partners are necessary if the burden is to be manageable. It is likely that this situation will extend as technology continues to replace labour. A similar argument (the fixed-cost problem) obtains for building and maintaining brand names: the cost of establishing a global brand awareness is high and critical mass penetration volumes are continually rising as competition intensifies. He also suggests that 'the past decade has seen a comparable movement toward fixed costs in sales and distribution networks'. To some extent these may be offset by using distributors (thereby meeting only the variable costs) but the sales force and sales promotional material costs remain, as do sales training and manuals, all of which are fixed costs.

■ Strategic Relationships in Logistics

The discussion thus far clearly establishes the strategic relationship as an option to be considered when developing logistics strategies. In the previous chapter the direction was to consider the concept of partnerships in both transaction and physical distribution channels. Indeed it could be argued that distribution and logistics decisions were more partnership orientated some years ago, when wholesalers formed an influential component within both structures. It was the move towards centralized organizations and control that changed this approach. However, as customers become more demanding and discerning it is possible that decisions within both transactions and physical distribution channels may increasingly require an approach 'across companies' in order that the most cost-effective *and* competitive response is made. Furthermore the changing nature of customer demand (and the response) is becoming service oriented, and frequently this implies the introduction of an intermediary if the prescribed level of service is to be delivered to all relevant customers. Dowling and Robinson (1990) refer to Bucklin and Schmalensee (1987) who suggested a number of important changes occurring in both consumer and industrial products distribution:

- Cooperation among channel members with a decrease in conflict; for example, the improvement in supplier/distributor relationships between large manufacturers and large food retailers.
- The necessity for manufacturers to develop new and improved products to reclaim (or maintain) brand loyalty and shelf space as the point of sale; for example, confectionery and breakfast cereal manufacturers.

- The increasing need for segmentation (by manufacturers and retailers) to meet specific product-service requirements of intermediaries *and* end users.
- The impact and importance of information technology within both transaction and physical distribution channels.
- The increasing diversity of delivery systems within the distribution of consumer and industrial products.
- The impact of increasing costs and virtually no growth in revenues put pressure on margins, thereby encouraging joint solutions which offer cost reduction or containment.

■ The Value Chain and Strategic Relationships in Logistics

An approach taken by Dowling and Robinson is to use the value chain (Porter, 1985) as a means to integrate product and service flows. A modified version of this is shown as Figure 13.3; a number of points are made. By using a distributor network there are benefits to be obtained by using the economies of scale accruing to specialist functions, thereby increasing the overall productivity of the network. By so doing there is also an impact on the value added to the product-service delivered to the customer. It is also likely that support activity costs (overhead, fixed costs) will be reduced due to the fact that each channel member specializes in those tasks at which they are most able, and focuses on the level of the channel required.

The divisions within the individual value chains, i.e. inbound logistics, operations, marketing and sales, outbound logistics and service, show the proportions of each member's costs accounted for by the relevant activity. For example, operations (manufacturing) is, together with marketing and sales, likely to be more extensive than those similar functions within the distributors' activities. Clearly, the objective of the channel (be it transaction, physical distribution, or a combination of both) is to develop an optimal situation whereby the value delivered to the customer or end user meets precisely their requirements, neither more nor less than that required to obtain a target volume of business.

Given the comments of Bucklin and Schmalensee (above), the value chain is obviously a useful model by which channel cooperation may be explored with a view to identifying key tasks, and then the location within the supply chain where each task maybe cost-effectively executed. The application of information technology to the task makes for an even more powerful approach, particularly with systems such as EDI (electronic data interchange).

EDI facilitates partnership activities by keeping each party better informed on a day-to-day basis via the database-to-database transmission of routine intercompany transactions such as purchase orders, order status, stock availability, etc. As well as improved and increased channel cooperation there are also direct benefits in the form of lower transaction costs and faster transaction response times. Increased operational capabilities are also being realized. For example, Wal-Mart's phenomenal 25 per cent annual growth rate is largely due to a strategy which includes a finely tuned network of some 5000 supplier partnerships, carefully coordinated with a sophisticated structure of electronic data systems. The systems enable suppliers to work closely with Wal-Mart in a strategic, long-term pattern to reduce their production/logistics costs.

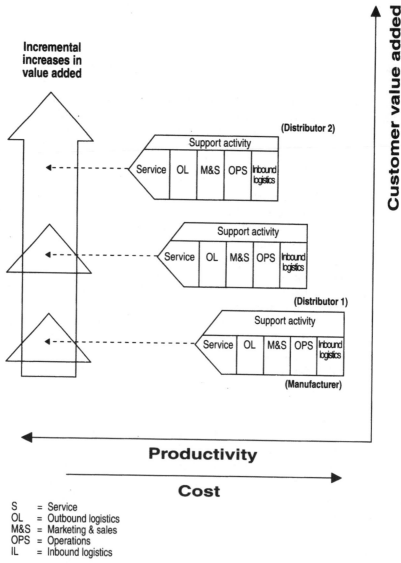

S   = Service
OL = Outbound logistics
M&S = Marketing & sales
OPS = Operations
IL = Inbound logistics

Figure 13.3   The value chain as an integrating mechanism in logistics

The current direction of supplier/distributor relationships in the fmcg (fast-moving consumer goods) industry is much more the strategic partnership marketing relationship. Cooperation has replaced conflict or competition for consumer loyalty. Between them manufacturers and retailers develop a unique assortment of products which best meet *both* sets of positioning objectives *and* those of target customer group. Areas for which cooperation are now beginning to occur include:

- Order processing and progressing procedures;
- Terms of trade and credit facilities;
- Packaging; sizes and unitization, handling issues and storage requirements;
- Point-of-sale and other selling aids;
- Quick response logistics systems;
- Joint product development projects;
- Joint advertising and promotions.

Typically, the benefits that accrue for both parties are: higher profitability, improved long-term planning, greater understanding of the objectives of the other partners, predictable transactions and cash flow, and improved forecasting.

■ Process Methodology

Any company considering strategic partnering should do so only after an analysis of what it sees as its critical strategic issues and how these may be resolved. Critical issues should first be identified and then prioritized by their likely *impact* (from low, significant, to high) and their *urgency* (from low (long term), significant (medium term), to pressing (short term) – the length of time is dependent upon planning cycles. Having completed this part of the analysis, the next step is to re-evaluate the critical issues by reviewing them alongside a prospective partner (or partners) to ascertain the impact of a partnership on the issues. Clearly, this should be done in conjunction with the other company. The required result is a potential situation in which both companies can minimize the impact of the critical issues through the agreed structure of a partnership or alliance. Criteria will be required and these should include revenue growth, profit growth, operating margins, cash generation and return to the shareholders. Assuming the results are positive, the partnership may be put into place. The criteria should include a review of the extent of the interdependence likely to occur. Figure 13.4 suggests some of these factors. The exercise should ascertain the nature of the interdependence. As Figure 13.5 shows, the response issues, and therefore the structure of the relationship, is dependent upon the pattern of the relationship between the potential partners.

Once having identified the 'cost and the benefits', and having taken a decision to formalize the structure, the overall process methodology found to be successful assumes the following pattern of events; refer Figure 13.6.

INTERDEPENDENCE INDICATORS

BUYERS	SUPPLIER
• % of business involved	• % of supplier's business this buyer represents
• Level of risk if supplier fails	• Impact if business lost
• Cost of changing suppliers ('exit-cost')	• Strategic significance of business
• Availability of alternative suppliers	• Number of direct competitors
• Strategic significance of business	• Degree of differentiation of product/service
• This supplier annual cost versus all suppliers	• Price advantage/disadvantage in relation to competitors
• Total category cost as a proportion of sales (e.g. distribution/cost/sales)	

INTERDEPENDENCE ASSESSMENT

BUYER

HIGH DEPENDENCE ☐

LOW DEPENDENCE ☐

SUPPLIER

HIGH DEPENDENCE ☐

LOW DEPENDENCE ☐

Figure 13.4   Strategic partnering

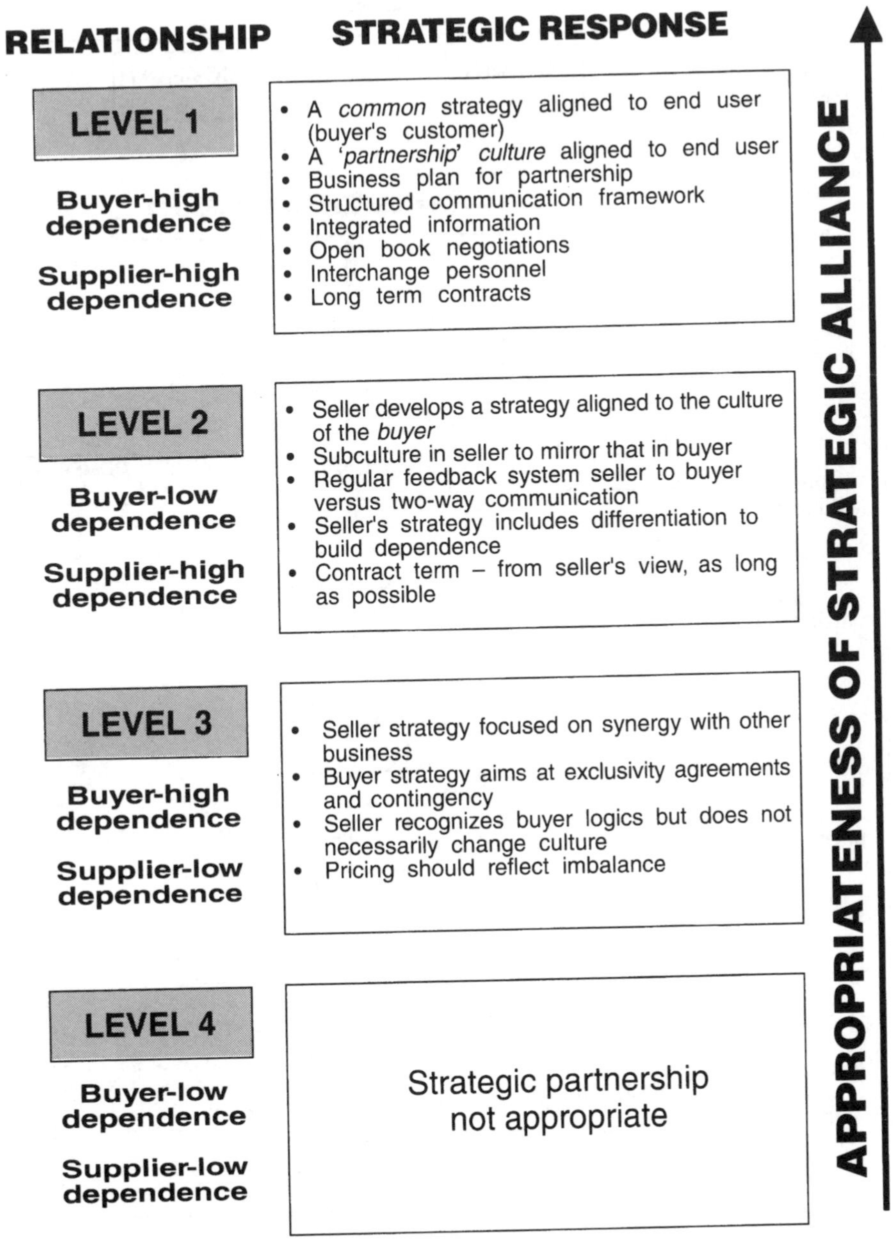

RELATIONSHIP   **STRATEGIC RESPONSE**

LEVEL 1 **Buyer-high dependence** **Supplier-high dependence**	• A *common* strategy aligned to end user (buyer's customer) • A *'partnership'* *culture* aligned to end user • Business plan for partnership • Structured communication framework • Integrated information • Open book negotiations • Interchange personnel • Long term contracts

LEVEL 2 **Buyer-low dependence** **Supplier-high dependence**	• Seller develops a strategy aligned to the culture of the *buyer* • Subculture in seller to mirror that in buyer • Regular feedback system seller to buyer versus two-way communication • Seller's strategy includes differentiation to build dependence • Contract term – from seller's view, as long as possible

LEVEL 3 **Buyer-high dependence** **Supplier-low dependence**	• Seller strategy focused on synergy with other business • Buyer strategy aims at exclusivity agreements and contingency • Seller recognizes buyer logics but does not necessarily change culture • Pricing should reflect imbalance

LEVEL 4 **Buyer-low dependence** **Supplier-low dependence**	Strategic partnership not appropriate

APPROPRIATENESS OF STRATEGIC ALLIANCE ↑

Figure 13.5   Relationship/response issues are a function of the extent of the relationship

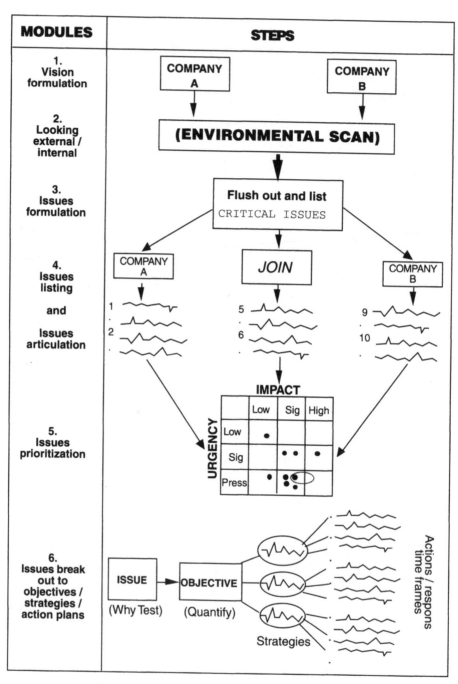

Figure 13.6   Strategic partnering methodology

☐ *Step 1: Vision Formulation*

This step produces vision or philosophical 'what we stand for' statements from both parties. The process significantly reinforces the awareness of the necessity to understand each other's business position and aspirations. It also prepares the way for an understanding of any conflict points wherein the companies may not fundamentally share the same objectives: yet both exist to serve the same customer.

☐ *Step 2: Environmental Scan*

This steps seeks to flush out and understand the various elements of the economic, government, consumer and organizational environment which do, or would, influence the proposed 'partnership/alliance'.

☐ *Step 3: Issues Formulation*

This step solicits and documents critical issues from both individual companies and jointly held perspectives. These issues are seen to be significant, inasmuch as they can have a major impact on the performance in a predetermined time frame.

☐ *Step 4: Issues Identification and Definition*

This step 'tests' each issue with pressure questions in an attempt to understand the rationale for its selection. The objective is to clearly sort out symptoms and causes.

☐ *Step 5: Issues Prioritization*

This step determines and graphically documents the position of the issues on an impact/urgency matrix to ensure that the resources available are allocated correctly. It also provides the key to the ongoing monitoring of issues which require attention when further resources become available.

☐ *Step 6: Articulating the Issues*

This step translates the issues (those selected as critical, given the resources) into:

● Assumptions
● Objectives
● Strategies
● Action plans
● Time frames

- Budgets
- Monitor points
- Responsibilities

Step 6 ensures that both parties in the 'partnership/alliance' understand and agree on what is to be done, by whom, and when, to achieve the jointly agreed results. The joint planning activities for a supplier/distributor are shown in Figure 13.7.

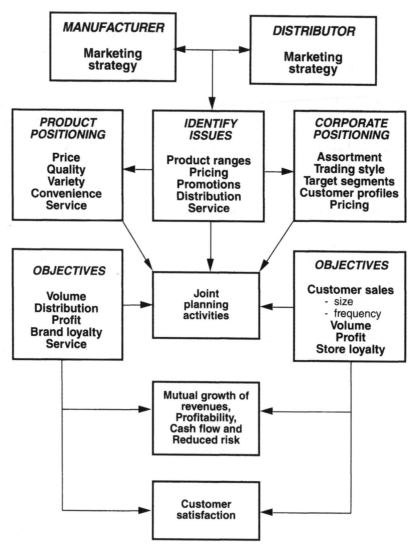

Figure 13.7   Supplier/distributor joint planning activities

It follows that once in place the partnerships should be reviewed constantly to ensure that what were prescribed as objectives and enabling strategies remain relevant. Inevitably changes will be required, and these will be effective if they are agreed and implemented jointly.

■ Summary

Interest in strategic partnerships and alliances has increased in recent years as a large number of companies have restructured their businesses around core products and activities.

This chapter reviewed the expanding literature in the area and applied the emerging concepts to supply chain issues. Examples of existing partnerships and alliances in the supply chain were provided.

The implications of strategic partnerships and alliances for value chain analysis were explored. A model for joint planning alliance and partnership activities was proposed.

CHAPTER 14

Customer Account Profitability and Direct Product Profitability

■ Introduction

The emphasis on productivity and profitability of recent years has brought back into focus the attempts to allocate costs to customers and products. The concepts of customer account profitability (CAP) and direct product profitability (DPP) reflect the desire to allocate as much of the indirect costs associated with the 'delivery' of the product or service. Hitherto, the emphasis has been on gross margin (or operating margin) as a measure of effective marketing. However, recent developments in information technology have made data capture easier, and this, applied to recent thinking in management accounting such as activity-based costing (ABC), has made both CAP and DPP realistic management ambitions. This chapter will discuss recent development in CAP and DPP and will explore the interface issues that concern both suppliers and distributors.

■ Servicing Customers: Profitability

Chapter 3 discussed in considerable detail the tasks involved in providing an appropriate level of service to customers. The point was made that for customer service to be totally effective it is preferable to offer a customized service package rather than a generic offer which may have broad customer appeal but may not address the total service requirements of any one customer. Indeed it was clear from the discussion that such a customer service policy is likely to be wasteful in terms of resources and, probably incapable of meeting the needs of those specific customers whom the company considers to be essential to its profitable operations.

The performance criteria that have sufficed for many companies have been few. Sales revenue is an obvious measure, with predictability of ordering patterns and payment record following in close order. Many companies have sufficient data accurately to calculate gross margins generated from transactions with large customers but beyond this the lack of sophisticated management accounting data inhibits detail.

It could be argued that during, and in the aftermath of, a recession, any customer is worthwhile. Clearly, if all cost data is available we may realize this is not the case. It follows that a structured approach to customer analysis is required.

■ Customer Analysis

There are a number of aspects to this task. We need to identify those elements of customer service and order handling expected by the customer; their relative importance; the cost of providing such services; any trade-off opportunities there may be between and among the service characteristics; and the customers' relative perceptions of competitive offers. However, before such detailed analysis is undertaken, other factors must be considered, such as the volume of business conducted with customers and whether there are indications that the customer base may be segmented in a way that facilities developing both service offers *and* methods by which they may be costed. A structured approach should be taken, commencing with an examination of a particular combination of customers; this may be on a regional basis, may be by size or, more likely, by channel of distribution. The segments or groups of customers are classified according to service needs, size, location (i.e. by variables other than those used for the initial classification) which are shared by the group but differ between categories. Within the categories individual customer accounts are reviewed.

As a guide, there are a number of principles which underlie the process and which are helpful if borne in mind during the analysis.

- *Principle 1*   *The individual customer order is the ultimate profit centre.* In other words, all costs incurred by the organization in supplying its goods/services are related ultimately to the customer's orders received. In an ideal world each order would be profitable or, at a minimum, the total trade with each customer would be profitable. Figure 14.1 identifies the stages and costs associated with a particular order.
- *Principle 2*   Within an existing product/market structure, *profitability is largely determined by what happens after the product is manufactured* – i.e. the effectiveness with which the product is passed along to the next stage of the supply chain.
- *Principle 3*   Costs incurred after manufacture can be directly related to the servicing of an individual order.
- *Principle 4*   Although the average cost of servicing a customer is easily calculated, *it is how such costs vary by customer, order size, order type, and so on, that is significant.* It is important to be aware of the customers who are at the extremes of the cost range.

- *Principle 5*   When considering costs and profits, we must realize that most cost elements have both fixed and variable components, and that the profit per transaction is influenced not only by customer-orientated costs but also by sales discounts, allowances, returned goods policies, and other revenue-influencing factors which produce gross margin per order.
- *Principle 6*   Profit is influenced by both costs and revenue producing policies.
- *Principle 7*   Customer profitability analysis requires a cost accounting system that attributes all costs forward to the revenue source, rather than applying revenues back to factories, products or their organizational units.

The analysis should include a checklist of costs. Christopher (1992) suggests:

Revenues	*Costs (attributable to customer)*
Net sales value	Cost of sales (product mix sold)
	Commissions
	Sales calls
	Key account management time
	Trade bonuses/special discounts
	Order processing costs
	Promotional costs (above and below the line)
	Merchandising costs
	Non-standard packaging and unitization
	Dedicated inventory-holding costs
	Dedicated warehousing costs
	Materials handling costs
	Transport costs
	Documentation/communication
	Returns/refusals
	Credit taken

See Figure 14.2 for a 'model' of customer account profitability.

The above list is extensive but also has the problem that many of the cost items are difficult to allocate with accuracy. Furthermore, the costs of performing service activities vary by customer, by order size, by type of order, order mix (product range), etc. The data below demonstrates Christopher's argument: while the average cost per customer may be easily calculated, there may be no customer that incurs the average cost. As he suggests, the problem concerns *the range of costs* that occurs:

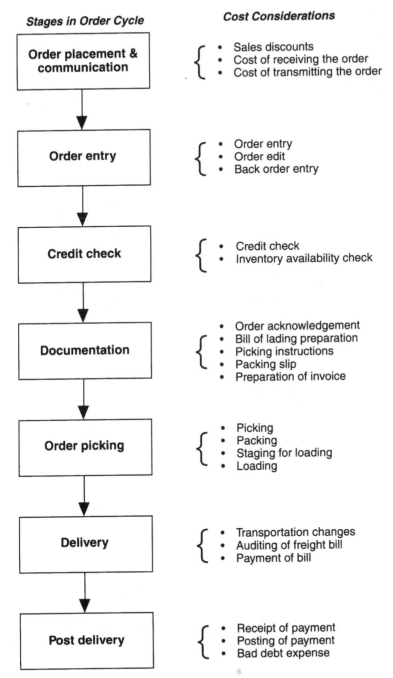

Figure 14.1   Stages and costs associated with an individual order

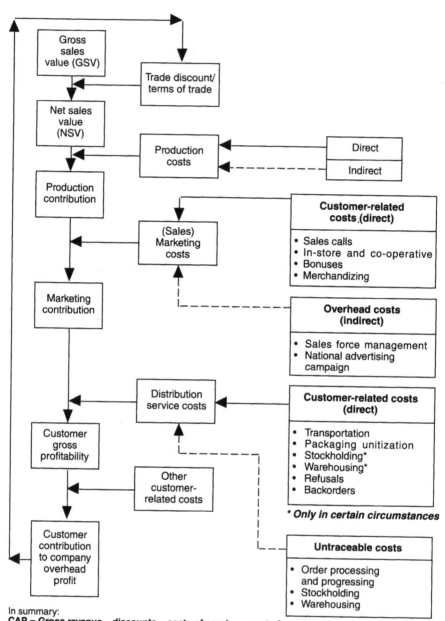

In summary:

CAP = Gross revenue – discounts – costs of service – cost of goods

Note: In terms of attributing costs, there is a primary recognition that costs are product-related in manufacturing, customer-related in selling and distribution, and 'below-the-line' when composed of administration and finance costs, which are not included in the CAP analysis.

Figure 14.2   Customer account profitability

	Customer costs as percentage/net sales		
	Low	Average	High
Order processing	0.2	2.6	7.4
Inventory carrying	1.1	2.6	10.2
Picking and shipping	0.3	0.7	2.5
Interplant freight and handling	0.0	0.7	2.5
Outbound freight	2.8	7.1	14.1
Commissions	2.4	3.1	4.4

Source: Christopher, M. (1985) *The Strategy of Distribution Management*, Gower Press.

There are a number of problems suggested by the data. The first concerns the range between low and high values, order processing, inventory carrying and outbound freight being particularly large. As Christopher suggests 'the need is to be aware of the customer at the extremes of the cost range because on the one hand, profits may be eroded by serving them and, on the other, although high profit is being generated, the business is vulnerable to price cutting. There is another issue. The data was generated in 1983. Since then there have been numerous technology developments and applications which, while they have improved effectiveness and lowered overall costs, have made cost allocation considerably more difficult.

The size of the problem can be appreciated when the costs of the service items are considered. The analysis of revenues and costs below are hypothetical but nevertheless based upon a realistic scenario:

		($000)
Sales revenue		400 000
Less: discounts	50 000	
Net revenue		350 000
Less: COGS	100 000	
Gross profit (margin %)		250 000
Less: Sales and marketing		
selling	15 000	
promotions	5 000	
merchandising	15 000	
	35 000	215 000
Less: Physical distribution		
order processing and communications	1 500	
storage handling	1 800	
inventory financing	2 500	
transportation	5 000	
packaging	1 700	
refusals	2 000	
credit financing	6 000	
returns	4 000	
		24 500
Customer contribution		190 500

Accepting the situation as hypothetical, but not unrealistic, it suggests that over half of the revenue available is absorbed by 'servicing' activities. Furthermore, we are uncertain the accuracy of the costs themselves and if, as suggested earlier, there is a wide range of values over which they may range, then the customer contribution may reduce further.

This raises some interesting issues concerning the collection of management accounting data and its allocation to customer accounts. As suggested earlier, while information technology provides more accurate, lower cost, rapid data it has some problems. One, of importance here, is that the application of these systems is seen as an increase in indirect overhead. This has been noticed with CAD/CAM (Computer aided design/computer aided manufacturing) and FMS (Flexible manufacturing systems) in manufacturing where the proportion of overheads as a proportion of total costs has increased significantly. Clearly, this makes the allocation of costs more difficult and increases the concern over specific customer profitability. We shall return to this issue at the end of the chapter. Meanwhile there are some alternatives that help.

Manufacturing costs attributed in the cost of goods sold should include 'fixed' or 'indirect' manufacturing overheads. If the cost accounting system excludes them from manufactured product cost, a simple basis for attributing them could be according to the 'value added' in manufacturing; that is, in proportion to the 'variable' or 'direct costs' of manufacturing.

Selling and distribution costs should be related to individual customers and based on the activities associated with servicing those customers. These costs are not a function of sales, and should not be attributed according to the sales volume.

Allocation of the costs should be based on a classification of physically identifiable activities. Typical physical activities might be:

- *Storage*: This is an identifiable physical activity in distribution, and the charge basis could be warehouse space in square or cubic metres for each customer or customer group, based on their sales throughput and stock-holding needs.
- *Despatch or delivery activity*: The basis might be a charge per sales order completed.
- *Order processing*: The charge could be based on the sales order (number, frequency, items per order).
- *Sales representation*: This is another typical physical activity and the charge basis could be on the sales call rate and time per call.
- *Promotion*: The charge could be based on direct sales promotion activities allocated to each customer or group being serviced.

A number of factors influencing CAP from a distribution, marketing and production perspective can be found in Tables 14.1, 14.2 and 14.3.

Clearly, there are many questions which need to be resolved, not only in terms of the technical issues involved in allocating costs, but also in actually implementing any of the changes which may be indicated by the analysis itself. Nevertheless, there are strong grounds for attempting to improve our knowledge of customer account profitability, because it enables financial performance to be measured and, therefore, acted upon in a way which traditional accounting and information systems fail to permit.

Table 14.1 Distribution-related factors influencing customer profitability

DISTRIBUTION-RELATED FACTORS
Cost of order processing
Mixed load versus full-load single product
Cost of packing materials
Time involved in order picking/packing
Returnable containers
Pallet hire/de-hire
Costs of broken lots – space, obsolescence
Differential transport modes
Remoteness of drop points
Number of drop points
Difficulty of access to customer's premises
Inadequate handling equipment
Costs of shipping documentation/insurance
Certainty of customer behaviour patterns

Table 14.2 Marketing-related factors influencing customer profitability

MARKETING-RELATED FACTORS
Position of product in life cycle
Level of discounts
Mix of products purchased
Level of technical support
After-sales service
Level of personal service - attention factor
Costs of administering accounts
Rebates, etc.
Credit/distribution terms
Customer payment record
Level of returned goods
Customer cooperation and flexibility
Customer loyalty factor

Table 14.3   Production-related factors influencing customer profitability

PRODUCTION-RELATED FACTORS
Multiple or single end-user products
Cost of special processes
Standard stock items versus special sizes/qualities
Cost of achieving quality standards
Inspection costs
Risk of rejected/returned goods
Time lost in production changes
Costs of customer-created bottlenecks
Stocking levels to support customer needs:
Quality demands
Target delivery schedules
Short lead times

Some of the actions which lead to improvement in performance, but which may be indicated only by a CAP analysis, are:

- An enriched product mix, which has the effect of increasing margins;
- Increased sales volume per customer, which will usually increase order size;
- Reduced delivery frequency, which in turn increases order and drop size;
- Application of 'minimum order' policy or a premium charge on small orders;
- Avoidance of 'balancing' follow-up deliveries because this adds cost;
- Lengthened order-cycle times;
- Intensified business conducted in each delivery area – again, this has the effect of increasing the drop size;
- Encouragement to use intermediaries, where appropriate, particularly for handling small orders;
- Reduction in level of service at the drop point – this increases the speed of turnaround and therefore reduces turnaround time;
- The search for a more cost-effective method of obtaining orders, e.g. using telephone sales methods rather than sales forces in the field, who often become no more than customer service reps, and who are therefore ineffective as 'order getters'.

In summary, customer profitability analysis helps an organization evaluate the impact of its prices (via the terms of trade offered) on the various customer groups, or individual customers, by measuring the relative profitability of these groups. From this it can develop a basis for taking decisions on prices, and the level and mix of service offered to each customer or group of customers. In spite of both conceptual and practical difficulties, companies that attempt to understand and introduce the mechanisms of CAP are likely to be amply rewarded at the 'bottom line', even with only limited application of the principles.

■ Direct Product Profitability

The focus of customer profitability analysis identifies the profit contribution from individual customers. The other concern for management is the profit contribution from individual products. Direct product profitability is a method by which the profit contribution from the sale of a product may be more closely ascertained. Essentially, the analysis attempts to allocate costs involved in moving the product from the point of manufacture through to the point of sale.

Two approaches have been taken; both aim to resolve the same problem, but in doing so take a different perspective. Manufacturers have considered the topic from the view of identifying total costs from point of manufacture, through finished goods storage and the physical distribution channel into retailing distribution systems and eventually onto the store selling fixtures. In many ways this has more to do with CAP, but the reality is that if costs can be identified and perhaps reduced then the resulting productivity can be shared with intermediary customers and used as a component of competitive advantage.

The retailers' approach is directed towards minimizing costs but is a component in the space allocation exercise. Thus while retailers' interests are clearly concerned with cost minimisation, there is also a concern to ensure that the financial return on space allocated to the product is maximized. It follows that if the rate of sale of a product related to the space utilized is attractive, the retailer may accept higher costs (lower DPP) because the cash value of the product (as opposed to the *percentage* of costs) makes a contribution larger than that of competitive products. Typically this situation occurs for brand leader products and often in complementary/support sales situations.

For many retailing companies the sales/space performance measure is easier to calculate, and many businesses focus on sales/space as the major performance criterion. As Figure 14.3 suggests, a merchandise strategy based in part on sales revenue/space and operating profit/space (a DPP variant) offers the retailer greater perspective than simply considering the direct product costs in isolation.

The decision to stock a brand/product by the retailer (and the ultimate profitability for the supplier) is influenced by two factors, the 'real' gross margin and the 'delivery' costs.

Gross margins may be leveraged by the addition of discounts and allowances based upon order size. For example, it is not unusual for mainline grocery brand margins to be more than doubled in this way.

Such methods for offering incentives are clearly directed towards large retail customers. However, some of the allowances may be illegal in some countries. For example, in the US, anti-trust law is very specific in this context and requires that all customers be made the same offer notwithstanding the fact that only a few could take advantage.

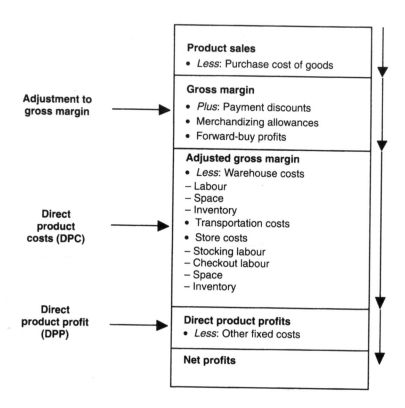

Figure 14.3   The 'DPP' model

	Percentage of purchase price
Basic gross margin	10.0
Cooperative advertising allowance	5.0
Merchandizing allowance	2.0
Quantity (volume) discount	2.5
Cash discount; prompt payment	2.5
Forward buying saving	2.5
'Real' gross margin	24.5

Direct product profitability is usually derived by identifying *direct product costs* such as warehousing, transportation, storage and head office (overhead costs). A typical example shows the delivered margin may approach 50 percent of the gross margin:

		Percentage of purchase price
Base gross margin		19
less direct costs of:		
Warehousing	2	
Transportation	1	
Storage	5	
HQ (overhead)	2	
	10	
Actual (delivered) margin		9

Clearly DPP is an important consideration for both suppliers and distributors. Christopher (1992) presented comparison data for a range of superstore products, some of these show quite revealing implications for both supplier and retailer:

	Gross margin (%)	DPP (%)	Average DPP/M^2%
Paper products	19	7.2	0.47
Frozen vegetables	34	23.1	2.60
Cigarettes	12	13.2	6.56
Dentifrice	31	18.6	1.42
Facial tissues	15	–	(0.01)

The wide range of margins is most noticeable, as is the range of costs and the impact on profit/space. Some products (facial tissues being one) are clearly sold at an accounting loss in order that customers' choice and range expectations are met.

There are a number of ways in which the DPP of both product ranges and individual products may be improved. Pack design is one favoured by many manufacturers: often pack design is a sales incentive feature rather than a design for cube economy. Adjustments to pack size in order to avoid pallet overhang eliminates damaged product costs.

Apparel retailers have eliminated a considerable cost penalty involved in pressing clothes prior to display by delivering products ready for immediate display. Additional equipment is required and a loss of transport cube occurs: however, the trade-off proves to be economically viable.

Range rationalization often resolves many problems. Boots (a UK chemist/pharmacy/retail chain) deleted the whole of its pet food and related products range following evidence from a DPP study. Woolworth (a UK variety chain) have made extensive use of DPP to trim their merchandise assortment. The technique was particularly helpful in weeding out unprofitable products in their 'garden centre' assortment. Clearly, there are numerous issues to be considered and Figure 14.4 summarizes the process.

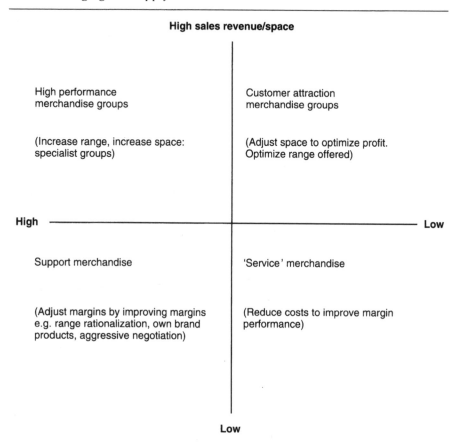

High sales revenue/space

High performance
merchandise groups

(Increase range, increase space:
specialist groups)

Customer attraction
merchandise groups

(Adjust space to optimize profit.
Optimize range offered)

High ——————————————————————————— **Low**

Support merchandise

(Adjust margins by improving margins
e.g. range rationalization, own brand
products, aggressive negotiation)

'Service' merchandise

(Reduce costs to improve margin
performance)

Low

Figure 14.4   Space and product performance: an issue for the retailer

■ Activity Based Costing: An Approach to Overhead Allocation

The fact that existing management accounting has limitations was mentioned earlier in this chapter. These problems are particularly noticeable in logistics decision-making. Logistics, like other service-based products, experiences a number of issues which management accounting cannot address due to specific problems:

- A general ignorance of the true and full costs of servicing different customer types/segments/channels;
- Costs are captured at too high a level of aggregation;
- Full cost allocation is the unrealistic ideal;
- Conventional accounting systems are 'functional' in their orientation rather than being 'output' orientated;

- Companies understand product costs far better than customer costs, despite the fact that in many supplier/customer situations the costs are higher *and* the fact that it is the customer transactions that account for profits.

It is for this reason that activity-based costing has considerable appeal. This chapter concludes with a discussion on the benefits of activity-based costing and its application.

Essentially, ABC relates overhead costs to the various activities which support the 'production' process. Activity-based costing moves away from the notions of short-term fixed and variable costs – the foundation feature of management accounting's traditional 'conventional wisdom' – and focuses on the variability of costs in the longer term. ABC advocates claim that all costs are variable and can be traced to individual products or product lines (including all common costs and those considered indirect and fixed in the short term).

As such, ABC has some appeal. It assumes that costs are best controlled by managing the workload, eliminating non-value-added activities, managing the factors that drive cost, continuously improving value-added activities and streamlining the management process. The emphasis is on effective use of resources. An understanding of the 'activities' of the business is the core of the approach. An activity describes how resources are used in the pursuit of the business objective: it describes how time, labour and capital are spent. Activities generate cost. How an activity is performed determines which factors of production are necessary: attaching costs to activities allows a firm to understand not only how much cost is being incurred but also how effectively the factors of production are employed.

Activity-based costing comprises a two-stage process. The first involves identifying the costs of individual activities and assigning them to activity cost pools: the relevant cost pools will be determined by examining the various activities which support the production and delivery of products. For example, a distribution function may be seen as: receiving, unloading, storage, order assembly, checking, loading and delivery, etc. These activities are the 'cost drivers' which give rise to indirect/overhead costs. The second stage of the process is to analyse cost drivers to determine the appropriate rates to be used in attributing indirect/overhead costs to individual 'products' and 'product lines'. It is essential that the activity cost pools are constructed in such a way to facilitate the use of the cost driver rates.

Our interest lies in the application of ABC in strategic distribution planning and control. Activity strategic cost analysis uses activity cost and performance data to develop enterprise strategies, translate the strategy into its impact on activities, and provides feedback to determine whether the anticipated results of the strategy were obtained. A strategic view of cost analysis decomposes a company's business mission and strategic direction down to its impact on specific activities – from concept design to delivery of the offer to the consumer – and determines where customer value may be enhanced or where costs lowered.

The vehicle by which activity-based costing may be implemented is activity-based management (ABM). Activity-based management reshapes how companies manage costs. By understanding its activities, a company can identify opportunities for performance improvement that conventional cost accounting systems seldom detect. Cost management is improved by identifying what the organization does, and providing a benchmark to judge how much better a company's performance might be. Cost accuracy is enhanced by tracing and allocating activities to the 'product'/customer offer.

Distribution is an interesting potential candidate for this approach. Many costs are difficult to allocate (with accuracy) to a specific product group or service 'offer' and the fact that many of the costs incurred are in support or service functions (or activities) suggests that management may find it helpful to view these from a different perspective. ABM uses the ABC approach to avoid the use of arbitrary allocations and apportionments by pooling indirect and overhead costs into activity-based cost centres or cost pools which are then directly linked to 'products' through a series of rates based upon the cost drivers. The ABM/ABC approach has gained increasing popularity due largely to the fact that it has provided a clear and convenient formula for achieving the two overhead costing objectives of cost pool homogeneity and cause/effect relationship between absorption bases and costs.

Activity-based costing can be extended to consider customer expectations. Attribute-based costing considers customer expectations within the context of a product/service to be offered. This differs from the conventional ABC approach which primarily focuses on current products and typically aims at identifying options for cost management either to improve profitability, by eliminating waste or non-value-added activities; or to adjust the product range and mix through promotion, discontinuance or possibly through price adjustments (due to improved product costing information). Thus, attribute costing brings an emphasis on proactive analysis. Figure 14.5 illustrates the relationship of the elements of the process.

■ Methodology

The usual procedure followed for developing and implementing activity-based management is by steps:

1. Activity analysis
2. Cost reduction
3. Product/service 'offer' profitability
4. Developing an integrated activity accounting system.

A customer/market orientation should be added if a more proactive approach is to be developed, together with the necessary critical success factors. To ensure that the implications of expansion are considered, an element which

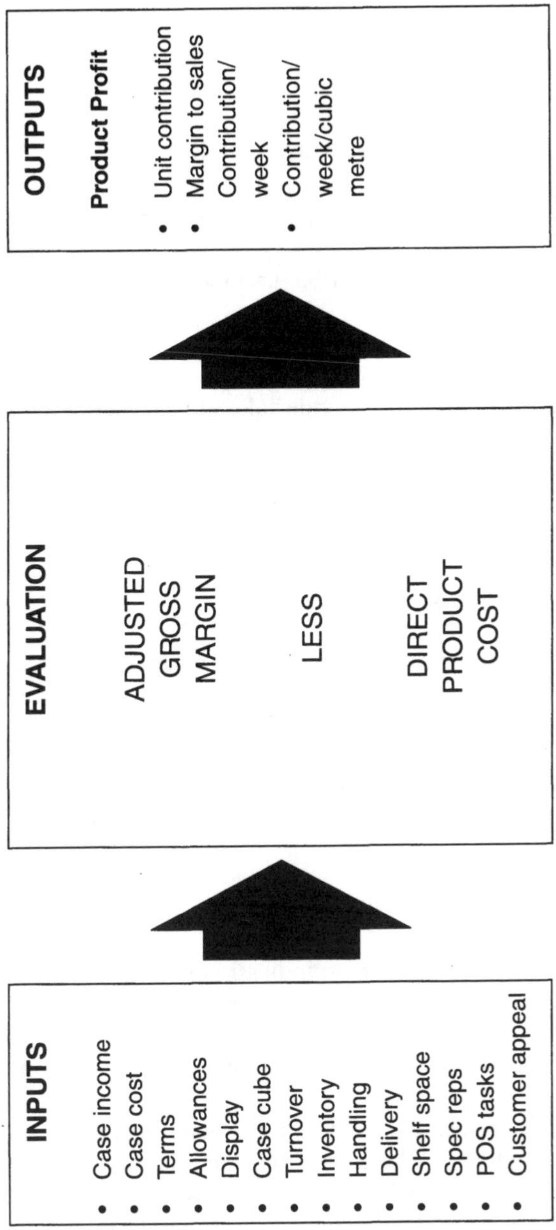

INPUTS

- Case income
- Case cost
- Terms
- Allowances
- Display
- Case cube
- Turnover
- Inventory
- Handling
- Delivery
- Shelf space
- Spec reps
- POS tasks
- Customer appeal

EVALUATION

ADJUSTED
GROSS
MARGIN

LESS

DIRECT
PRODUCT
COST

OUTPUTS

Product Profit

- Unit contribution
- Margin to sales
- Contribution/ week
- Contribution/ week/cubic metre

Figure 14.5   The DPP process

explores the likely impact of the expansion of the business on the activities is also included.

Thus the process to be followed comprises:

1. Evaluating customer expectations
2. Identifying critical success factors
3. Identifying and developing 'activity' analysis
4. Exploring product/service 'offer' profitability
5. Exploring the 'real' value of expansion of the business
6. Developing an integrated activity accounting system.

See Figure 14.6. Each element will be discussed briefly.

■ Evaluating Customer Expectations

A customer research programme is undertaken to determine:

- Customer's service expectations (by user segments)
- Customers' perceptions of competitors' service offer
- Customers' product-use behaviour patterns.

■ Identifying Critical Success Factors

The customer research is reviewed to identify critical success factors (CSFs). These will be discussed with senior management and will be reviewed within the context of existing competitors. CSFs identify the means by which customer satisfaction may be achieved and maintained; it follows that in so doing the nature of the requirements for developing sustainable competition advantage is established.

■ Exploring Customer Expectations

The initial requirement is to obtain an indication of customers' expectations. If the company has recent research evidence of service expectations (and perceptions of service currently delivered) this would be extremely helpful. Failing this, it is usually necessary to mount a research exercise to obtain the necessary data.

The findings of the research would be used as input data for developing the customer service attributes. These will then be analysed using existing costs together with the activity-based cost items that will be formulated in parallel with the customer research. The research topics should include:

- Order cycle times
- Delivery frequency

- Delivery reliability
- Inventory availability and continuity of supply
- Order processing and progressing procedures

Figure 14.7 illustrates a detailed attribute costing model.

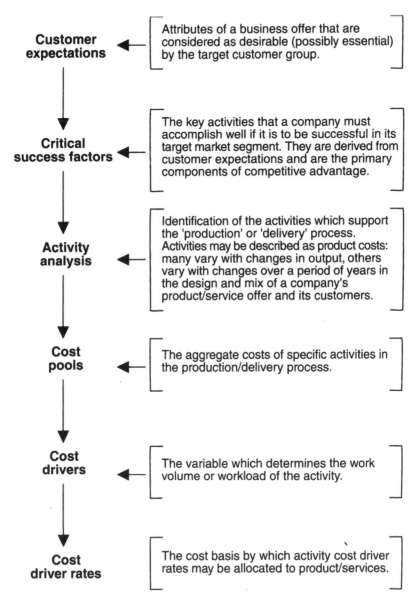

Customer expectations
Attributes of a business offer that are considered as desirable (possibly essential) by the target customer group.

Critical success factors
The key activities that a company must accomplish well if it is to be successful in its target market segment. They are derived from customer expectations and are the primary components of competitive advantage.

Activity analysis
Identification of the activities which support the 'production' or 'delivery' process. Activities may be described as product costs: many vary with changes in output, others vary with changes over a period of years in the design and mix of a company's product/service offer and its customers.

Cost pools
The aggregate costs of specific activities in the production/delivery process.

Cost drivers
The variable which determines the work volume or workload of the activity.

Cost driver rates
The cost basis by which activity cost driver rates may be allocated to product/services.

Figure 14.6   The attribute/activity based management process

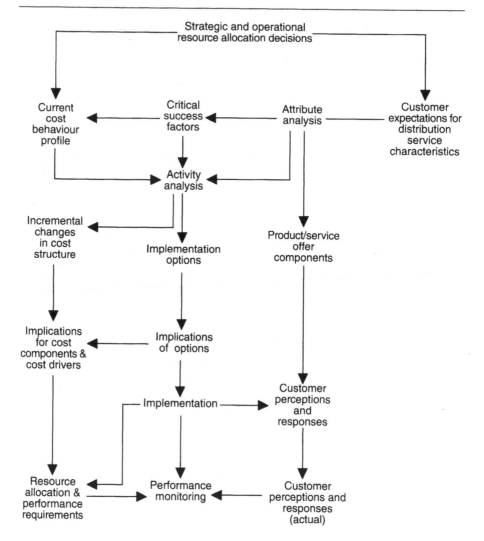

Figure 14.7   A detailed attribute costing model

■ The Value Chain as a Means by which Costs may be Identified

The well-established concept of the value chain makes a useful contribution. Figure 14.8 shows how the generic value chain can be modified to describe the *activities* involved in delivering the product and service offer. It is usual to consider inbound logistics and manufacturing activities. However, for our discussion the inbound logistics are omitted and 'manufacturing' will be considered as 'operations'.

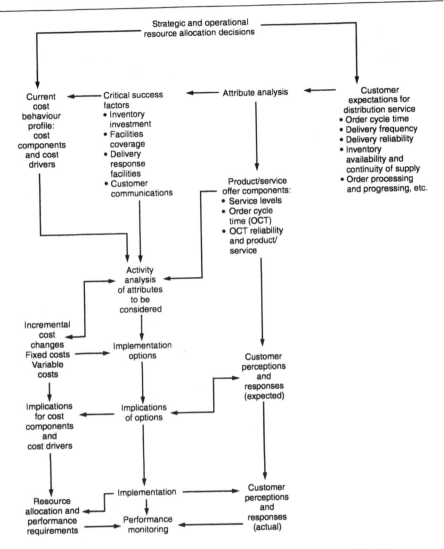

Figure 14.8   An attribute-based costing model in detail

The focus for identifying customer-related costs will be upon the *primary activities* (logistics) and the *primary activities (marketing channels)*. These are the vital areas of both cost and competitive advantage which may be undertaken by the producer, intermediaries, or perhaps a combination of both. How these are configured is a fundamental strategic decision. In the context of Figure 14.7 the issue concerns strategic resource allocation such that customer service expectations are met as are corporate profit contribution objectives.

The value chain, apart from identifying activities, gives an indication on the relative importance of activities, see Figure 14.8. By allocating costs to activities

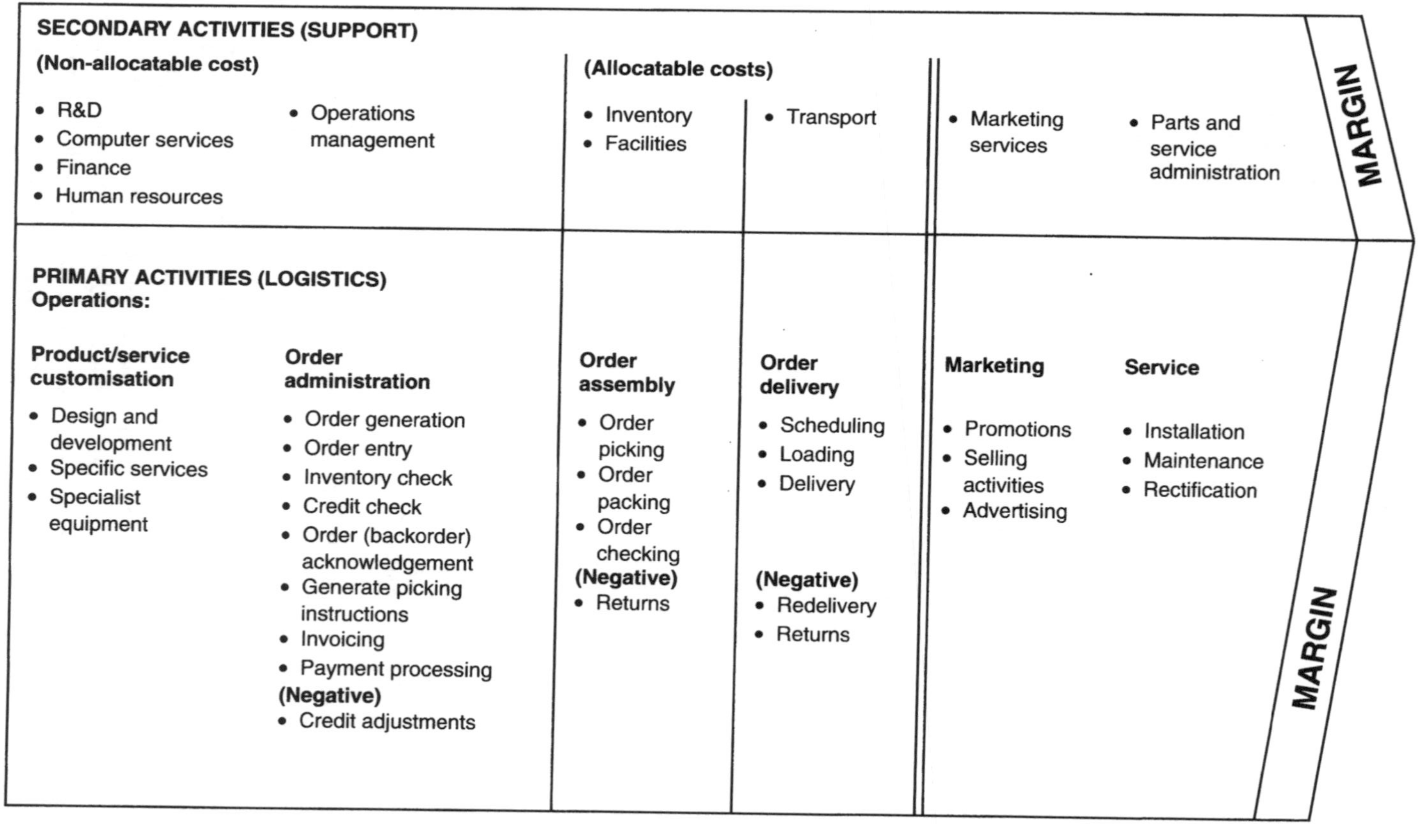

SECONDARY ACTIVITIES (SUPPORT) (Non-allocatable cost)		(Allocatable costs)			
• R&D • Computer services • Finance • Human resources	• Operations management	• Inventory • Facilities	• Transport	• Marketing services	• Parts and service administration

PRIMARY ACTIVITIES (LOGISTICS)
Operations:

Product/service customisation	Order administration	Order assembly	Order delivery	Marketing	Service
• Design and development • Specific services • Specialist equipment	• Order generation • Order entry • Inventory check • Credit check • Order (backorder) acknowledgement • Generate picking instructions • Invoicing • Payment processing **(Negative)** • Credit adjustments	• Order picking • Order packing • Order checking **(Negative)** • Returns	• Scheduling • Loading • Delivery **(Negative)** • Redelivery • Returns	• Promotions • Selling activities • Advertising	• Installation • Maintenance • Rectification

MARGIN

MARGIN

Figure 14.9   A value chain approach

Exhibit 14.1   Attribute activity-based costing: terminology

An *attribute* is a feature of a product or a service which adds value for the customer.

An *activity* describes the way in which resources are allocated/employed to achieve a company's objectives.

A *primary activity* contributes directly to the purpose of the department or organization.

A *secondary activity* supports an organization's primary activities, including 'head office functions' such as administration, supervision, training, secretarial support, etc.

Functions are aggregates of activities related by a common purpose, such as procurement, distribution, marketing, etc.

A *business process* is a network of related and independent activities linked by the outputs they exchange.

A *cost driver* is a factor that creates of influences cost. Cost-driver analysis identifies the cause of cost, e.g. the number of customer orders received in a specific period. A *positive cost driver* results in a revenue, production or support-related activities that generate profit. A *negative cost driver* causes unnecessary work and reduces profitability.

The product of an activity is its *activity measure* – the number of activity occurrences per period.

Critical success factors are those characteristics, conditions or variables that when properly sustained, maintained or managed can have a significant impact on the success of a firm competing in a particular industry.

Activity-based costing focuses on *cost behaviour patterns* which relate input cost with the changes of output volumes over a range of relevant activity levels.

Attribute-based costing first identifies customer expectations of a product/ service by its components (its attributes); the cost (to the company/ organization) of providing the combination of attributes is derived by using the techniques of activity-based management (i.e. the effective use of the organization's activities).

A *cost pool* is a grouping of costs caused by related cost drivers and activities. For example, *order assembly* may be designated as a *cost pool* for order picking, packaging, checking and returns handling.

rather than functions we identify the true costs involved in service delivery and apply these when determining the cost of (attributes) customers' expectations.

Similarly, we may also identify the largest area of costs which, if reduced, would provide economies. To do this effectively we need to know what causes the costs activities and these are known as cost drivers. Suggestions for these have been made in Figure 14.9. Clearly they need some discussion prior to adoption in order that their relevance is appropriate.

Exhibit 14.1 provides a glossary of ABC terminology.

■ Summary

Previous chapters have discussed the principles and tasks involved in providing customer service. In this chapter the topic was revisited and the ways and means of providing service were discussed together with problems of determining the costs of doing so.

The problem of identifying and classifying costs was seen as a major issue confronting management, and activity-based costing was introduced as an aid to resolving many of the cost issues and decision-making. Activity-based costing can be developed further to identify the costs of specific attributes of customer expectations. The problems of accurate cost allocation is shared by customers and products, and the chapter discussed the implications of both and introduced the topics of customer account profitability and direct product profitability.

The value chain was reintroduced as a potential vehicle for cost analysis. The value chain approach (i.e. breaking down the overall company activities into primary activities and secondary/support activities) provides a useful 'model' with which to identify more detailed activities from which cost pools and cost drivers can be developed.

COST DRIVERS		
PRIMARY ACTIVITIES (LOGISTICS)		
Product service customisation		

Product service customisation		
• Design and development	} Costs allocated to specific customers	
• Specific services		
• Specific equipment		

Cost pool: Order administration

Activities	Cost driver	
• Order generation	• No. of orders received	
• Order entry	• No. orders processed	
• Inventory checking	• No. of items	
• Credit check	• No. of customer accounts	
• Order (backorder) acknowledgement	• No. of orders and backorders processed	
• Generate picking instructions	• No. of picking documents	
• Invoicing	• No. of invoices	
• Payment processing	• No. of items per invoice	
• Credit adjustments	• No. of cheques, etc.	
	• No. of credits	

Cost pool: Order assembling

Activities	Cost driver	
• Order picking	• No. of items picked	
• Order packing	• No. of items packed	
• Order checking	• No. of items returned	
• Returns (handling)		

Cost pool: Order delivery

Activities	Cost driver	
• Order scheduling	• No. of orders	
• Order loading	• No. of customer deliveries	
• Order delivery (redelivery)	• No. of unit loads	
• Returns (pickup)	• No. of deliveries	
	• Distance/delivery	
	• No. of return journeys	

Cost pool: Marketing

	Cost driver	
• Promotions and advertising	• No. of enquiries	
• Selling activities	• No. of sales calls	

Cost pool: Service

	Cost driver	
• Installation	• No. of installations	
• Maintenance	• No. of maintenance calls undertaken	
• Rectification	• No. of rectification visits	

SECONDARY ACTIVITIES

Cost pools	Cost driver	
• Inventory	• No. of items held 'in stock'	
• Facilities	• No. of order movements through the facility	

Figure 14.10   Identifying activities, cost drivers and cost pools within the value chain

Best Practice and Benchmarking

Introduction

The effective companies are those who deliver customers' service expectations to a level of satisfaction that will ensure them a position of 'first choice' supplier with the customer, but, at the same time, maintain very high levels of production and profitability, thereby maintaining satisfactory returns to the shareholders. Two concepts are noticeable and operate in these companies: best practice and benchmarking. Best practice is widely considered to be about doing things in the most effective manner, usually focusing upon a specific activity or operation (a critical success factor) such as inventory management, customer service, and so on. Best practice is identified by searching for companies who, in similar product-market situations, excel, and then analysing the reasons for that success in terms of processes and functions conducted within the business. In order to assess best practice, some form of measurement criteria needs to be applied: for example, inventory management might be reflected by stock turn, gross or operating margin performance (actual/planned).

It is here where benchmarking is useful. Benchmarking helps understand the business, its process and performance, and identifies 'gaps' between 'best practice' and the current operating environment. In so doing, benchmarking focuses on understanding how the 'best practice' companies achieve superior performance as well as understanding their objectives. Clearly we must consider the level at which the benchmarking is to be undertaken, what our own objectives are, and then decide upon whom and which of their activities we should benchmark.

Best Practice and Benchmarking: Definitions and Interrelationships

Best Practice

Best practice is accepted as being 'about doing things in the most effective manner'. Usually, this implies that the focus is on a specific operation such as inventory management (at a detailed level) or distribution management (at a broader level), and then examines organizations who have been identified as being expert in that particular area.

An essential first step is to identify strategic or operating congruence between two companies. For example, if we assume we are manufacturers of a fast-moving consumer good, seeking to improve effectiveness, we should first identify successful companies in similar product-market sectors whom we judge as market leaders. This requires us to keep the search for *best practice* activities within a realistic context. It should be recognized that the achievement of best practice is within the context of a specific set of circumstances, relevant and appropriate to the company's situation.

A company will pursue best practice as a philosophy with one overall view: to become a *world class* organization. World class in this respect implies an international reputation for overall effectiveness. There are a number of characteristics which distinguish world class companies (see Figure 15.1). Overlying the four critical elements of customer focus, flexibility, continuous improvement and the effective use of information technology is the need for equally effective management of human resources which energizes creative decision-making and problem-solving.

Customer focus is usually achieved by maintaining a relatively flat organization structure; in this way, everyone is kept close to the customer base. Apart from the service aspect there is the additional benefit of information from customers concerning current and future needs. These organizations typically create new demands for products and services, aside from offering rapid response to current demands.

For long-term success, continuous improvement is the key to differentiation and, therefore, to achieving sustainable competitive advantage. Successful organizations do so by responding faster, more effectively and efficiently than competitors, but doing so on a global basis. Much of the continuous improvement process is through *internal learning*. Typically this is achieved through process re-engineering (the reorganization of the operation by process rather than by functions). There are some clear parameters for process re-engineering to be successful, such as:

- Focus on a process that can be clearly defined in terms of cost or customer value, such that it improves performance across the entire business.
- Present a design which permeates the entire company, challenging the critical organizational parameters of:
  - roles and responsibilities
  - performance measurement and reward
  - organizational design
  - organizational culture
  - information technology

In order to achieve continuous improvement there are additional supporting concepts the organization should introduce and implement:

- Benchmarking (to be discussed in following pages);
- Empowerment of employees;
- Corporate strategies designed to expand the organization's *knowledge* asset base;
- Outsourcing where it can be seen to *add extra value*;
- An incentive-led innovation policy.

Flexibility and responsiveness are essential if the organization hopes to respond quickly and decisively to changes in the environment with appropriate responses. 'World class organizations' know their core business well and resist the burdens of excessive investment in peripheral activities: their flexibility is a key feature of their success, they know what type of response to make, for how long, and the nature and extent of its added value.

Figure 15.1 Distinguishing characteristics of a world-class organization

The use of information technology offers four key attributes:

- Accurate and reliable information input for decision-making;
- The ability to respond rapidly;
- Greater knowledge and therefore understanding of the marketplace;
- A means of differentiating the business to reinforce its competitive advantage.

It should be noted that information technology is a means to an end; it is not the end in itself. It offers the dynamic business the facility to maintain each of the other characteristics (i.e. the customer focus, continuous improvement, and the flexibility and responsiveness); on its own without creative use of IT, the organization cannot hope to become a world class organization.

Best practice is a first step toward long-term success. For maturity the process must become a dynamic component of the company's strategic and operational activities. Furthermore, to ensure success continues, the world class organization monitors marketplace and competitors and is aware of processes that could enhance its position through the process of benchmarking.

■ Benchmarking

Benchmarking has been variously defined. Macneil *et al.* (1994) suggest benchmarking to be 'a method for continuous improvement that involves an ongoing and systematic evaluation and incorporation of external products, services and processes recognized as representing best practice'. The authors suggest that there are some key terms in their definition.

Method describes benchmarking as a management method or tool which their research suggests is often used alongside 'other performance enhancement tools or philosophies, such as total quality management (TQM) or competitive analysis'. Their experience and research suggests that the compatibility between benchmarking and TQM creates a synergy which enhances the competitive advantage.

Continuous improvement is clearly an integral part of benchmarking. As we found earlier in this chapter, continuous improvement is a vital component in permitting flexibility for rapid response to opportunity. The philosophy of benchmarking is to create a change-oriented workplace culture (Macneil *et al.*) within which 'participative, people-driven approaches to benchmarking create an outward looking, cooperative, and responsive organisation'.

Benchmarking is a *systematic*, structured approach to searching for best practice. Experience suggests that successful implementation occurs when a formal approach is adopted. Macneil *et al.* illustrated this by outlining the models used in Australia. An interesting point in their description is the comment that organizations using advanced models retain the fundamental principles of benchmarking but adapt them to match environmental and internal changes that are ongoing.

Clearly, the principle of benchmarking is *evaluation*. Benchmarking exercises should contain two ingredients. One is the measurement and understanding of the company's performance. The second is identifying, measuring and understanding external best practice (Macneil *et al.*, 1994). Perhaps there is a third component and this concerns the ability to direct the search for best practice. Often the best practice examples are occurring in entirely different sectors and may be peripheral to the central process or core product.

The definition of benchmarking is extended by Miller *et al.* (1992) who suggests 'strategic benchmarking provides strategic data and information that can be compared to similar information from other global manufacturing companies . . . [strategic benchmarking] is just one of several ways to benchmark – an activity that varies depending on whether a product, a process, customer needs or global strategies are being compared'. They then describe four different types of benchmarking and outline procedural steps for their implementation. Their four types of benchmarking are:

- Product benchmarking
- Functional or process benchmarking
- Best practices benchmarking
- Strategic benchmarking.

Product benchmarking has been part of the practice of competitive evaluation for many years. Automobile manufacturers have practised benchmarking by dismantling competitors' products to identify not only performance differences but to understand design and production methods: 'By using the product as directed, a designer may be able to deduce how a competitor thinks about design tradeoffs, or learn a new way to satisfy a customer's need from a non competitive product (Miller *et al.*, 1992).

Functional or process benchmarking differs from product benchmarking in two ways. First is the emphasis on comparison of a functional process such as order entry, assembly, set-up activities, and so on. The other is the nature of the process: it requires permission of the company being benchmarked, if it is to be effective. It is also necessary for the organization to accept that some company, somewhere 'can do it better'. Functional benchmarking became current practice in the mid-1980s.

Best practices benchmarking extends functional benchmarking by directing management focus on management practices as well as the elements of the functional processes that managers supervise. The purpose is to understand the philosophy and practices that enable good processes to perform exceptionally.

Strategic benchmarking begins with the proposition that unless the strategic direction of the targeted benchmark company is understood it is unlikely that the exercise will prove to be successful. It is obvious too, that the company must itself have a clear view of its own strategic intent.

This is essential because then 'there is consensus within the organization about basic directions and key performance measures, as well as a common language for describing them' (Miller *et al.*, 1992).

Miller *et al.* use a process developed by *Industry Week* (1990) in a survey of current practices to indicate the typical steps followed in a strategic benchmarking procedure:

1. *Identify the function (or best practice) to benchmark.* Clearly the identification of issues and opportunities are a starting point.
2. *Identify the best-in-class company.* Once the factor is identified, the best-practice company should then be identified and cooperation sought.
3. *Identify the key performance variables to measure and collect the data.* Agreement is reached with the cooperating company on the type of data to be collected.
4. *Analyse and compare the data to what happens in your own company.* Differences in data and key management opportunities should be identified between the companies. Critical success factors should be identified.
5. *Project future performance levels of the benchmarked company.* The implementation of many of the observed techniques will take time, by which time the benchmarked company will have 'moved on'. The benchmarking company should estimate what that performance may become over the period and plan to match or exceed the level of performance.
6. *Establish functional goals.* To implement changes there will be recommendations on what these should be if performance goals are to be achieved.
7. *Communicate benchmark findings.* If the remainder of the organization is to buy into the changes that have been recommended, the benchmark study findings should be made available to employees.
8. *Develop action plans.* The benchmarking team should assume responsibility for developing specific action plans for each objective.
9. *Implement specific actions and monitor progress.* To ensure that changes made are relevant and are working as planned, ongoing performance should be monitored with changes introduced as and where necessary, if goals are not being met.
10. *Recalibrate benchmarks.* As the project matures the benchmarks should be re-evaluated and modified to ensure that current data and revised targets are utilized.

■ The Role of Critical Success Factors

The concept of best practice suggests there are a number of characteristics or features that are essential to a business if it is to compete successfully. Leidecker *et al.* (1984) suggest:

Critical success factors (CSFs) are those characteristics, conditions or variables that when properly sustained, maintained or managed can have a significant impact on the success of a firm competing in a particular industry. A CSF can be a characteristic such as a price advantage; it can also be a condition such as capital structure or advantageous customer mix; or an industry structural characteristic such as vertical integration.

The authors provided examples of critical success factors in a number of industries:

☐ *Automobile Industry*

- Styling
- Strong dealer network
- Manufacturing cost control
- Ability to meet EPA standards.

☐ *Semi-conductor Industry*

- Manufacturing process: cost efficient, innovative, cumulative experience
- Capital availability
- Technological competence
- Product development.

☐ *Food Processing Industry*

- New product development
- Good distribution
- Effective advertising.

Hofer and Schendel (1978) had earlier applied the concept to strategic analysis. They suggest that critical success factors are important at three levels of analysis: specific to the firm, to the industry, and to the business environment. Analysis at each level can identify a source of potential critical success factors.

■ Critical Success Factors and the Benchmarking Process

The conclusion that can be drawn is that for any company the critical success factors that will facilitate the successful implementation of any selected strategy should be identified and related *across the business*. The process requires that growth objectives are first established; second, a current profile of the activities and functions of the business (manufacturing, logistics and marketing) is established; and thirdly, the critical success factors that underlay the successful companies (those who may be benchmarking candidates/colleagues) are then qualified. An example of what some of these may comprise is suggested in the table:

Critical success factor	Strategic implementation and action characteristics
	Price
● Low price	Ability to exploit experience effects, profitably, across a wide range of volume activity
	Flexibility
● Design flexibility	Ability to incorporate product/service modifications to existing products
● Flexible capacity	Ability to adjust throughput volume
● Order processing management	Ability to respond to order changes
● Augmentation capability	Ability to offer complementary products and/or services
● Innovative and creative product design	Ability to develop and introduce new products/services to meet customer performance specifications quickly
	Quality
● Dependability	Low level of defect rates
● Product performance	Ability to produce 'high performance' products or services
● Reliability	Ability to provide 'reliable/durable' products and services
	Delivery
● Quick response	Ability to provide fast deliveries
● Accurate response	Ability to meet delivery and picking accuracy promises
	Service
● After sales service	Provision of after sales support
● Field support	Ability to provide complete product support
● Distribution coverage	Provision of widespread product availability
● Customized service	Ability to provide specific aspects and levels of service

It is unlikely that all of these critical success factors will be required in any one situation. The key task for management is to identify which are important prior to the development of its corporate strategy. It follows that the critical success factors thus elicited are an important input into logistics strategy decisions. At both the corporate level and in the supply chain the CSFs become the basis for identifying best practice and then for benchmarking. The examples given above have clear linkages between the 'macro' issues of corporate strategy and the more detailed CSFs required for directing thinking on logistics strategy. The essential points to be made are that:

- Successful strategy requires identification of relevant CSFs.
- The CSFs should be addressed across the company.
- Companies with obvious competitive advantage features should be identified and their 'best practices' benchmarked.

- The best practice characteristics should become critical success factors if persistent monitoring establishes they have a strong influence on success and they are medium- or long-term characteristics.

■ Best Practice, Benchmarking and Supply Chain Strategy

Formulating supply chain strategy was considered in Chapter 11, and Figure 11.2 described the components of the supply chain strategy and items to be included when the strategy is being developed. We use Figure 15.2 to illustrate how both best practice and benchmarking may be used in the strategy development process.

Behind the corporate objectives is an influence of the environment and industry critical success factors. These are likely to include an ability to offer environmentally sympathetic products and services and reflect industry-specific requirements (these may be based upon industry-agreed specifications for quality, and so on).

The objectives and the environment and industry CSFs will influence the corporate strategies. It is at this point that best practice and benchmarking should be used. The critical success factors will provide benchmark topics from which key processes and activities will be identified. These should form the basis of the company's internal critical success factors, and the purpose of these will be to ensure that; functional strategies are developed which are congruent with the corporate and marketing strategies, and that key performance indicator (internal benchmark criteria) are agreed.

■ Best Practice Benchmarking Criteria for Supply Chain Management

Essentially, we require a set of benchmarking criteria that report time, cost and quality performance. From each of these we are able to develop productivity and profitability performance criteria for corporate internal performance. To these we would add criteria which measure the level of achievement of customer service performance. It is possible but not necessary for a company to benchmark more than one best practice company.

Examples of *time* best practice criteria would include:

- Time from order to delivery
- Response to customer order progress enquiries
- Advice on non-availability
- Stock turnover rate.

Examples of *cost* best practice criteria would include:

- Order processing cost/per order
- Order progressing cost/per order
- Cost of transportation/tonne/km

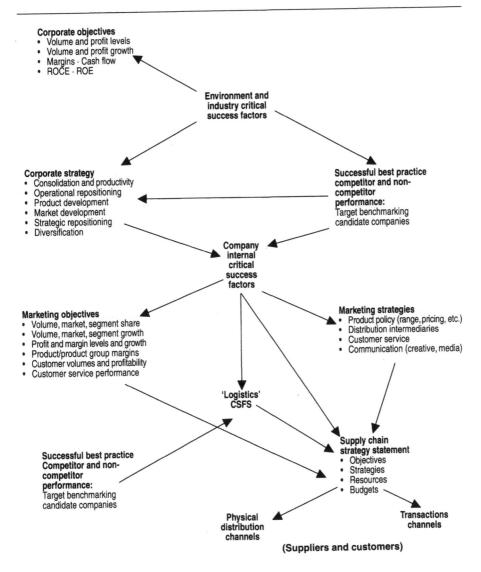

Figure 15.2 Using best practice and benchmarking in the strategy process

- Costs per transaction
- Costs per tonne/warehouse throughput.

Examples of quality best practice measures may include:

- Picking accuracy
- Availability; orders filled completely

- Reliability of delivery
- Frequency of delivery
- Emerging response.

Clearly, the importance of these criteria (and others that may emerge) can only be determined following an analysis of critical success factors and best practice followed by benchmarking successful companies. In addition the intra-industry and -sector research of customers' responses to company customer servicecan provide benchmarking criteria. One final point. During the process in which best practice is identified and quantitative criteria established it is important *not* to lose sight of the need to maintain a strategic perspective. The best practice that is emulated and the companies benchmarked should be future oriented. Furthermore, as commented above, the performance sought may require more than one benchmark candidate company.

■ Summary

Best practice and benchmarking are two of the more recently developed management practices. Both offer an organisation the opportunity to identify and replicate the practices and methodologies of successful, superior, leading companies. Well-implemented best-practice activities enable an organisation to emulate the successful companies, while benchmarking ensures that the high levels of performance that are implemented are maintained and updated.

Best-practice and benchmarking in the supply chain were discussed in detail and a procedure developed (based upon identifying external and internal critical success factors and relating these to supply chain activities) whereby these may be applied to supply chain management decisions.

CHAPTER 16

International Supply Chain Management: Issues and Implications

■ Introduction

The move towards global operations by a number of companies has implications for supply chain management. There can be no doubt that the expansion of the European Union which will eventually include some, if not all, of the former communist comecon countries, and the North American Free Trade Area, with its future possible inclusion of many South American countries and the growth of an Asian/Pacific economic entity, can only have huge implications for supply chain management. As a consequence, supply chain management should be prepared to cope with *expanding* markets which are more *interactive* and which *penetrate* one another. Markets are becoming increasingly *competitive*, with producers/suppliers seeking to minimize costs, and further, they are *converging*, as business practices are benchmarked and replicated. As global marketing becomes a 'norm', so it becomes necessary to seek sources of competitive advantage which are based upon identifying opportunities for differentiation. Two vectors are potentially available to the business: one a cost-led productivity vector, the other is customer- or market-led, which identifies features that add value, or augment the product offer. However, it should be added that increasing flexibility in manufacturing and logistics operations is enabling many companies to compete effectively along both vectors. The direction adopted should be a response to the characteristics of global competition, particularly the move towards standardized yet customized product/service offers, shortening product life cycles, outsourcing and offshore manufacturing and the convergence between marketing and manufacturing strategy. Within this environment, supply chain management should respond to developments in which it is not unusual for the market life of a product to be less than the time it takes to design, procure, manufacture and distribute.

■ The Move to International and Global Marketing

There are some terminology differences that should be noted before discussing the topic in any detail. The reason for doing so is that the implications for logistics decisions do differ. For example, *export marketing* covers all activities involved when a company markets its products beyond its domestic base, and where these products are physically transported across international boundaries.

International marketing takes the activities beyond exporting by becoming more directly involved in the local marketing environment. The company will have sales subsidiaries and operate specific marketing strategies for these markets. To be successful requires an understanding of local cultural, economic and political differences and developments.

Multi-national marketing is characterized by extensive overseas operations. Each market is managed quite separately and operates with its own dedicated asset base. Such companies operate as though they are 'local' companies with individual strategies and a considerable degree of localization. While this is, in many ways, an advantage, it often results in resource duplication and, consequently, less than optimal effectiveness.

Multi-regional marketing considers (and attempts to gain) economies of scope by developing regional, integrative, strategies. Politico/economic developments make this strategy option realistic. Developments in the European Union, North America (North American Free Trade Area) and the Pacific Rim countries have caused many countries to focus their operations on one region rather than across a number of countries within different regions.

A *global marketing* strategy differs from each of the three foregoing options by virtue of the feasibility of being able to create a single strategy for a product, service or company which is equally applicable to all target market countries. Whereas each of the other alternatives require specific individual strategies, the global marketing company aims to develop one general strategy and apply it universally. The reality of global marketing is that there are very few companies and products that have such an opportunity. However, it should be said that, as many consumer preferences now show evidence of convergence, so the opportunities for global marketing strategies become larger. The implications for supply chain management are not difficult to see. The exporting company manufactures and distributes from its domestic base while the other strategies (other than the global marketing business) require both manufacturing and logistics facilities operating in the territories. We will discuss these issues in detail.

■ Patterns of Internationalization

Jeannet and Hennessey, in *Global Marketing Strategies* (1995), write: 'Whether to compete internationally is a strategic decision that will fundamentally affect the firm, including its operations and its management.' The authors identify some nine motives for extending overseas. The implications for logistics management vary with each.

Opportunistic development is suggested to be the most common reason. Typically, the events leading to this type of expansion are a series of orders from overseas that may, or may not, have been solicited. Servicing these orders is usually difficult. If the company persists with the additional administration, then quite often the business expands such that some systems may be put in place and the company may then pursue more business actively. Until the business is formalized, logistics tasks are primarily concerned with export packaging and possibly administration.

Following customers abroad in order to preserve the business and the goodwill is another motive. Usually the situation is one in which a large customer moves abroad and the decision is then for suppliers (usually specialist and small in comparison) to follow. The logistics implications are not large. The supply chain may be extended (geographically), but essentially the service issues remain unchanged as do the supplier/customer relationships. Clearly distance problems will accompany the move unless the supplier manufactures locally. This may be the situation for some time, but may change if the supplier begins to expand his own interests and supplies local customers. Examples of 'following customers abroad' are typically found in the automotive and durables industries where component suppliers seek to secure their business.

For many companies, having all or a large proportion of their revenue in one country may be seen as high risk, particularly in product-market sectors in which sales are dependent upon a buoyant 'consumer confident' economy. To pursue *geographic diversification* reduces this risk, but does invite additional problems to be solved. If the growth occurs through acquisition the supply chain management problems are small, but if the diversification is organic then entire networks must be established with both inbound and outbound supply chains. Profitability may be increased incrementally by international expansion. Companies with high fixed-cost operations and who have made substantial investment in products can improve the recovery of the investment by introducing the product into overseas markets. The issues and implications for supply chain management may often be overlooked, particularly if the customer service demands are higher in the market to be entered due to the existence of indigenous expectations for high levels of service.

Growth rates for markets differ and may well exceed those of a competitive domestic market. In such situations overseas expansion becomes attractive. An interesting point to consider from a supply chain management aspect is the need to establish a strong customer-service-based advantage. It is likely that the market will be targeted by other companies taking the same view of the comparative growth rate opportunities.

Product life cycle stages have been seen to differ from one country to another: a product well into maturity in a domestic market may be in the growth, even introduction stage in a less developed market. Clearly, these situations offer opportunities. Jeannet and Hennessey (1995) illustrate this example using Coca Cola, where the US market, at 189 servings per capita was saturated (no pun intended) compared with the UK at 35, France 26 and the Republic of China at 0.3 per person. In such a situation, *exploiting product life cycle* differences can be very attractive. However, such situations do require careful analysis. Often the reason for success can be due to the infrastructure support (roads and rail transportation) that makes distribution cost-effective. Without this support, costs would be such that large parts of the market could not be serviced at a satisfactory level of operating profit.

As economies expand and disposable income increases, many markets become attractive for low cost large volume products. Recent expansion of fmcg manufacturers and brewing companies (not to mention Coca Cola) in the Pacific Rim countries are examples of how companies may *pursue potential abroad*. The comment made in the previous paragraph is also applicable here. Clearly low-value products are dependent upon efficient infrastructure systems for success.

Jeannet and Hennessey (1995) suggest that overseas expansion often occurs because the companies concerned do so for *defensive reasons*. They do so by entering the domestic market of a company who enters their own domestic market. They argue that such a strategy can prove effective by causing the new entrant to undertake reactive competitive steps (i.e. increase its customer service and other costs), which dilute profitability and require cash which would otherwise be devoted to market development in the new market. An alternative strategy is to increase the costs of being competitive by making effective supply chain management a critical success factor. Yet another strategy is to close down access to markets by use of exclusivity agreements in the channels of distribution.

A *global logic* is present in many industries. The IT/Communications industry is one such example, in which the locations of manufacturing and logistics facilities are viewed with a global supply chain management logic, so a US-based company will regard an offshore activity in no different way than that based in its domestic market. Such companies operate their support functions in context, and therefore global procurement and sourcing, manufacturing and physical distribution are managed as a network. The fact that the network is international and not domestic presents no difficulties whatsoever.

■ Managing International Supply Chain Operations

■ Market Entry Options

There are several alternative entry options available to the company seeking overseas expansion. The supply chain management implications vary with each.

☐ Exporting as an Entry Option

This option has a number of concerns. First of all it has appeal for companies confronted with low volume opportunities and who wish to take advantage of it without making major commitments of fixed and current assets. A second point concerns the unpredictability of future volume growth. This has two supply chain management concerns. While there may be a high probability of growth, some indication of rate of growth and likely volume on maturity is necessary if the supply chain system structure is to be effective. Without a reasonably firm idea of market volumes it is very difficult to plan both the nature and size of the logistics infrastructure. As a consequence there may be sound reasons for initially pursuing an exporting-based strategy.

There are two options here. *Indirect exporting* has very little if any investment requirement. Often there are domestic-based intermediaries with specialist market knowledge who offer market maker/merchant specialisms to companies who have neither the knowledge or expertise to undertake operations in a market. Typically, these businesses take title to the product and sell the product on into the markets in which they are established. Inchcape is one such marketing group that offers these services to major brand manufacturers throughout the world.

Direct exporting is the other option. Here the company does need an administrative structure to work with market-based intermediaries. Success requires both company and intermediary to build a close working relationship in which a large amount of time is invested. Furthermore direct investment requires an additional investment of working capital, because often the product remains the property of the supplier until sold to the end user.

The supply chain management issues are not particularly complicated for indirect exporting. There is a need to ensure that the intermediary offers reliable levels of service to end-user customers and that faulty products are returned for service (if applicable). This does require the supplier to be aware of the supply chain issues, but once the products have been sold to the intermediary the ability to exercise control to ensure that service is given to the customer is not likely. However, the direct exporting option is different. Here a number of supply chain management tasks are required. The packing and transportation of products is a responsibility of the vendor. While the storage of product at the intermediary's location is clearly a task for the intermediary the supplier should be concerned to ensure that, if there are specific storage and transportation requirements, the intermediary is both aware of the needs and is capable of ensuring they are attended to.

☐ *The Company-Owned Sales Subsidiary*

The sales subsidiary operates in much the same way as the export agent would do in the previous paragraph. However, here the company manages the sales operation and assumes the role of the distributor by stocking product, selling to customers and assuming the payment risk. This option requires a major commitment of capital to finance inventory and customer credit. It also requires a supply chain operation. This may comprise a third-party activity for both storage and transportation rather than a company-owned activity. It is preferable for the company to use service company activities provided. They are capable of meeting service requirements (which is likely, assuming they have been established successfully in market for any length of time). The advantages are that volumes are not predictable with any degree of certainty and nor, therefore, are capacity requirements. In addition there is the benefit of local knowledge that such an arrangement offers. All this notwithstanding, there remains a management task to ensure that appropriate service is offered at competitive costs to the business.

☐ *Licensing*

A number of companies license an overseas-based company to operate a process or brand. Again the company gains low-cost entry and market presence without an investment in fixed and current assets. There are a number of manufacturing and marketing reasons for licensing. Mostly they relate to synergy. If the licensee has a successful existing business (and this is assumed to be the case) then there are clear cost benefits to the licensing company. This may also apply to the supply chain activity, though it may be that this activity is a third-party service arrangement. This raises the problem of control, or lack of it, as a major consideration. Not only is product quality a concern (or could possibly be) but so to is the entire range of customer service attributes. Thus, while licensing may have apparent attractions the management of 'quality' may be expensive and be a problem. Another disadvantage is the possibility that the licensee may eventually become a competitor.

This possibility may be controlled to a degree by limiting the licence period such that the licensee would not be able to establish themselves either with the product/process technology or the distribution channels infrastructures.

☐ *Franchising*

Franchising is a special form of licensing. The franchiser makes available a marketing and operations management programme. The programme is more comprehensive than a licensing agreement and often involves input supplies as part of the franchise agreement; if this is so, then the implications for logistics management can be extensive. For example the McDonald's experience is that in order to ensure that product quality delivery meets their requirements they have found it necessary to become involved in an extended supply chain management task.

☐ *Local Manufacturing*

While local manufacturing may offer favourable terms for foreign companies seeking to manufacture and market their products in an overseas market, there are increasingly wider reasons for undertaking local manufacturing. The large international companies are locating offshore to take advantage of benefits such as lower labour costs and raw materials. Having reduced their manufacturing costs, they transport the finished product to markets elsewhere.

There are a number of alternatives available. *Contract manufacturing* uses local companies to undertake manufacture of products to meet specific volume requirements. Contract manufacturing is used for countries with low-volume sales potential and possibly high tariffs; in either situation the company finds no incentive to build and operate a manufacturing unit. The marketing task is assumed by the principal, which clearly involves the supply chain function.

Assembly operations are another alternative. Typically, this is undertaken to use low-cost labour in a situation where to undertake the complete manufacturing task would require a large capital investment. In addition, to obtain cost advantages from the labour savings (and possibly interest charges on investment), two other economies are realized. By using an integrated facility in one location, both economies of scale and experience effects operate, but additionally there are savings from the transportation of products in 'kit' form. There may also be economies available from purchasing some components locally. Automobile manufacturers use this approach extensively.

Fully integrated production requires substantial capital investment and commitment to the local market. Such a decision is usually undertaken after extensive research into market potential *and* market support infrastructure (i.e. transaction channels and physical distribution channels, and so on). There are four principal reasons for considering local fully integrated production: to establish local operations to *gain* new business, to establish foreign operations in order to *defend existing* business, moving with and to service an *established customer*, or to locate overseas *to save manufacturing costs*.

In each instance there are significant implications for supply chain management activities. *Contract manufacturing* requires an efficient inventory management programme operating in the markets serviced by the manufacturing location, together with cost-effective transportation if the economies obtained from contract manufacturing are to be maximized. The supply chain management implications of an *assembly* strategy are larger. Here we see the need for a total supply chain management approach, managing the inbound flow of component kits, their storage, the storage of finished products and the outbound flow of finished items to end-user markets. The tasks confronting logistics managers when fully integrated production takes place in overseas locations requires extensive knowledge of corporate and customer markets. In addition to this knowledge, the supply chain management activity must also be fully aware of the availability of logistics facilities and services locally and in the territories serviced by the manufacturing unit.

■ Risks Involved in International Marketing: Implications for Supply Chain Management

Apart from the usual risks from competitive actions and reactions, the international marketing company is particularly vulnerable to political risk, and this primarily depends upon government actions and the political climate that prevails. Clearly, the company contemplating an overseas venture will undertake a comprehensive review of not simply political influences but the entire range of issues that have an impact of these decisions. A detailed discussion of these issues is outside the scope of this text, our concern being with those having a direct impact on the supply chain management function. Many of the issues will have wide-ranging impact on the company's investment strategy, and it follows that any perceived threats that may put the company at risk will be offset by either forgoing the opportunity or continuing to pursue it but with a lower risk alternative.

■ The Political Climate

Political philosophy and stability are the two major indicators of potential risk. Extreme political views (be they right- or left-wing) can be difficult for international business to operate in. From such views can stem a number of goals. These may be as extreme as the underlying philosophy and may be damaging or, at the least, inhibitive for guest businesses. Often the extreme philosophies result in equally extreme xenophobia, expressed as prestige, ideological or security (in its broadest sense) goals. Quite clearly, if a country's philosophy is suspect then it is unlikely that the venture would not get very far. Similarly, signs of instability should prompt similar responses. Frequent changes of government or perhaps a government of long standing but one which is unpopular (and the unpopularity is made manifest through civil unrest) will be unhelpful to the incoming business. Furthermore the political ideologies that exist may influence supply chain infrastructure components. For example, the Chinese government makes use of its railways mandatory. Such issues can be costly.

■ Host Government Actions

Given that a company has made a decision to commence operations in an overseas location there are a number of actions that may be taken by the host country at one time or another. Again, if the guest company has concerns it is unlikely to pursue the opportunity, particularly if the concerns are strong over the impact on the company's investment and its activities. Not all the actions that may be taken by a host country are negative, indeed some may be attractive and are the reason for undertaking the venture.

'*Buy local*' *restrictions* may be imposed by governments. These may have two influences. One occurs when the government (typically a large customer within any country) favours domestic suppliers. Depending upon the nature of the guest business, this could have a very damaging effect on its activities. Not only may sales and profit be reduced but under-utilization of plant, equipment and the logistics system could easily occur. The other aspect of 'buy local' restrictions are equally damaging. Here the government may have, or introduce, regulations to the effect that foreign companies are required to ensure that a significant proportion of inputs are from local suppliers. The impact on cost recovery may be damaging and the impact on margins significant, often due to low quality inputs or non-standard sizes, and so on, all of which creates costly penalties.

Non-tariff barriers are not official customs duties but do inhibit the free flow of products between countries. The restrictions may equally affect inputs or inbound components as well as finished items for sale. The common type of barrier is the import restriction or quota.

Subsidies may be both positive and negative. Positive subsidies are those offered to attract foreign country companies. They may be offered for numerous reasons. Overseas companies generate employment and foreign exchange and are clearly attractive to the developing country. Conversely subsidies may be used to protect local, domestic industries from competition from large multinational businesses, and to protect employment.

Operating conditions can have both direct and indirect influence on non-domestic businesses. They may comprise restrictions on operating hours of work, on vehicle sizes, promotional methods and sales activities, they may require mandatory use of distribution intermediaries and many other elements. If the restrictions are equally applicable to all firms, domestic and international, the competitive threat is lessened. However, it is possible that if the restrictions are such that the company's normal operating methods cannot be utilized then the international companies will be disadvantaged.

Ownership conditions vary markedly. Many countries have restrictions on incoming businesses. Usually these restrictions impose a national ownership content on the guest company which quite often implies that overall control is exercised locally. Many international companies find these constraints to be to difficult to operate with, and avoid entry into countries where they exist, or withdraw if the regulation is subsequently introduced.

Takeovers of international companies by host country governments are not unknown. They may take a number of forms. *Expropriation* occurs when the operation is acquired, possibly with compensation but not necessarily. *Confiscation* is expropriation without compensation and *domestication* describes the restriction of specific activities to domestic companies.

It is quite clear that there are a number of potential problems that the international business could find itself dealing with. Typically, the political (and economic) climate are evaluated well before any decision to pursue an overseas opportunity is made. As and when it is made, the entry strategy reflects the perceived levels of risk.

From a supply chain management viewpoint the issues are interesting. Clearly the higher the level of perceived risk then the lower will be the commitment of investment in fixed assets. Consequently, the role of supply chain management may be increased as the company follows an export-based strategy in high risk locations. If we add the competitive dimension to the decision it becomes quite clear that the activity will be primarily responsible for maintaining competitive levels of customer service. In such a role the logistics function plays a major role in the planning process. Figure 16.1 suggests how this may be managed.

The logistics decisions follow the corporate decision on market entry method. Both depend much upon the company's overall strategic direction and the means by which this will be implemented. A company intent on pursuing an aggressive international strategy will probably undertake a strategy which locates much of its activities in the designated markets or market regions. Conversely a conservative company may prefer to centralize its activities in its domestic markets and pursue international opportunities in an opportunistic manner, in which case the focus will be more on localized efficiencies with a reliance on outside companies and suppliers.

The scope of its activities will be influenced by both the economic and political environment of the target markets. From these the company will be able to determine a view of likely constraints that will be imposed by the host country government, and the implications that follow for logistics planning and control.

Throughout the process, management should consider their decisions against the overall *corporate direction* planned for the business and the logistics function. Therefore, at each step, the decisions taken should be evaluated against acceptable levels of risk. Finally, prior to implementing an international supply chain management strategy, its 'strategic fit' should be examined. These steps are identified in Figure 16.1.

■ Summary

The ability to compete on a global basis is becoming an essential consideration for a number of companies. This does not suggest that global operations are essential for overall corporate success, but rather that an understanding of its implications for the business should be investigated.

This chapter approached the issues of international operations and their implications for supply chain management by identifying the patterns of internationalisation typically pursued by companies involved in this type of business and therefore the implications for supply chain management. The factors considered in a strategic context are equally as important for supply chain management decisions.

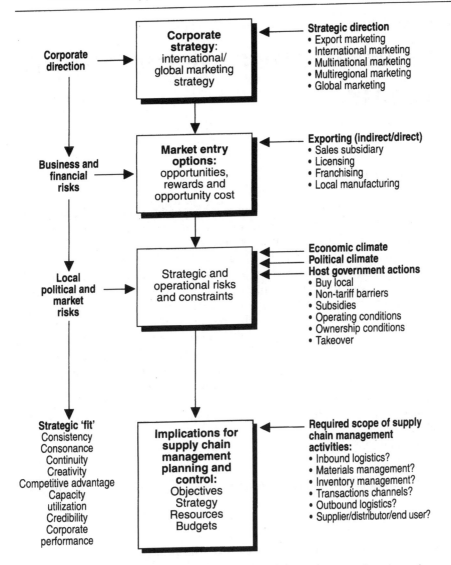

Figure 16.1   Logistics planning and control: international perspectives

CHAPTER 17

Optimization of the Supply Chain

Introduction

In an economic environment dominated by little opportunity for volume growth and with strong competitive pressures on operating costs, resource allocation issues gain priority consideration. Any business activity requires four resource inputs: physical resources (land, buildings, equipment, inventories, and so on); financial resources (cash, receivables, creditors); human resources (management and employees) and information resources (data, hardware, software, and so on). Clearly, resources have particular characteristics, some of which are shared and others which are specific to the resource. Resource allocation takes cognisance of these characteristics such that when resource allocation is considered, a number of issues should be considered. They are the *scarcity* of resources, their *flexibility* (or perhaps lack of flexibility), the *multiplicity of requirements* confronting the business and the *resource allocation priority* that evolves within the business, based upon the relative desirability of competing requirements for resources. Increasingly, business is turning to optimization models to provide the answers to questions of *when*, *where* and *how much* resource should be allocated, given a clearly defined objectives set.

Problems of Complexity Confronting Supply Chain Management

The Basic Problem

As we have indicated throughout this text, the primary problem for supply chain management is the management of stocks and flows of material and information such that specified service performance is achieved at acceptable, predetermined (budgeted) costs.

For some time the choice facing management was one of maximizing service or minimizing costs. The problem facing logistics managers was how to evaluate alternative solutions and in fact how an optimal solution might be found that resulted in both service and costs reaching acceptable levels; acceptable, that is, to customers (the service offered) and to the company (the levels of cost required to achieve the service offer).

Bender (1990) describes how 'the basic distribution problem is characterized by a flow of finished products between *sources* and *sinks*'. *Sources* are facilities that despatch freight, such as company-owned distribution centres, finished goods stocking points and service company facilities. *Sinks* are facilities that only receive freight customer locations (warehouse facilities and stores) or service company facilities. Figure 17.1 illustrates this concept.

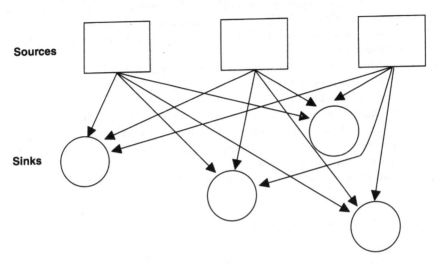

Sources

Sinks

Source: P. Bender 'Development of optimum logistics strategies' in *The Gower Handbook of Logistics and Distribution Management*, 5th edn, ed. J. L. Gattorna, Aldershot: Gower, 1990

Figure 17.1   A basic distribution network

Bender continues by describing the 'basic distribution strategy development problem' as:

Given:

Sinks, characterized by:

- locations
- demands by product, as points, ranges or demand responses (due to changes in price and service)
- the frequency distribution of order size by product;

Sources, characterized by:

- locations
- capacity constraints for each location, including
  - maximum and minimum by product
  - maximum and minimum for the location

- costs associated to each product, to each process within the facility, and to the facility itself
- constraints such as maximum inventory investment allowed (or desired) in the system
- customer service requirements, in terms of response time, availability, order accuracy, reliability of shipment time and shipment condition
- conditions of a technical legal or operational nature that must be respected to ensure a practical solution
- order constraints (complementary and joint products)
- order handling requirements
- transportation flows
  - predetermined or acceptable transportation mode combinations linking sources and sinks and involving product characteristics
  - unit cost of each link, i.e. transportation costs, together with associated handling and service costs
  - constraints on flow levels for any link such as maximum/minimum flow levels

From the given data, *determine*:

- How much of each product should be shipped from each source to each sink, such that the profit contribution of the operation is maximized (or put another way – its cost minimized), while respecting the constraints and conditions established.

Given the following conditions, the problem stated above is the simplest type of supply chain management problem since it involves only direct shipments from sources to sinks. However, even then there may be conditions:

- The size of most shipments is large enough to guarantee low transportation rates;
- The 'market coverage' is sufficiently small to enable an acceptable order cycle time to customers;
- Final distribution to customers is effected through service operations which become sinks in the system.

■ Problems of Complexity

Shipment sizes vary, they are often smaller than optimum 'container' load size and, because of service requirements, inventory allocations are necessary between suppliers and their customers. The logistics solution requires intermediary stocking locations; see Figure 17.2, which describes the *transshipment problem*.

Solutions are then required which permit the shipment of large complete loads to intermediate warehouse points, thus *enabling low transport costs to be obtained*, and from the warehouses, smaller (often heterogeneous) shipments to be made for shorter distances to customers.

- *Improvements in response times* are resolved by locating inventories closer to customers.
- *Reliability of service is enhanced* by the strategic allocation of inventory such that local problems do not result in total system failures.
- *Improved inventory availability* is achieved by increasing inventory levels of products for which customers are particularly service sensitive.

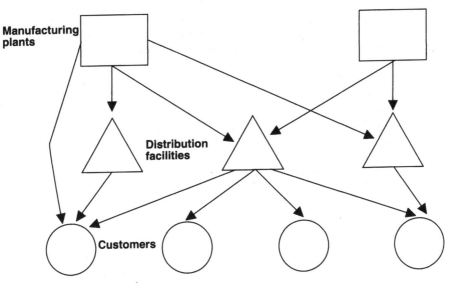

Source: P. Bender (1990) 'Development of optimum logistics strategies' in *The Gower Handbook of Logistics and Distribution Management*, 4th edn, ed. J. L. Gattorna, Aldershot: Gower

Figure 17.2   The distribution problem gains complexity

It is not surprising to find that both inventory carrying costs and warehouse costs can escalate unless both inventory cover and the number of warehouses are kept to an optimum number.

Bender also identifies the problem of servicing a wide product range within which selected items are very fast moving, frequently demanded products. This introduces another issue, the multilevel problem. To resolve this complexity the favoured solution is to introduce another storage/service function into the system between the manufacturing/storage locations and the warehouse system.

These units (distribution centres) carry a complete range of inventory while the field warehouses, closer to customers, carry only the fast-moving items. The distribution centres are responsible for replenishing the field warehouse stocks.

The multilevel approach enables the supplier to take advantage of bulk shipment transportation rates between the plants and the distribution centres; it also offers the facility to increase the level of service response and its accuracy. However, as with the transshipment solution, there are cost penalties involved.

The *international problem* introduces the complexity of identifying the most suitable 'ports' for loading and unloading products *and* the consideration of customs constraints.

Bender also lists sourcing as an additional consideration under the heading *logistics system problem*. We would add another problem, one creating considerable interest – the *international supply chain management problem*. While many of the issues have been considered above, the international supply chain management problem can be larger. Not only must it consider the movement of products from a domestic manufacturing plant and distribution system, it also needs to take into account the type of international marketing strategy the company selects and additional factors such as the effectiveness of overseas distribution infrastructures in overseas markets.

■ The Role of Modelling

Advances in computer technology and within the discipline of operations research now permit the application of custom-built computer-based models to the problems we have outlined.

Computer-based models offer significant advantages. First, they handle uncertainty and complexity by using the speed and capacity of the computer to identify alternative scenarios and then evaluate each one by comparing the costs involved in allocating resources in such a format that the service requirements are met within the specified constraints. They handle conflict situations effectively by initially establishing an optimal solution against which all possible solutions are matched. Computer models can be modified rapidly to accommodate change and explore *all possible* solutions, not just the intuitively obvious options.

■ Modelling Parameters

To proceed with the resource allocation modelling process, it is necessary to define, for each market segment, the following parameters:

- *Strategic direction*, specifying whether penetration of the market segment should be expanded, maintained, contracted, or abandoned.

- *Demand characteristics*, including the forecast demand by customer or geographic area as a function of price, service, and promotional intensity.
- *Supply characteristics*, including the location of each supplier of raw materials and other purchased items, their price structure, including discounts and minimum quantities and maximum quantities to be purchased from any one supplier or location.
- *Facility characteristics*, including for each existing and potential facility its location, its role, production or logistics operations, all costs involved, material balance equations which relate the amounts of inbound materials needed for each unit of outbound product, minimum and maximum capacity acceptable, plus any other practical conditions that may have to be respected in the production or logistics processes.
- *Financial conditions*, such as total capital available for investment and operations, rate of return to be used, inventory carrying cost, depreciation schedules, and replacement policies.
- *Overall conditions* that must be met when allocating resources, in order to account for contractual obligations, personnel agreements, engineering conditions, and others.
- The *objective* to be met by the allocation of resources. This may be profit maximization, cost minimization, throughput maximization, service maximization, or a combination of those and other such factors.

■ Resource Allocation Modelling Data

Any organization that allocates resources by some formal method already has the necessary information to do so. The most typical problem with resource allocation data is not so much its availability, but its accessibility and accuracy.

When an organization allocates resources by informal means, some of the data are estimated or implicitly assumed. Furthermore, in many organizations the only systematically developed data are accounting data: such data are usually developed to comply with legal and auditing requirements. As is the case with most data developed in transaction processing systems, they are not adequate to support the decision-making process. The main reason for this is that *transaction processing* and *decision support* have *different objectives*.

Transaction processing systems, such as accounting systems, are concerned with such things as record keeping, variance measuring, tax considerations, and risk minimization, for example. Decision support systems (DSS), such as resource management systems, are concerned with representing the real world in a reasonably accurate way. For example, depreciation of assets is treated in a totally different way in each type of system.

In an accounting system, depreciation is normally calculated to amortize the greatest allowable amount of the original cost as soon as possible. The purpose is to create the maximum cash flow allowed by law and to minimize risk. Thus the annual amortization figures shown in accounting books do not necessarily have any relationship to the physical, actual depreciation of the asset.

In a decision support system, an amortization charge typically will be calculated by transforming the actual expected amortization stream into an equivalent payment series that represents the asset's expected life and deterioration. In some instances, when evaluating the replacement of assets, their replacement values instead of book values may be used. Although different organizations follow different policies, the important point is that in a decision support system the data used can have a value that is significantly different from the equivalent data in a transaction processing system. Despite such differences, both sets of data may be correct for the purposes for which they were developed.

■ Data Types

For the purposes of processing data in a resource allocation modelling project, it is essential that a decision support information system be used to afford the necessary flexibility.

For a given time period there are three types of resource allocation data:

1. Costs
2. Constraints
3. Conditions.

Costs, from a decision-support viewpoint, must always be considered as variable, in that they are always a function of a facility's activity level; these can be continuous or discontinuous (varying in steps). When the activity level reaches a maximum, additional investment can create additional capacity through expanded or new facilities, or accelerated or additional equipment.

An efficient way to avoid arbitrary cost allocations is to define operational costs in 'tree' structure form (see Figure 17.3). Thus, continuous and discontinuous costs can be described in relation to facilities, processes and products. Every cost relationship is developed by itself, relating activity levels to total cost, without allocating costs. Since the cost relationships are described by equations, it is not necessary to select any particular set of conditions to arrive at cost figures. The cost equations form a tree structure because they are related to one another by the condition that all costs are added at every branching point. Thus, all product-related costs are added to their common process costs, and all process-related costs are added to their facility-related costs.

Since accounting data are not a good source of decision support data, such data must be developed independently. The two most common approaches in identifying decision support costs are:

- *Engineered costs*, developed by costing out an engineering description of process behaviour;
- *Regression costs*, developed by fitting a curve to a sample of observations.

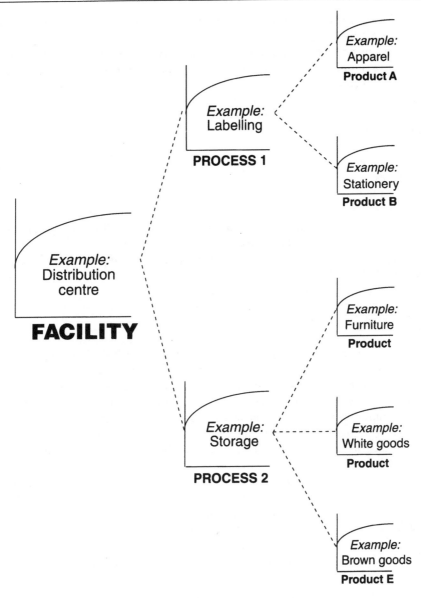

Figure 17.3 Defining operational costs

Constraints are numerically expressed characteristics that must be respected in developing the optimum allocation of resources. They usually reflect physical limitations or targets inherent in the situation considered. Typically, constraints are maximum and minimum values of activities within which the solution must lie – the limits defining the relevant range, for example. Other types of constraints are usually expressed as ratios among resources, such as material balance equations.

Conditions are logical, non-numeric characteristics that must be respected in developing the optimum allocation of resources. They usually reflect business considerations, such as policies, contractual obligations, or customer service needs.

Conditions can be described in terms of expressions involving logical operators, such as:

- If-then/else
- And/or
- Not/nor.

An example of a condition found in practical resource allocation problems is: 'If project 1 is funded, then project 2 must also be funded.'

Examples of the sort of data required for a resource allocation model can be found in Table 17.1.

■ **Network Descriptions**

The most efficient way to state and solve a resource allocation problem is to describe the system under consideration as a network model. In such a model, the nodes in the network represent entities involved in the problem: these represent fixed places, with resources whose levels are continuously varying. For example, nodes can be such entities as plants or warehouses containing material inventories that are being augmented through production or receipts and diminished through shipments. Nodes can be described as static inventories of variable levels.

The links in the network represent relationships involved in the problem; these represent movements of given resources between entities. For example, links can be such relationships as movements of materials, cash or information between two nodes. Thus links can be described as flowing inventories of constant levels.

The structure of a network model can be seen in Figure 17.4.

■ **Resource Allocation: Basic Questions**

By considering a company's structure and processes, we can answer a series of questions that defines the best allocation of resources. Such questions revolve around the need to optimize benefits. This may take the form of maximizing profits or return on investment, or minimizing cost, for example. Under those conditions, there are four types of questions that must be answered.

Table 17.1   Data requirements for computer-based modelling

1. PRODUCTS
    – What are they?
    – How can they be grouped?
    – What are their logistics characteristics?

2. SUPPLIERS
    – Who are they?
    – Where are they located?
    – What products do they supply?
    – How can they be classified?

3. DCs
    – Where are they?
    – What are the relevant fixed costs?
    – What sort of processing do they do?
    – What products do they handle?
    – What are the relevant capacity constraints?
    – What resources exist at these facilities?
    – What inventory costs are incurred?

4. STORES
    – Where are they?
    – What sort of processing do they do?
    – What products do they stock?
    – What are the inventory holding costs?
    – What are their sales?

5. TRANSPORT
    – What modes of transportation are used?
    – Which products are carried by the various transport modes?
    – What are the usual shipment sizes?
    – Which different routes are used?

1. *Strategic questions*, including:

    • What market segments should be served and to what extent?
    • What prices should be charged in each market segment?
    • What are the optimum levels of vertical, horizontal, and lateral integration? This defines the enterprise's external portfolio.
    • What is the total capital investment required?
    • How many facilities of each type are needed and where?
    • What are the major characteristics of facilities? This includes their locations, missions, products handled, capacities and costs.
    • In what sequence and when should facilities be added, expanded or closed?
    • What are the delivered costs expected at each market segment?

The model is structured as a *3-level model*, defined by a series of links and nodes as depicted below. *The flow of product in the Network would be taken from the raw materials source through to customers/markets as depicted below.*

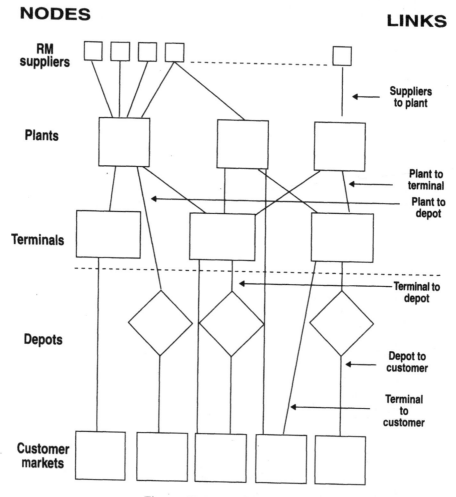

Figure 17.4   Model structure

2. *Tactical questions,* including:

   • What part of the sales that have been forecast should be sold and where? This question is important when available capacity is insufficient to meet forecast demand.
   • What supply sources should be used and how?
   • What products should be produced, where, and in what quantities?

- What products should be put in inventory, where, and in what quantities?
- What transportation arrangements will be needed to move materials into, through, and out of the company?

3. *Operational questions*, including:

- Where should each customer order be produced and shipped from?
- What suppliers should be made available, where, and when?
- What transportation rates and routes should be used to move what products?
- What production plans are needed to provide the necessary inventories in the right places and at the right times?

4. *Analytical questions*, including:

- What is the sensitivity of the optimum solution to changes in input values?
- What are the penalties associated with non-optimum solutions?
- What conditions could be relaxed slightly to increase profit substantially?

These questions are of two types: problem-related questions, including strategic, tactical and operational questions; and solution-related questions, or analytical questions.

Problem-related questions deal with the optimum structure for the enterprise to fulfil its mission and meet its goals and objectives. Such questions examine the enterprise's structure from the standpoints of its financial and physical resources structure. Thus, the financial and physical resources aspects of a resource allocation problem are modelled together, because the answers to questions about the structures of financial and physical resources generally reveal different aspects of the same problem.

To facilitate the modelling task, it is usually practical to describe the problem in physical terms and include in the problem statement all relevant financial entities and relationships.

Solution-related questions deal with the sensitivity of the solution to changes in input values or problem statements. Thus they deal with the effects of uncertainty on the solution.

■ The Use of Optimization Techniques

A model can be used as a means of describing the essential features of the problem under consideration. That use in itself makes it a valuable tool because of the completeness and precision it offers. In fact, the construction of a model alone provides enough discipline and understanding about the problem under consideration that it generally requires no further justification.

However, descriptive models represent only a fraction of the value that can be obtained from modelling and simulation. The greatest value of such techniques comes from the fact that a properly structured model can also be used to determine an optimum solution to the problem under consideration.

Many years ago, optimization models could not be run without the use of large, expensive computers. This limited their value and applicability and forced many users to settle for heuristic/simulation approaches to answer the types of questions discussed above.

The current performance and cost of computers has made it unnecessary to use heuristic/simulation resource allocation planning. The cost-effectiveness of available data processing systems allows users to make extensive use of optimization techniques at low relative costs. From a managerial point of view, the use of optimization techniques in resource allocation problems eliminates two serious limitations of heuristics, namely:

- The need to rely on an arbitrary selection of an approach;
- Reliance on past performance to evaluate the adequacy of an approach.

The difference between optimization and simulation can be seen in Table 17.2. The key variance is the use of mixed integer, rather than linear programming (see Figures 17.5 and 17.6). It is important to realize that, in solving resource allocation problems, the power of optimising techniques cannot be matched by the existing alternatives. The use of large-scale optimization models based on mathematical programming techniques has proven to be a powerful, effective technique for resource allocation. Although most applications have related to problems requiring the allocation of financial and physical resources, they can just as surely handle the allocation of human and informational resources. Thus technology currently available enables the allocation of all relevant resources involved in a problem to be considered simultaneously.

The three main benefits of optimization modelling are:

- Gaining an understanding of total logistics costs and network
  – used as diagnostic aid;
- Generation of potential 'counter intuitive' strategies;
  – used as a strategy suggestive tool;
- Evaluation of different strategic alternatives
  – used as a strategy assessment method.

Generally, optimization models would be used to address:

- Network complexity
- Decentralization/Centralization decisions
- Overseas expansion (sales or manufacturing)
- Rationalization
- Product launches
- Entering new markets
- Mergers and acquisitions
- Consolidation.

Table 17.2   Optimization and simulation models: the differences

Optimization vs Simulation	
TECHNOLOGY: RELATIONAL DATABASE MIXED INTEGER PROGRAMMING (SLIM & FOCUS)	SPREADSHEET (LOTUS 1-2-3)
FEATURES:	
• Mixed integer programming	• Trial and error
• Optimal allocation of resources	• Arbitrary allocation of resources
• Powerful	• Easy to use
• Complex	• Simple
• Processor intensive	• Labour intensive
• Dynamic	• Static
• Multi-variable optimization	• Multi-variable modelling
• Capable of counter-intuitive solutions	• Limited to management intuitive solutions
• Multi-period modelling	• Single period modelling
• Complex problem-solving	• Simple problem solving
• Good approximation to reality	• Relatively poor approximation of reality
• Piecewise linear relationships	
• Identifies key relationships in data	• Linear relationships
• Simultaneous multiple problem resolution	• Analyses stability of a given system
	• Single problem resolution

■ Methodology

Using artificial intelligence techniques, such as expert systems, we are able to optimize any logistics system that can be described by way of a network of nodes and links, and the costs, constraints and conditions that relate to them.

Given the completion of the first stage of the process – definition of the network (see Figure 17.7) the next step is to proceed to base year data collection and formatting. We now have the foundation to move towards our objective of *optimization for tomorrow's demand*.

**Avoids the problem of most optimizers,
i.e. over-simplification**

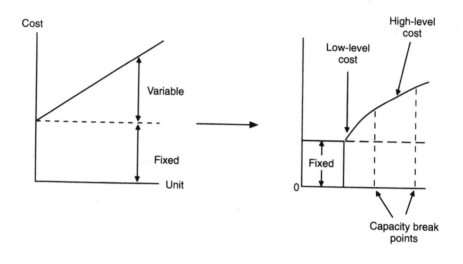

LINEAR   **PIECEWISE LINEAR**

Figure 17.5 Mixed integer programming instead of linear programming

Prior to constructing the model it is essential to define the overall goal:

- Should we minimize the total pipeline supply chain costs?
- Should we only minimize the company-controlled network costs?
- Are we interested in revenue maximization?

It is also extremely important to define the scope of the model in order to focus the data acquisition process:

- Where does the supply chain management function end?
- Where does responsibility for the pipeline begin?
- Should buying costs be included in the model?
- What is the overlap between sales and logistics?
- What activities are relevant and logistics related?

TAKES ACCOUNT OF:

1. ECONOMIES OF SCALE

e.g. Transport/inventory centralization

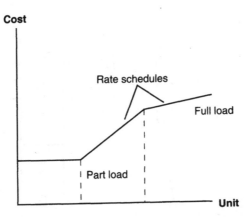

2. DISECONOMIES OF SCALE

e.g. *Increased product range*

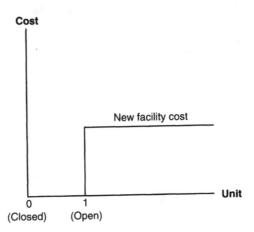

3. BOUNDED OPTIMIZATION

e.g. *Feasible physical locations*

Figure 17.6   Mixed integer programming

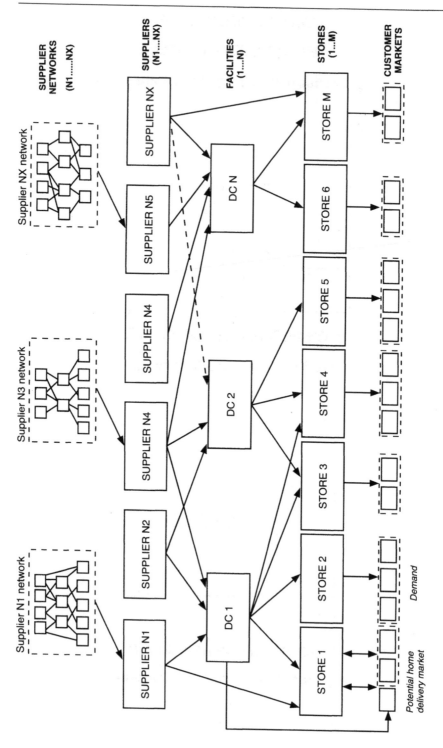

Figure 17.7 Defining a retail network: the complexities of the logistics pipeline

Because of the turbulence of today's environment, it is best to look toward optimization three to five years into the future. If considered any further, the variability range broadens too much. Although properly structured resource allocation models have the ability to cope with degrees of variability and inexactitude, they still rely upon the overall integrity of the alternative nodes and links that have been put into the model.

A design year is chosen and all issues relevant to structural changes in the logistic network over the projected design year period should be examined. All viable alternatives need to be considered and built into the model with relevant costs, constraints and conditions nominated. All input data should be thoroughly checked and validated.

Upon completion of the design year data-collection stage, which will have taken into consideration the relevant data that describes the characteristics of the situation to be modelled, the next step is to generate a *customized* model of the problem at hand. A model generator, using high level modelling languages, scans the data in predetermined formats, deducing from it the characteristics of the problem and generating the mathematical expressions needed to represent it.

A series of runs of the model is conducted, representing alternative scenarios worth studying to arrive at a practical system. This situation allows the user to focus on the *optimum solution* and on a few quasi-optimum solutions worth exploring. It is worth reinforcing here that the optimum solution is all about trade-offs, which may mean increased costs in one area, leading to a greater reduction in another (see Table 17.3).

Table 17.3   An example of a supply chain study results

	(Costs in $000s)	
	Current	Optimal
Transportation costs	6 226	5 498
Facility fixed costs	1 360	818
Facility variable costs	577	879
Facility shutdown costs	0	159
Inventory cost (safety stock)	281	319
Total	8 444	7 673

A by-product of the optimization process, known as *sensitivity analysis*, is an extremely valuable means to analyse complex situations characterized by high uncertainty. It allows the user to determine the impact on the optimum solution of simultaneous variations in several inputs. System-wide sensitivity analysis is essential to arrive at an answer that will be valid in the long term under varying conditions.

The modelling phases are shown as Table 17.4.

Table 17.4   Modelling Phases

1. DATA ACQUISITION PHASE
    - Scope Project
    - Data Specification
    - Data Availability

2. MODEL DEVELOPMENT PHASE
    - Data Management
    - Model Construction

3. VALIDATION PHASE
    - Last year's Financial Performance
    - Compare to Actual Data
    - Provides 'Benchmark' for Scenarios
    - Iteration

4. OPTIMIZATION PHASE
    - Identify Potential Quantum of Cost Saving
    - Typically 5-20% (Average = 11.63%)

5. SCENARIO PHASE
    - 'What-If' Analysis
    - Five Major Areas Investigated
    - Sensitivity Analysis

Optimum allocation of resources today can be a potential means of designing a logistics network to deal with tomorrow's demands.

■ Summary

Increasingly organizations seek to maximize the return on investment received from resources allocated to supply chain activities. Hitherto companies were confronted with two options: they either attempted to maximize their service offer, or they opted to minimise the costs involved in offering a predetermined level of service. Optimization modelling improves the choice of the options by allowing management to model the supply chain and build in specific demand situations and structural constraints and then use the model to evaluate all of the feasible options and combinations of institutional and physical facilities available to the company within the supply chain. Optimization identifies combinations of resources, indicates likely economic performance and leaves the responsibility of selection to managers.

Information for Supply Chain Management

■ Introduction

Information has become a central feature of management planning and control. The application of information technology to the process of planning and control of supply chain activities is well documented and the focus of this chapter is on how information can make logistics decisions more effective. The chapter first considers the role of information management in the development of supply chain strategy, and then discusses the issues from an operational perspective. The discussion dealing with operational issues will look at requirements planning and the role of information.

■ Information for Strategic Supply Chain Decisions

In Chapter 11 we discussed the issues and activities surrounding the formulation of supply chain strategy alternatives. In that discussion a number of points were made. Two points in particular are important in our opening discussion on information requirements.

To be effective the strategy eventually selected should clearly demonstrate advantages over and above the alternatives. To do this effectively requires a sophisticated information base which addresses the interface issues between the macro issues of corporate and marketing strategies *and* the supply chain support requirement, for which a strategy should be developed prior to allocating capital resources. From Figure 11.2 (Chapter 11) it is quite clear as to how and where resources should be allocated once the roles of the elements in both the physical distribution and transactions channels strategy are determined. However, before we can make these decisions, the overall role of the supply chain function must be determined. This requires a number of questions to be asked. A method by which this may be approached is suggested in Table 18.1 in which three strategic tasks are identified, as are their marketing and supply chain implications, together with the information requirements necessary if an effective supply chain response is to be developed. There are, of course, other strategic tasks that will emerge during the overall process and each should be dealt with in a similar manner. Clearly, there will be some overlap and the information that evolves is likely to have multiple application.

Table 18.1 Developing the supply chain strategy information requirements

Strategic task	Marketing strategy	Implications for marketing	Supply chain management implications	Information requirements
1. Responding to the needs of existing customers	• Product modification	• Product design and formulation changes	• Handling, storage, transportation requirements: facilities transportation	• Customer identification, volumes, patterns of demand • Delivery frequencies • Storage requirements; space characteristics, etc.
	• Product-service development	• Before, during and after sale activities, e.g. design service, installation maintenance • Distributor profile/specification	• Delivery requirements • Service parts • Stocking and delivery capabilities	• Forecast number and destinations • Volume of product to be stored and transported • Product to be carried by company and amount to be carried by distribution network • Distributor service requirements
2. Expand customer base. Identify and respond to needs of new customers	• Market development	• Review channels of distribution • Margins and costs; cost effectiveness/revenues generated	• Additional deliveries and destinations • Capacity and capability of existing system	• Number of distributors • Distances • Order sizes • Utilization of existing logistics system

3. Extend supply chain membership backward to integrate suppliers	• Strengthen company/supplier relationships	• Improve buying margins by supplier rationalization	• Evaluate the potential for lowering system inventories
			• Evaluate the potential for using own transportation for raw material deliveries
				• Locations and amount of inventory between supplier and company
				• Review levels of availability
				• Review ordering frequency:
				  – all suppliers
				  – selected suppliers

We can consider the overall task by referring to Figure 18.1 which describes a supply chain audit model. The model would consider all of the proposed (or determined) corporate and marketing strategy intentions and evaluate each to determine the impact on the current capacity and capability of the supply chain system. The benefits of an audit system are that it uses an ongoing approach to data collection, review and dissemination and monitors both external and internal information.

■ Designing the Information System

■ Identifying Customers' Service Requirements

It should be clear from Figure 11.3 (and Table 18.1 and Figure 18.1) that the design of a supply chain information system should begin with a survey of customer needs and determination of the performance standards required to meet these needs. Figure 18.1 then suggests that customer needs be matched with current capacities and capabilities of the supply chain system to identify the logistics areas that will require monitoring.

The basis of any information system is the decisions made by the information system users. It follows that interviews with the users should be made and the type of decisions each makes at both strategic and operational levels and, therefore, the type of information each requires should be identified. Given that both strategic and operational decisions are customer-service-led, the review of information requirements should commence at this point. The *customer service characteristics* (Figure 11.3) provide the focal point and the information may be developed across a matrix format such as that described by Figures 18.2 a, b and c.

Figure 18.2a presents a format for use in gathering the necessary information. It should consider all of the strategic and operational issues and activities required to deliver the supply chain offer. Figure 18.2b uses inventory availability to give an applications example. Given an inventory availability profile, the information requirements necessary to reach a cost-effective solution which meets the prescribed performance requirements can be identified, assembled and evaluated. This may be quite detailed in its coverage but is necessary if management is to ensure that both the service requirements are met and are done so as the most effective cost to the business.

Figure 18.2c continues with the availability example. Here the performance and cost parameters have been established and the purpose of the matrix is to ensure that appropriate performance measurements are in place and *are used* to monitor the activities involved in delivering the customer service requirements. It will be recalled that performance criteria for each of the major activities, i.e. facilities, inventory, transport and communications management were detailed at the end of their respective chapters (Chapters 7, 8, 9 and 10).

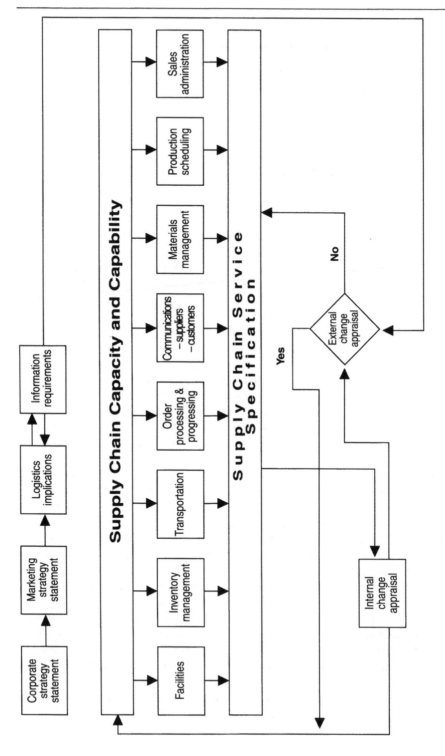

Figure 18.1   Supply chain audit model

■ Developing the Data Base

The next stage is to review the existing supply chain system, across each activity and function, in a survey to identify the precise amount of data currently available in the system. The most likely sources of data are the order processing system, company records, industry data and management data.

From the *order processing system* it should be possible to obtain information detailing customer locations, their ordering patterns (volumes, items, frequencies, and so on), revenues generated and the pattern of transactions over a period of time sufficient to be able to determine sales trends that may occur in customer businesses. A particularly useful item of information is the average transaction profile which can be used to calculate customer accounts profitability.

Company records should provide both financial and management accounting data. These sources should identify cost structures, depreciation and overhead recovery, in manufacturing and logistics, interest payments, cost of capital and service charges such as insurance, damage rates and taxes.

Industry data sources can be both formal and informal. The formal sources include marketing data from companies such as Nielsen which provide market-share information. In some industries there are data services which offer data comparison facilities, such as the Centre for Interfirm Comparison in the UK. Trade associations and professional bodies may also publish comparative performance details. On an informal basis there is often an interchange of data which, while limited, does enable management to form a view of how it is performing in broad and general terms, for example, benchmarking.

Management can augment this information by assessing competitive activities and responses to marketplace changes. In addition, they are able to judge the likely outcome of alternative strategies. They also maintain informal contacts within their industry scope.

This review of existing information may now be compared with the decision/information matrices developed from a review of the supply chain manager's activities. Any gaps found to exist may then be addressed. The additional information that is required may well be available within the company, simply being generated and used elsewhere. Should this be the situation it is not difficult to include relevant managers on the distribution list of recipients. However, for any information not currently available, arrangements should be made for its retrieval.

Computer-based information systems have four characteristics: data retrieval, data assembly, data analysis and report generation.

Data retrieval is the capability of recalling data items and allowing rapid and easy access. Typically the data are still in their basic form. The design of the data base should attempt to identify all data requirements and initiate their collection *at this early stage* in the development. This facilitates the servicing of subsequent data/information requirements. It should be said that data can only become useful as *information* and subsequently as *intelligence* if its collection is

Supply chain system components / Decision type	Facilities	Inventory management	Transportation
Strategic Customer service requirements: implications for performance and costs			
Operational Customer service characteristics: Performance Costs			

Figure 18.2a   A strategic and operational decision/information matrix

Supply chain system components / Decision type	Facilities	Inventory management	Transportation
Strategic Customer service requirements: Inventory availability – response cover by product group (product item) – response time – percentage of orders to be serviced *(QR: quick response)	Determination of number of facilities, locations and size. Identify alternatives – company owned – service company Design/layout Equipment alternatives	Identify 'core' products for QR* category. Identify market location for inventory supporting inventory category for *all* items	Evaluate transport needs. Evaluate cost of alternatives to meet availability objectives

Figure 18.2b   An 'in use' example of the strategic and operational decision

Supply chain system components / Decision type	Facilities	Inventory management	Transportation
Operational Customer service characteristics: Inventory availability Performance Cost	Picking levels Picking accuracy Time to process order Cost per order(s) QR standard Capacity utilization	Percentage of orders serviced 'first time' Inventory carrying cost – by category Capacity utilization	Delivery reliability Delivery time (by mode used) Cost per tonne/km Cost per customer delivery Capacity utilization

Figure 18.2c   An 'in use' example of the strategic and operational decision

Order processing & progressing	Communications	Materials management	Production scheduling	Sales administration

Order processing & progressing	Communications	Materials management	Production scheduling	Sales administration
Determine response times. Evaluate response alternatives for both QR and standard availability offer	Evaluate cost-effectiveness of alternatives e.g. Phone Fax E-mail, etc. for customers and supplier links	Identify and select key suppliers. Establish QR systems. Establish inbound materials programs to meet overall availability offer.	Establish schedules that are capable of servicing the overall inventory availability offer	Inform sales-force of the availability offer program

(strategic decisions) information matrix

Order processing & progressing	Communications	Materials management	Production scheduling	Sales administration
Response time achieved: order received/ order delivered to customer cost per order entry	Response time by mode Cost per transaction by mode	Stock levels In-company availability Stockholding costs – materials – work in progress – finished goods	Production cycle times Actual/ budgeted costs	Sales call frequency cost per sales call – routine – service inventory availability complaint
Capacity utilization	Capacity utilization	Capacity utilization	Capacity utilization	Capacity utilization

(strategic decisions) information matrix

in an appropriate form and frequency, thereby meeting management's requirements.

Data assembly is the capability to transform the data into information and thus to offer utility to management. Data assembly structures the items of data into specific formats. For example, data from facilities order processing and progressing, inventory management, transportation and communications will provide a customer profile that outlines the ordering pattern of the customer, the service response from the company and the costs of the response, thereby enabling management to measure the profitability of the transactions with the customer.

Data analysis extends the benefits of data assembly by applying the data to market and other models from which management may make both strategic and operational decisions. Chapter 17 described the process of optimization as a means for evaluating customer service and supply chain service (and therefore cost) options. It will be recalled that data availability, assembly and analysis are crucial in the construction of optimization models that evaluate optional logistics systems.

■ The Application of Supply Chain Information Management: Materials Management and Requirements Planning

Strategic and operational information requirements can overlap. As the responsibilities of logistics expand to include supply chain coordination, management time horizons become blurred, and short-, medium- and long-term planning horizons merge. This is clearly so when the roles of information management and materials management combine under the auspices of logistics management. In order that the supply chain may be managed effectively, the short-term requirements of manufacturing are integrated with the longer-term planning horizons of materials supplies. Indeed the current focus of business on JIT and QR (quick response) are good examples of how this occurs. The remainder of this chapter considers the application of information to the management of materials and information flows into and within the business, and onto customers.

■ Information Systems and Materials Management

Materials management concerns itself with the input of materials necessary to satisfy distribution outputs. The materials management task includes working with other subsystems, such as design and marketing, to ascertain the types and quantities of components and raw materials, purchasing, handling and inspecting receipts, quality control, inventory and production. Distribution is, of course, the other end of the pipeline, where customer service is actually delivered. Central features of the integrated logistics concept are the bonding of previously separate functions and a singleness of purpose through an understanding of the overall system.

Materials management has become an important field, not surprisingly when purchase costs consume at least half and often up to 60–70 per cent of the total income of a typical manufacturing organisation. Much leverage is therefore available in the materials area for profitability improvement. However, although the potential for profit from materials exists in all industries, the extent to which it can be realized varies. Industry characteristics which tend to affect the ability to improve profitability through materials management include:

- The proportion of sales revenue spent on materials;
- The existing profit margin;
- The nature of the production process;
- Product features.

Company considerations include:

- The role assigned to the materials management function by company policy;
- Organization structure;
- Materials management techniques and efficiency in use;
- Staff personalities, relationships and training.

An important point to grasp is that materials should 'add value' as they flow. By moving inventory through an *integrated system*, we add the maximum value to it.

■ Objectives of Materials Management

The materials management function is that part of the overall logistics task which ensures that *inputs* are fed into the production process.

The broad *objective* of materials management is to maximize profits by obtaining the required quantity of the *materials* of prescribed *quality* from designated *sources*. This objective, however, implies internal conflicts which must be resolved to maximize overall corporate profitability. For example:

1. Within the materials management area a low price might be obtained only at the cost of quality or delivery.
2. Within the logistics function, low levels of materials stockholding might be achieved only at the cost of interruptions in production.
3. Within the organization, savings from quantity discounts or speculative buying might be more than offset by high costs of financing, handling and storage.

In each of these areas there will, in turn, be conflicts between short-term and long-term objectives. Therefore, basic to the achievement of profit is the need to avoid sub-optimization by means of trade-offs within and beyond the function itself.

Profit from materials management can arise through:

- buying at comparatively low prices;
- timing deliveries to optimize stockholdings according to the inventory, distribution and customer service policies in place;
- ensuring quality;
- tapping the most advantageous sources (e.g. to ensure continuity of supply, or taking profit from making rather than buying at a later phase);
- obtaining (just) the required quantities at the right price (e.g. balancing opportunities for price speculation against supplier relationships, and maintaining market intelligence to watch for line ends and alternatives).

■ Reducing Conflict

A total systems approach to materials management demands participation in setting corporate objectives to ensure that profit potential is fully taken into account in company decisions relating to regrowth, diversification, capital investment, and so on.

Materials management also must relate to functional areas and subsystems:

Design: value engineering and value analysis; product standardization and simplification.

Production: avoiding excessive or inadequate stocks, obsolescence and new or alternative materials.

Marketing: ensuring adequate supplies of finished goods, meeting price structure requirements and enabling reciprocal trading agreements.

Finance: capital expenditure, stock evaluation and working capital management.

■ Materials Requirements Planning (MRP)

Materials requirements planning (MRP), and the now more common manufacturing resource planning (MRPII) offer an approach based on future needs, product design and production cycles and above all, information feedback. MRPII can be defined in the following way:

> MRPII is a software supported, time-phased management programme used to plan, schedule and coordinate a company's resources.

MRP derives its demand from a master production schedule. The schedule is created from customer demand, market intelligence, forecasts and production requirements. It has been through a rough-cut capacity assessment and is the plan for production to meet needs. The master schedule must be realistic and have integrity. MRP makes assumptions about goods inwards, directly on the basis of the integrity of the master production schedule.

Demand is 'netted off' against stock and forward orders to determine net requirements, which become planned purchase orders. Planned receipts are offset by the lead time to become planned purchases, which in turn become the demand for component items. These items are netted against the open orders and inventory, and so on through a bill of materials (BOM) system. An example of a bill of materials is shown as Figure 18.3.

A typical system, of necessity computerized, will produce invoices and picking lists, production schedules and inputs for costing. Such a system encourages and, indeed, demands greater integration of the functions of purchasing, warehousing, production, distribution and finance. MRP plans and controls inventory, charts open order priorities and provides input to capacity planning. Managers can try different resource allocations in 'dry runs' on the computer before setting the plan. The MRP process is depicted as Figure 18.4.

The basic logic of MPR is as follows:

$$N = G - R - O$$

Where:

N = net requirements
G = gross requirements
R = scheduled receipts
O = inventory on hand

The requirements and key concepts relating to a MRP/MRPII system are set out below:

- *Dependent demand*
  Demand depends on the demand for another item;
- *Fixed time periods*
  Fixed period for production schedule related to material lead times, e.g. one week;
- *Bill of materials*
  List of all components/materials that are used to make the product;
- *Inventory accuracy*
  MRP needs accurate and up-to-date inventory records;
- *Predictable lead time*
  Assumes lead times are known and unvarying;
- *Schedule regeneration*
  Reruns of schedule and MRP – may be only by exception, i.e. 'net change';
- *Input for capacity planning*
  MRP indicates capacity requirements for each period and gives ability to smooth

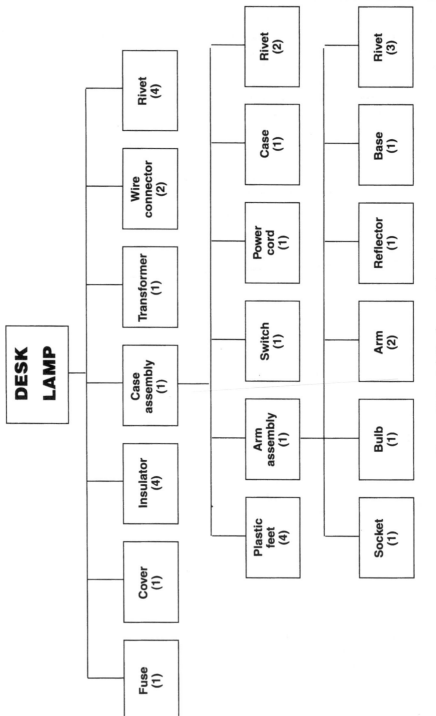

Figure 18.3   A bill of materials

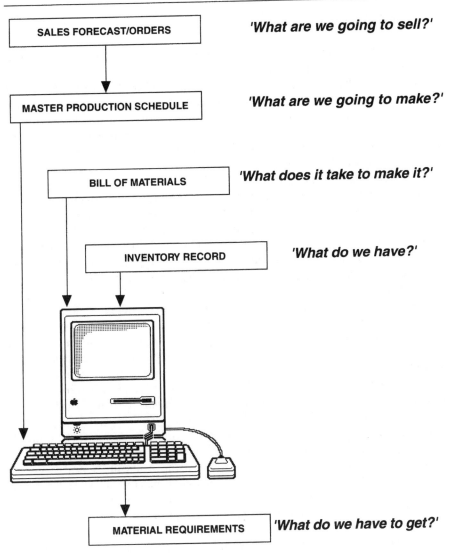

Figure 18.4   The MRP process

In drawing together not only the logistics functions of a company but also its other departments and teams, an MRP/MRPII system provides a powerful tool to drive towards lower costs, fewer stoppages and fewer surplus conditions. Many organizations are now using MRP/MRPII to generate a more disciplined approach to supply chain management.

Of course, there is an investment cost in implementing MRP/MRPII. As with any new technology, users have to undergo a learning curve, and changes are necessary in internal procedures, standards and documentation.

■ Radical Changes

There have been some radical changes in attitudes to inventory and requirements planning in recent years.

Separation of flow: Sales and marketing once used to deal with information and materials. Many companies now separate these activities into 'customer service' and 'delivery'. The sales function supports customer service by concentrating on promotion, demand data, sector intelligence and negotiation. New divisions, or combinations of old divisions, control the materials flows, based on MRP/MRPII. Materials flow directly from manufacturer to retailer or customer. Agents increasingly deal only with information.

Distribution network integration: This is a trend towards reducing the nodes or levels in distribution. Inventory may be held in what still passes for bulk at a single distribution centre which supplies small local warehouses. The task of a local warehouse is to break bulk and avoid odd lots, which can, however, cover express orders or defective deliveries. The forthcoming change is in the scale of direct delivery, with production and packaging geared to the single lot for the single customer.

Sophisticated service for customers: Customers increasingly require variety in the service channel as well as in products, so suppliers have to select *appropriate* distribution channel strategies. The large increase in non-store retailing (visiting sales, telephone orders and computer down-load sales, for example) has obvious repercussions in inventory and requirements planning. The phenomenon is bound to expand with the perfection of integrated network systems, which combine all the communication media into one line carrying telephone, telex, facsimile, data, and so on.

Flexible manufacturing systems: Flexibility implies a capacity for multiple processing, a mixed flow line. Such production can only be based on a comprehensive production control system using computers and accurate information, enhancing the case for robot installations and automated production technologies. Some processes are becoming so precise that they are impossible to execute manually. Robot technology offers many benefits: increased capacity (24-hour shift), reduced human loadings, increased safety and improved quality. Some automated factories now operate automatic warehouses, automatic carriers and processing cells 'employing' cutting robots, welding robots, painting robots and assembly robots. Inventory and materials requirements are of quite a different order in such an environment.

■ Distribution Requirements Planning (DRP)

What is the implication of this for the supply chain and information management? In order to cater for less volume per product, more variety and quicker response, the trend is towards integration, coordination and flexibility.

Inventory, far from being an asset, is increasingly viewed as a liability. Customer service – providing a service in all respects to the customer – rather than 'selling' is the principle external aim of the organization. The techniques of MRP establish and control the programme of acquisition, handling and production.

As we have extended the supply chain by adding raw materials we will now move towards the customer end by discussing distribution requirements planning (DRP) (see Figure 18.5).

The demand forecast, representing the needs and requirements of customers, drives distribution. The nature of the demand is significant: independent demand for an item is demand unrelated to that for any other item, like the demand for spoons. Although you normally use a spoon with a cup, a dish or some other vessel, demand for the spoon is not actually related to demand for the vessels. Dependent demand occurs when the demand for an item derives directly from the demand for another item, for example, special thermal printout paper of a non-standard size for a particular portable computer.

Distribution strategy for the two kinds of demand will be very different, but distribution requirements planning (DRP) provides a general method for either type.

DRP is defined as:

Software supported, time-based planning of distribution resources in order to satisfy demand at all stages of the distribution channel.

The use of DRP is shown diagrammatically in Figure 18.6.

DRP begins with identification of the time and place at which product SKUs (stock keeping units) will be required. DRP analyses demand for individual SKUs at each customer-service location and produces aggregated, time-phased requirement schedules for each level in the distribution system. These schedules then feed into the master production schedule.

One method to improve performance is to have managers think about and implement demand management, which seeks to modify customers' behaviour while closely forecasting demand. Another tool is scheduled distribution: specifying closely the conditions, especially the timing, under which deliveries must be made. The most important feature of DRP, however, is the coordination of the manufacturing and distribution functions of the company to provide the following benefits.

- Lower finished-product inventories;
- Better customer service;
- Opportunities for timely replanning as market conditions change;
- Production schedules with valid priorities, with;
- *Common bases of information to enhance communication* and help build the company-wide plan.

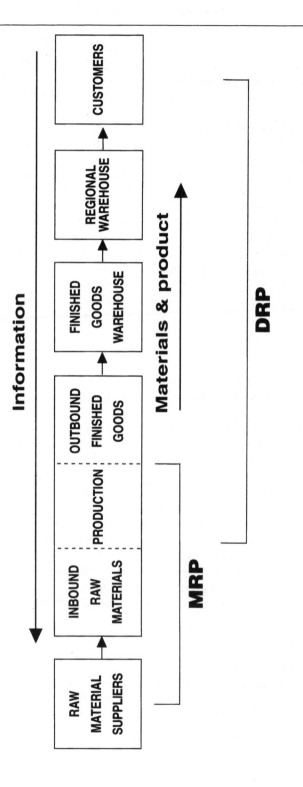

Figure 18.5   MRP and DRP

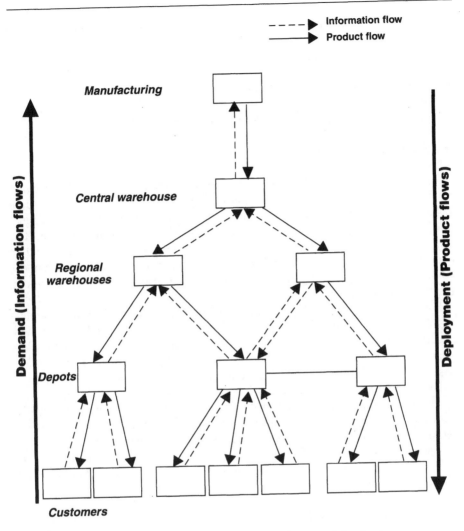

Figure 18.6   Using demand information to produce and deploy resources throughout the supply chain

■ From Control to Coordination

By moving away from separate control of departments, and towards overall coordination of effort, all the major movement activities, both of information and materials/products, are brought together in a single system; *supply chain management*. Its objectives are:

● Reduced pre- and post-production inventory levels, tending towards a minimum;

- Maximum efficiency in using labour, capital and plant throughout the company;
- Flexible planning and control procedures;
- Controlled customer service performance;
- Minimum variance (reduced uncertainty);
- Minimum total cost;
- Product quality, in other words, preservation of added value.

■ Approach to a Flexible System

Implementing MRP, MRPII, DRP and other techniques and methods does not, of itself, produce or guarantee a sound flexible supply chain management system. Implementation is itself a major innovation, not just a matter of small improvements. It produces many conflicts with the conventional system. The critical problem is the interface with the environment: an organizational and an educational problem. All the relevant personnel must understand what the company is trying to do and the role of each subsystem. Key points in implementation are:

Small lot size: Brand loyalty in some product groups is becoming less significant. Distribution lot sizes (and eventually production lot sizes) will necessarily become smaller to prevent losses from unsold stock and to allow flexibility through switching. Small lot sizes decrease the changeover time and ease handling. Common parts, modular product ranges and a strict line of balance help to solve the dilemmas in seeking flexibility.

Accurate information for control: The weakest point in modern logistics planning is the accuracy of the information used for control of the system. The required information accuracy level is said to be at least 98 per cent for a system to run smoothly. Mistakes frequently occur in obtaining or processing information, and most of them are caused by carelessness. To avoid human error, 'foolproof' systems need, for example:

- automation and robotics
- bar coding
- computer communication for ordering and billing
- cycled stocktaking
- statistical expertise
- education and training.

However, it should be remembered that all performance is achieved by humans. Generally speaking, an excellent system run by less understanding staff is worse than a good system run by understanding, participative staff. Quality circles and employee involvement schemes are time consuming but represent a long-term investment in committed staff.

Controlling distribution: We saw that suppliers need to be brought into and made part of the input subsystem. At the output end, distributors should be integrated. Company or associated distribution echelons are amenable to logistics planning of location, routing, inventory, packaging and bulk-breaking. Handling methods can be aligned with storage, transit and trucking systems. However, independent agents and distributors can be managed by effective dealership agreements, incentives and penalties, inventory guidelines (allowing for local variations) and suitable monitoring and control arrangements. The aim is to add control of distribution to the system. To do this requires an effective information system which permits planning and control of the entire supply chain.

Corporate strategy must reflect the importance of quick response and flexibility to survive the competition not only from within the country but from abroad, where different cultures, histories and circumstances may enable sudden breakthroughs or abilities to occupy significant niches in a market. 'How to realize the concept' is the challenge. The logistics manager is well placed to maximize co-ordination and minimize conflict in companies rising to meet the challenge, provided accurate, relevant and timely information is made available.

■ Summary

The importance of information management in the supply chain has been discussed throughout this text. This chapter has considered some of the issues raised in earlier chapters in more detail.

Information inputs for strategy decisions, and for operational and implementation decisions, were discussed with the emphasis placed upon data requirements, sources and generation.

Specific information-based systems and applications such as materials requirements planning (MRP) and distribution requirements planning (DRP) were discussed in detail within the context of supply chain management.

CHAPTER 19

Organisation Design and Management of the Supply Chain

■ Introduction

The notion of having to be a customer-driven company is widespread, however, realization of this concept on the ground is not without its difficulties. In Chapter 2 we introduced the concept of strategic alignment. It will be recalled that the thesis of the strategic alignment approach is that to be successful the 'logics' of the marketplace and of the strategic response should be aligned. The alignment concept extends beyond this into corporate culture and leadership style and the discussion of these issues and the linkages with the marketplace and the strategic response are dealt with in this chapter. The chapter commences with a discussion on the issues involved in achieving a customer focus in the organization. It will argue that the customer orientation is not easy to implement. The discussion considers the problems of overall implementation, not simply those functions of the business that are in contact with the customer. The chapter also discusses issues in labour relations. Clearly, the nature of labour relations tends to be country specific and it follows that the chapter can only address international trends; however, some of these are of common concern to *all* supply chain managers; for example, the trend among many businesses to focus only upon core activities has led to the divestment of 'service' functions such as the distribution service activities of transportation and storage. So too information technology has led to the restructuring of many tasks, and in some situations has resulted in considerable labour redundancies.

■ The Customer-Led Business

The 'customer led' business is in many ways a manifestation of the marketing-oriented business. The marketing literature identifies production, sales and marketing orientations. Each claims to have customer satisfaction as its prime objective, indeed function, but close examination suggests that this may not always be the end result.

A *production orientation* suggests that companies give their major attention to developing 'world class' technology-based products. The result is often a product with too many capabilities, excess quality or capacity, such that the customer neither wants or needs the characteristics. The firm is then left to ponder its lack of success with a product superior in all respects to its competitors, other than price.

Another production orientation feature is the cost-led business. Here the firm assumes customers have only one criterion – price! The low cost/price offer is one easily imitated and one which offers little opportunity to differentiate the product. In a market characterized by consumers increasingly seeking choice, quality and exclusivity, the cost-led orientation limits the flexibility of response.

The production orientation has implications for supply chain management. The philosophy can extend into the logistics 'production processes' of order handling, transportation and delivery. Typical symptoms of the approach are the bulk handling of orders through a batch processing system, together with a similar approach to transportation and delivery. Orders are held to ensure that a full truck load (FTL) can be guaranteed; deliveries are made to meet the convenience of the firm rather than the customer.

The *sales orientation* typifies a business which has either an excess capacity/high fixed cost problem or a product range offering little opportunity for differentiation. The approach is to use aggressive sales methods to obtain volume sales. As Levitt (1960) suggested 'Selling tries to get the customer to want what the company has; marketing on the other hand, tries to get the company to produce what the customer wants.'

A sales orientation influences supply chain management, usually in the area of the cost to service customers. Often the sales organization, anxious to firm up an order, will offer a service response which may be difficult to 'deliver' and usually totally uneconomic in the context of revenues that the order generates.

A *marketing approach*, as usually espoused aims at understanding the customer well enough to be able to respond with a product/service offer that meets rather than exceeds the customer's needs and wants, sells itself and makes an acceptable contribution to profit. This suggests that a business is most likely to be successful when it organizes itself to meet its customers' current and potential needs more effectively than competitors. This is the customer-led business, although when to say 'no' to customers is also an important ingredient of the whole equation.

The implications for supply chain management are not difficult to identify. It suggests that the customer-led business is aware of service needs as well as product requirements. It follows that a logistics customer service offer should be planned to meet, where feasible, specific service requirements. It is not unusual for companies to offer a generic service to all customers, missing the point that service differentiation can result in considerably greater added value for the customer and consequently enhanced profitability for the business.

■ Issues for Organization

A number of lessons have been learned in recent years. The first is quite simple: a customer-led organization does not simply materialize from the chief executive officer's statement. It has to be built, with each function identifying both external and internal customers. The second lesson that has been difficult to accept is that customers prefer to deal with suppliers who have a quality and service reputation. Reputations are only built over time but can be lost very quickly. The third lesson that has been learned by a number of companies is that for customer service to be delivered at the 'point of sale' it is necessary for it to be delivered at a number of 'points of sale' internally. In Chapter 3 we quoted the problem experienced by a large food retail multiple. A considerable budget had been allocated to sales staff training in customer service; customers were taken to product displays in response to enquiries, purchases packed at the point of sale, etc. However, there was no attention given to the internal points of sale (stores and distribution centres) and consequently no 'extra efforts' made by staff in these areas to meet the demands for rapid delivery of items for which unpredicted shortages had occurred.

It is now clear that traditional organization structures are unhelpful in developing a customer service ethic. Traditional pyramids suggest hierarchies of importance as well as power and authority. Consequently the members of an organization who typically have contact with customers appear in the levels of the pyramid.

Doyle (1994) discussed the 'right-side-up company approach of Pepsi Cola'.

Today's leading companies are attempting to change dramatically by turning the pyramid upside down and flattening it. By flattening it, they aim to take out layers of management and so slash overhead costs. By turning it upside down they seek to create a customer-led business with front-line employees motivated and empowered to satisfy customers. These new organizations recognize, first, that everything should start from a customer perspective. Second, those employees closest to the customer are at the top of the organization. They should be empowered to exercise their freedom to act within their areas of competence – to take responsibility, to accept accountability, to exercise initiative and to deliver results. . . see themselves as owner operators. . . Third. . . see the primary role of staff, middle and senior management as helping the front line by providing the right products and resources and removing obstacles.

Christopher (1992) considers the need for the business to be 'market facing'. This reintroduces the mission approach of the 1970s (see Christopher, Walters and Gattorna, 1977). In this early approach the mission approach was developed out of the corporate objectives and the product-market mission (see Figure 19.1). Much of this early work was developed from the PPBS (planning, programming, budgeting systems) literature that itself was developed during the late 1960s and early 1970s. Subsequent thinking and developments in corporate and marketing strategy shifted the focus from objectives to the qualitative concept of vision (or mission). This can be seen (in retrospect) to have been both helpful and necessary. By establishing an agreed view of what

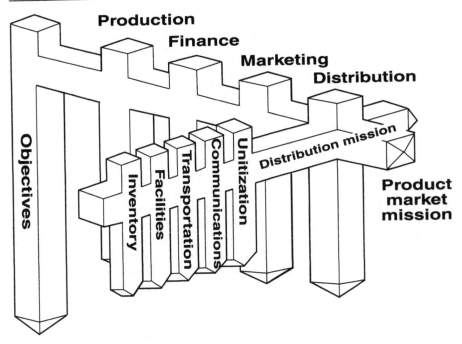

Figure 19.1   Objectives, product-market missions, functional missions

the business aims to be (or to be seen as being) in the marketplace, so the main foundations of the organization structure can be put in place. The approach of the 1970s was itself a considerable step forward because it required a coordinated approach across a range of functions, each tasked to commit resources to meet an overall output objective. Thus the emphasis was shifted away from being primarily concerned with inputs (and their costs), towards creating outputs primarily concerned with customer satisfaction. The use of a corporate vision enables the company to take a more focused view of its relationship with the marketplace (i.e. customers, suppliers and competitors) and to identify the important components of competitive advantage, in essence the *critical success factors.*

A number of influences have impacted on the organization design decision. An obvious influence is that of information technology which has provided control and flexibility together with detail and speed. Thus equipped, management can identify and respond to customer requirements more accurately and with greater speed of response, and create greater added value for the customer, often using resources which the company does not own. This introduces the second important influence. The notion that it is necessary to *own* the largest resource base has been replaced in the more advanced thinking organizations by a view that prefers to *coordinate* those resources that are not essential to the 'operational' processes of the core elements or products of the business.

Christopher (1992) identifies a number of problems inherent in conventional organizations. An obvious problem is the *functional* organization structure which is typically vertical, which encourages budgeting and performance measurement along the same structures. We have discussed this problem and the solution, suggested in the 1970s of becoming output rather than input oriented. More interesting problems identified by Christopher are logistics based.

The *build up of inventory at functional boundaries* is one such problem. If functions are encouraged to maximize outputs or minimize costs it is usual for the problems to be distributed *across* the organization. Many of these issues were identified in the interface chapter (Chapter 5) and included the implications of long production runs to reduce average costs of production, the implications of offering customers excessive choice options, and so on.

Cost transparency is another problem. Here the concern is that many costs are not identified or revealed. If the costs are identified on a functional basis only, there is a risk that the costs of activities which take place across functions may well not be identified. Our earlier discussion (see Chapter 6) on value chain analysis and the use of activity-based costing (ABC) is helpful in allocating costs to throughput processes in both manufacturing and logistics. As we identified in Chapter 6, a major issue is to find those activities which account for both influencing the decision to purchase, and a large element of total costs. Given both, it is then possible to be selective with the allocation of resources.

Fragmented processes with artificial boundaries impede the management of customer satisfaction as a 'through process'. In many respects this also reflects the problem presented by functional management. In this instance the problem is more likely to be an intra-functional problem, not an inter-functional problem. By this we mean that many functions within an overall function, for example, order processing with its components of order receipt, acknowledgment, credit checking, etc, create a series of processes within an overall process, with excessive documentation and delays.

The focal point of customer contact should be one area within a company. This is not so for a large number of businesses who permit *multiple points of contact* between themselves and the customer. This results in an uncoordinated presentation of customer service policy, often with promises made by one area of the business which have to be delivered by another. To make the situation more difficult, often the area responsible may not be aware of the commitment, nor may they have the resources available to meet the 'delivery' promise made.

■ Developing the Logistics Organization for Effective Supply Chain Management

From the foregoing a number of issues concerning logistics organization structures emerge.

First there is the clear need for the business itself to adopt a customer perspective, and for customer satisfaction to be pre-eminent in the planning of the business. The acknowledgment of the role of customer satisfaction should be reflected in the structure of the customer service role and in the specification of customer service functions.

The traditional, vertical, functional structure typical of most business organization clearly has limitations, in that a number of problems exist such as effective coordination of logistics order flows, inventory surpluses at functional boundaries, and a lack of visibility for important cost elements.

Christopher suggests a return to the mission concept of the 1970s and proposes a 'market facing' organization structure, the right-side-up approach, but differing in that it crosses functions in order to capture the benefits of coordination and improved resources allocation. It also emphasizes the planning aspect of logistics. Christopher suggests the key lies in the recognition that the *order and its associated information flows* should be at the heart of the business: 'Everything the company does should be directly linked to facilitating this process and the process must itself be reflected in the organizational design and in its planning and control'. The vehicle suggested for this is a *customer order management system*. This system becomes a planning framework that links the information system with the stocks and flows process required to satisfy demand.

There are other improvements suggested to the customer order management process. One is to *eliminate* the 'non-value'-adding activities. It will be recalled that in Chapter 1 (Figure 1.2) we identified a number of value added activities performed by distribution and marketing activities. The generic value added entities attributed to effective distribution activities are time, place, assortment and information. It follows that any activity that reduces value rather than enhances it should be eliminated; by commencing with these 'entities' the scope for eliminating unproductive activities and procedures often is quite large.

Christopher describes the digital approach to cross-functional-cross-departmental order processing and handling, the *order fulfilment group*. This approach groups activities in logical structures which reflect order management processes rather than the departmentalized structure described and discussed earlier. The benefits accruing are related to reduced order cycle times and accuracy.

We suggest that, while this approach eliminates a number of issues, a few remain. The first raises concerns introduced in Chapter 2: the need to consider differences in alignment between the market environment and the organization. The suggestion made in Chapter 2 was that strategy (i.e. corporate response) should recognize competitive conditions, and that strategic fit considers the degree of alignment that exists between competitive situation, and organization culture, and leadership should also reflect this understanding. Figure 2.3 (Chapter 2) illustrated marketplace logics, and a review of Figure 2.3 will emphasize the point. A market characterized by uncertainty and high competitive intensity clearly requires quite a different response to one showing opposite characteristics, i.e. market certainty and low competitive intensity. Figure 2.4 suggested that the former would have customer expectations which would respond more to creative offers of unique features (i.e., in a logistics context, innovative service activities). Conversely the market with characteristics that suggest low competitive intensity and market certainty would expect service responses characterized by reliability, predicability and consistency.

Thus any organization design which would group activities into an order fulfilment group should in fact designate a number of groups, each of which would be 'aligned' with the logic of its target market. Not to do so may result in sub-optimal performance with inappropriate resource allocation and equally inappropriate responses.

One other suggestion is to use the value chain as a vehicle for analysis. We have discussed both the value chain and the concept of partnerships and strategic alliances. This can be developed further. Figure 19.2 illustrates a supply chain management situation in which there are two coordinating activities. The *internal coordination function* is a customer order management system which works across functional boundaries and eliminates many of the cost and resources allocation problems identified by Christopher. An *external coordination function* extends the role of the logistics function by seeking to reduce further unnecessary costs and inventory allocation *between* supply chain members. Figure 19.2 identifies the information and decision flows that are likely to occur if the supply chain is to be integrated and if optimal revenue and profitability are to be achieved.

For this approach to be effective it does require some empathy between marketplace and strategy, and therefore alignment between customers and suppliers. It does extend the notion of the order fulfilment group towards the national or major account management concepts, but adds a logistics role to their functions. By operating across value chains the potential for eliminating the problems discussed by Christopher may be extended from the intra-organizational level into a broader, inter-organizational perspective.

■ Issues in Labour Management and Labour Relations

A detailed discussion of the issues affecting labour management and relations on an international scale is clearly beyond the scope of this text. While many of the issues and problems have much in common across international borders, the solutions are usually country specific. With this in mind, we will identify the issues that are common and review some of the more important aspects of contemporary industrial relations.

In the past decade there has been a progressive retreat from full employment, and a fundamental change in the labour market away from physical production work towards the service sector. There have been changes in the structure of industry and the workforce, changes in the nature of work, and changes in the size and composition of trade union membership. The tourist industry, the fast-food industry and the information industry are the growth areas for employment.

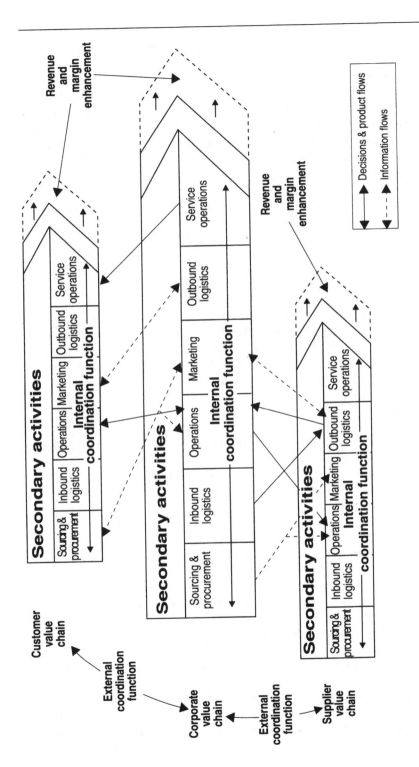

Figure 19.2 Integrating value chains to enhance revenues and margins throughout the supply chain

Three significant trends in the labour market have been observed:

- An increase in the participation rates of women in the paid workforce;
- An increased growth of the casual and part-time workforce, both in absolute numbers and relative to the 'full-time' or permanent workforce. (For example, the 'full time' proportion of the UK labour force has reduced by 20 per cent since 1977.) This is most pronounced in the service sector.
- An increasing application of information technology in higher labour-content industries.

Banks are employing increased numbers of part-time tellers, usually female, whose positions have been limited and deskilled by the expansion of electronic funds transfer systems. A similar pattern is found in the retailing industry. Major retailing firms have replaced full-time positions with an army of part-time and casual workers, including schoolchildren. In the past decade, night work and weekend trading, including Sundays, has expanded.

These trends are creating a secondary or 'marginal' labour market in which both full-time and casual/temporary/part-time workers are confronted with a situation where they are required to decide whether or not to enter arrangements geared to the flexible organizational needs of the business enterprise rather than their own needs. The introduction of night work and weekend trading in the retail industry are examples of new employment patterns as a response to labour market flexibility.

Other responses include:

- The introduction of continuous shiftwork, longer hours and fewer penalty rates (e.g. in essential services);
- Early retirement schemes (e.g. in the public service);
- Higher average-age levels for entry to the workforce (associated with extended schooling);
- The attachment of microprocessors to production machines;
- Employer attacks on 'restrictive practices';
- A political debate over immigration policies;
- Less legislative protection in employment;
- A growing debate over deregulation in the labour-market;
- Political debate about the privatization of state-owned enterprises.

■ **Contemporary Industrial Relations: Some Issues**

The debate about industrial relations is conducted in the following context:

- The manufacturing sector is shrinking and selling to a domestic market.
- The service sector is expanding, with financial services, fast foods and tourism the largest activities for many countries.

- There is a transformation in the make-up of the workforce, in particular an increasing participation rate of females.
- New employment patterns are emerging: part-time, casual and temporary work; job-sharing and 'workers on a long-leash'.
- There is a growing demand for workforce 'flexibility'.
- There is a worldwide decline in trade union membership.
- The population is ageing and birthrate is declining: the 'baby boom' is over.
- The welfare state is in crisis in all industrial countries.
- Challenges to the traditional protective and promotional functions of labour law are taking place.
- There is evidence of growing employer 'militancy'.

Underpinning these trends are the pressures of accelerating technological flexibility, institutionalized inflation and institutionalized unemployment at unprecedented levels.

The questions, therefore, are the effects of the observed trends on the four major institutions associated with industrial relations:

1. *Trade unions*: the challenge of 'de-industrialization' (i.e. decline in the 'smokestack industries', with associated job losses); accommodation of female members; maintaining real wages; maintaining job security; redundancy; award restructuring; demarcation disputes; amalgamations; impact of technology on skills; white-collar militancy; changes in bargaining structures; decentralization and shift of power to the shop floor; human resource management.

2. *Employers*: how to remain competitive and reduce on costs; 'flexibility' in the use of labour; use of non-employees; fewer tiers of management and flatter structures; smaller plant sizes; geographical diversity; shorter product runs; choice of anti-union or union-substitution policies; complex technology creates job-description problems.

3. *Governments*: tariff policies and protection from foreign competition; taxation policies; debates over such matters as privatization of public-owned enterprises, deregulation of the labour market, provision of social security and the user-pays principle; role of government as largest employer (is it the model employer?); role in ensuring minimal standards in employment legislation; concern to minimize industrial conflict; an interest in regulating the economic outcome of collective bargaining.

4. *Labour and industrial law*: the challenge will be to balance the conflicting demands for flexibility and unregulated use of labour with employees' demands for minimal protection and job-security; three questions raised are:

    (i)   How far should the state intervene between employer and employee?
    (ii)   Does labour law have both a protective and promotional/educative role?

(iii)   What is the future of traditional conciliation and arbitration – status quo, deregulate, tightly regulate?

A broader question is the impact of the changes on society at large: is it likely that the part-time, casual, intermittent worker will cease to regard work as the control element in his/her life? If so, this raises questions about education for leisure, educational policies generally, skills and training. Population ageing raises questions about early retirement (and its reversal?), superannuation and pensions, the social system. Most important of all – what is the social cost of unemployment at each end of the age spectrum?

■ Implications for Supply Chain Management

The changes in the labour market, together with changes in corporate strategy and structure are in parallel.

For example, the downsizing of many companies has been implemented in a number of ways. One obvious reason has been the removal of layers of management in an attempt to reduce costs and increase the efficiency of processes. Another reason has been the preference by many companies for outsourcing many of their activities. The return to the core business has released large amounts of capital locked into fixed assets in 'service' activities from which the returns are less than those used in producing the major product of the business. The result has been a move towards outsourcing service functions and, in the process, a reduction in the number of employees. A third factor has been noticeable: the introduction of IT-based systems has eliminated a large number of tasks in many companies, and one area of the business affected more than others is logistics. The full implications of IT applications to supply chain management is probably yet to be seen.

If we consider the effects of these changes in an overall context we can see further implications. As firms concentrate increasingly on core products and activities, leaving 'service' companies to fill the role of less profitable activities, those companies are likely to seek economies of scale and scope within their own activities. The use of capital-intensive systems are very attractive when high fixed costs may be amortized across an increasing volume of activities. The potential for decreasing, rather than increasing, the number of jobs becomes even greater.

The concentration of manufacturing and logistics operations is continuing. It is encouraged by international economics/politics; the growth of the European Union, NAFTA and the SE Asia/Pacific Rim unions are encouraging the growth of larger cost-effective operations. Add to these the cost and flexibility benefits offered by AMS and FMS systems (advanced manufacturing and flexible manufacturing systems) and the prospects for job creation in both manufacturing and logistics are increasingly becoming limited.

■ Summary

As companies become more aware of the importance and the influence of their customers in designing their organization structures the issues of customer service design and management take precedence in the overall organization design process. Supply chain management is essentially a customer-led process, and to make decisions more effective the process of identifying and applying customer market logics has been shown to offer a great deal.

The chapter also discussed the components of an effective logistics organization which include a customer-order management system which offers a planning framework, an order-fulfilment group and an external coordination function (it will be recalled that a similar structure was reported to work well for Dow in the USA). Together these activities provide a customer-led organization structure for supply chain management activities.

The chapter also considered issues in labour management and labour relations that have international similarities and implications for supply chain management. The increasing trend towards part-time work, the impact of information technology and the increase in the number of women in the workforce are among the more significant global trends. Other international issues concern the concentration of business, the shift towards service-based industries, the requirement for labour to be flexible in all aspects, the decline of trade union membership and the retreat by almost all governments from providing a welfare state were issues that will have either direct or indirect implications for all business activities.

CHAPTER 20

Retailing Management and the Supply Chain Interface

■ Introduction

To be successful in today's business environment, retailing management have become more aware of the leverage offered by effective logistics management. It is interesting to see how the successful companies are using logistics to improve profitability. J. Sainsbury, the UK food multiple, reported in November 1993 that their increase in profit was due in no small part from improvements in distribution. In the first half of 1993–4 distribution costs fell by 0.1 per cent of sales: this suggests that with sales in excess of £5,500 million the contribution to net profit of £5 million was indeed significant.

Increasingly, successful retailers are improving the cost-effectiveness of their marketing, finance and operational activities. Marketing effectiveness has been developed by moving away from the conventional view of market segmentation which combined socio-economics and demographics with lifestyle variables. More recently we have seen the notion that customers not only differ from each other demographically but that they demonstrate a range of buying behaviour which often offers marketing opportunities.

Financial management is becoming concerned with the utilization of fixed assets and working capital. Trends suggest that management is taking a polarized view: either non-retailing activities are seen as part of an 'integrated delivery activity' or they are non-core activities which, while essential, can be considered as service functions which may be purchased from a specialist supplier. Either view does not detract from the importance of such functions: it merely points to the growing concern that management has for performance.

The operational activities within retailing have typically focused on management of the 'delivery function', the link between purchasing and sale to the consumer. However, this is now regarded as a somewhat narrow view. Increasingly we are aware of retailing management expanding its activities to incorporate supply chain management. These activities are involved before and during purchasing and procurement and consider issues upstream in the supply chain. Figure 20.1 suggests there are two components of the retail supply chain: an external supply chain which influences gross margin management, and the internal supply chain which has a large impact on the management of operating margins. For both there is a large logistics influence.

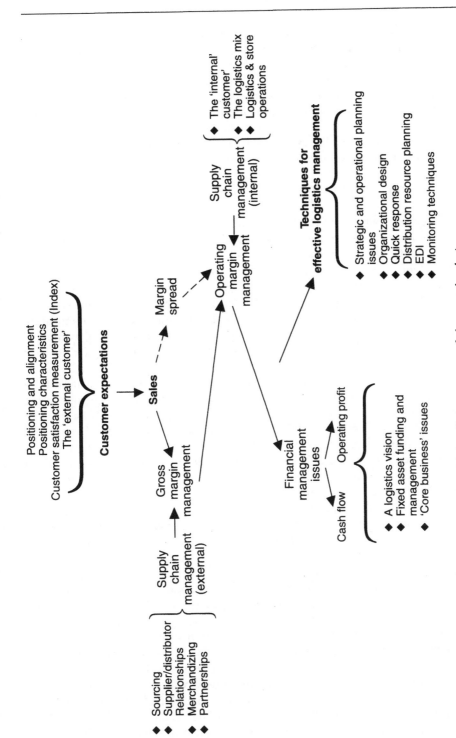

Figure 20.1 Components of the supply chain

In addition to the expanded influence of the logistics function across the activities of retailing there has been an equally important expansion in the technologies used and available to logistics managers. These have a number of aspects. There is a philosophical view which influences the structure of management and organizational design as well as an operational view in which an increasing range of computer-based modelling techniques have facilitated the evaluation of various alternative system structures and corresponding cost and service configurations. These have been important to the growth of the credibility of the logistics function as well as increasing its influence.

■ Customer Expectations: A Moving Target

Much has been written concerning the role of marketing in identifying customer needs and wants (their expectations). Retailing, being so close to the consumer, is required to respond to changes in expectations and preferences at very short notice. One of the most favoured approaches has been to use segmentation techniques to identify 'target customers'. Having identified a target customer (and a target customer profile) a more specific and focused positioning response can then be evolved which include elements of merchandise characteristics, customer service, store environment and customer communications, combined in such a manner that customer expectations are met to a high degree of satisfaction.

More recently it has been suggested that customers are likely to demonstrate quite different behavioural responses, depending upon the category being purchased and the circumstances. One of the authors developed the concept of shopping missions to explain and expand the notion. In brief terms the concept suggested that consumers demonstrate a range of shopping missions which match their needs at a specific time: it is the shopping missions which should determine the particular combination of merchandise, customer service and other features (see Walters, 1994).

Gattorna has developed a longer-term approach (discussed earlier). The authors suggest that through the process of *strategic alignment* a more satisfactory fit may be achieved. The detail of this approach was discussed in Chapter 2, so here it is sufficient to remind the reader of the approach. Essentially strategic alignment considers there to be four key elements of concern for management, and proposes that the 'logics' that exist at each level canf be identified. Thus the *marketplace* has its own 'logic' (or underlying dominant processes and practices) and determines 'the rules of the game' for competitors in the market. Company *organization strategy* then becomes 'how we will play the game' and is a planned response to the opportunities and the structure of the market. However, this alone is unlikely to work unless *organizational culture* develops an atmosphere within which the company develops a sufficient 'capability to play the game'. Finally, the entire process needs to be driven by a *leadership style* which 'builds a team vision' capable of delivering stated objectives. The successful retailing companies are those which identify the logic of the marketplace and align the logics of their strategy, culture and leadership style to match that of the marketplace. This approach goes beyond the lifestyle and demographics/socio-economics methods which are essentially a short/medium-term response between the retailer and the customer at the point-of-sale: strategic alignment proposes a long-term and in-depth (for the company) approach by which it improves upon existing approaches to customer satisfaction by ensuring an overall alignment of the business.

Customer satisfaction is achieved by demonstrating an understanding of the 'logics' of the target customer and responding in such a way that customers tend to consider the company as first choice for a specific need set. The point we make here is simply that it is no longer viable to attempt to be an 'all round' supplier or mass merchandiser. Consumer sophistication has increased to the extent that a high level of expectations exists in almost every purchase situation. It follows that, to be successful, every attempt should be made by retailers to understand the composition of customer expectations, identify the dominant expectations and what motivates particular decisions and selections.

There is an important role for logistics here. Indeed, for many of the characteristics that constitute a retail offer and that currently motivate consumer decision-making, logistics is a significant influence. For example, the response to consumer preferences for choice and quality in produce (fruit and vegetable product ranges) has resulted in an increasing range of fruit and vegetables at very high levels of quality. It is primarily the development of logistics systems that has made fulfilment a possibility. Cost-effective and rapid-response logistics facilities have enabled produce buyers to source from increasingly expanding supply markets. Without the technology of chilled transportation and storage facilities which operate cost-effectively over large distances, the existing levels of customer satisfaction would not be possible.

Clearly customer expectations and levels of satisfaction should be researched. Again, the example set by successful companies suggests that tracking studies and customer satisfaction indices are well worthwhile if close control over response to customer needs is to be maintained.

■ Gross Margin Management: Managing the External Supply Chain

The management of gross margin is vital for success in retailing. The gross margin should cover all the expenses of the business (including interest and tax), and the residual is then available to the shareholders.

The roles played by logistics are numerous and collectively we suggest they comprise the external aspects of the supply chain. From Figure 20.1 we see these to include: sourcing, supplier–distributor relationships, merchandising and strategic and operational partnerships. Some examples of the scope of the role of logistics in this respect may help.

Sourcing should consider the cost component of delivery of the product into the business and beyond, to the customer. Logistics management should be responsible for working with buyers to identify suppliers who can optimize the costs of storage, transportation and packaging, such that the tasks necessary within the supply chain are the responsibility of the most appropriate member of the supply chain. Furniture retailing has battled with lead times and damage in transit as major problems for some time. These problems have been considerably reduced by delivery directly from the suppliers' facilities. This example identifies the increasing involvement of logistics considerations in sourcing and supplier–distributor relationships.

Merchandising is also being influenced by logistics decisions. A number of retailers for whom promotional activities are important have developed alliances and partnership relationships within the supply chain which plans the delivery and display of promotional packages of manufacturer and retailer branded products. Other examples exist in which the need for minimizing inbound costs and those for in-store merchandising has resulted in packaging developments in which 'outer' packaging becomes display material. It is interesting to note that the cage pallet activity initiated by Asda in the early 1970s was concerned with this issue. This was an early attempt at creating partnership arrangements in the distribution channel. However, in this case the benefits were not shared equally and the success of the initiative was limited.

Strategic and operational partnerships in the supply chain are now becoming more common. At a strategic level partnerships operate on what might best be described as 'piggy-back' arrangements. Here we see a specialist (usually low-volume) retailer reach an arrangement whereby all (or some) of its merchandise range is sold within the offer of a larger host retail business. For many retailers this offers the means by which high delivery and storage costs are reduced by a partnership arrangement. Often this is a method used for evaluating market opportunities, but increasingly it is being seen as a long-term relationship. There is marketing appeal, as well that of reducing logistics costs, in strategic partnerships of this nature. The 'packaging' of merchandise items that may be purchased at the same time but which have quite different sourcing (such as confectionery and greeting cards) offers synergy in marketing and logistics terms.

Operational partnerships are often short-term expediency arrangements. The use of near-competitor's distribution facilities has often enabled low-volume retailers (and manufacturers) to achieve profitable low-volume penetration (and thereby customer satisfaction).

■ Operating Margin Management: Managing the Internal Supply Chain

The topics of current interest in retailing include 'internal customer service' relationships. The internal supply chain has as its central thesis the notion that the stores are the 'customers' of the distribution system. It follows that, given specified levels and characteristics of service requirements by the stores, it is the responsibility of the distribution activity to meet these at budgeted costs.

The retail logistics mix comprises: facilities (and materials handling); transportation; inventory; the capacity utilization issue; and information management. The logistics management function may be responsible for maintaining an extensive logistics system of distribution centres, vehicles and inventory.

Conversely the management function may be more one of a coordinating activity within which it is responsible for ensuring that an extensive (but external) system (which may be owned by numerous 'suppliers') meets the service requirements within the internal supply chain.

Typically, most retail logistics systems are a combination of owned and leased functions supported by third-party service companies whose expertise, together with advantageous costs, is integrated with the company-owned facilities. It is becoming increasingly the case that corporate management views the retailing activity as its core business and channels investment into the core business, preferring to use the facilities of 'specialist' service companies. The benefits of this approach are that capital is made available to invest in the mainstream business and that services are purchased as required, therefore becoming operating (or variable) costs.

The service requirements of the stores are related to the company's marketing and financial objectives. The marketing objectives specify volumes (and market share) *as well* as specifying the characteristics and the levels of customer service required if these are to be realized. The implications of both are clear for logistics management. Volumes indicate planned merchandise throughput by product range and by store location. Availability levels prescribe the levels of stockholding and delivery programmes required to achieve the marketing objectives and to achieve customer satisfaction. The financial objectives will infer the levels of investment (and return on investment) that should be deployed (and achieved) by the logistics activities. Hence the issues for fixed capital and working capital are made explicit.

Store operations and the corresponding resources involved also interface with logistics. The productivity (and the profitability) of space, staff and stockholding can only be maximized if an overall view of operations management is established. This is seen as particularly important in retailing activities for which visual merchandising is a central and critical activity, for example in apparel and furniture retailing (particularly in the high-price point sectors).

Often creative visual merchandising restricts merchandise density, which influences the availability levels of sizes, colours, styles, and so on, and it is here where a well-managed logistics activity can reinforce the positioning statement by ensuring that customers are able to obtain their selected items as and when they are required. Similarly, staff utilization may be improved if store deliveries are planned to meet off-peak times for sales activity and can use the staff time to replenish stock and fixtures. Clearly, logistics as an activity is closely concerned with the decisions of stockholding levels and locations.

■ Financial Management: The Role of Logistics in Maximizing Profitability and Cashflow in the Retail Business

The role of logistics in maximizing profitability and cash flow is one not to be ignored. Much of the working capital of a retail business can be tied up in inventory. Often the expertise used by buying and merchandising to develop assortments that meet customer requirements for choice (but also at minimum levels of inventory cover) can easily be thwarted by poor logistics service. Having set the range width, depth and availability necessary to maximize customer transactions, it is the role of the logistics function to ensure that a cost-effective means of delivering the offer is devised – and maintained.

Thus it follows that logistics management should be aware of their role in meeting target working capital cycles, particularly for slow-moving merchandise items.

The role of effective logistics management in making significant contributions to the financial management of both manufacturing and retailing business was discussed in Chapter 4, together with the concept of inventory/cash flow profiles and how they may be used to determine which supplier offers may meet both marketing and financial objectives more effectively. The Du Pont/strategic profit model approach in which the retailer identifies and outlines issues of concern to its own logistics function and that of the supplied, is proving very useful.

Of particular importance is to define the 'logistics vision' of the business. Retailing adds value for the consumer by offering appropriate merchandise in locations, and at times, convenient to the customer. This suggests that effective retailing is concerned with the management of 'stocks and flows'. These 'stocks and flows' should be planned such that they clearly respond to customer needs, but do so without consuming unnecessary financial and other resources. It follows that the chief executive should view the business in this context: it is simply a system of nodes and links which either hold or move inventory during the process of maximizing customer satisfaction. It is here where the management of both gross and operating margins can be seen as important because the logistics activities involved in managing the 'stocks and flows' of merchandise impact on costs and profit contribution. The margin spread (Figure 20.1) can be defined as the overall margin that remains once these activities have been accounted for.

■ Techniques, Methodology and Models: Current Developments in Supply Chain Management

Effective logistics management requires the support of models and computer-based planning and control systems.

During the 1970s, attention was focused on the development of operational systems such as vehicle scheduling programmes: the strategic aspects of logistics planning and control were largely unaddressed. The same could be said for viewing the logistics function as an integrative activity. Indeed during the 1970s and 1980s physical distribution was more likely to be found as an activity in companies than was the larger more pervasive and integrative logistics. The latter part of the 1980s saw the growth of the logistics function across manufacturing industry and to a lesser degree in retailing.

An important influence in the changes in the retailing/logistics interface that have occurred during the past ten years has been the impact of information technology. There are three aspects involved here.

The first is cost: initial applications required large amounts of capital investment due to the high cost of IT equipment. This was significant in the context of that time. Many companies were expanding rapidly to take advantage of the growth opportunities of the 1980s; both organic growth and growth by acquisition were available and they each required capital. A second aspect was the effectiveness of the systems available. They were often limited in capability and capacity, usually requiring manual support systems, either to complete their functioning or for verification of output.

Furthermore their flexibility was minimal, and often companies found that subsequent to their adoption a number of structural or procedural changes within the company were necessary if even limited benefits were to be obtained. A third aspect concerned the philosophy and perhaps attitudes of management. There was concern over accuracy and reliability and consequently reluctance to 'hand over' important operational features of the business to a largely unproven computer-based system.

Competitive requirements and a deepening recession during the latter 1980s was by no means the sole reason for an expansion in the application of IT-based systems. Clearly, with pressure on both volumes and margins, cost-effective solutions were sought. By this time IT systems had matured significantly. EPOS (electronic point of sale) systems were commonplace. They were accurate and had shown significant impact on costs, particularly stockholding and labour costs. Moreover they were being extended into the realm of supplier–distributor negotiations and operations, i.e. into supply chain management, and did so with startling success.

Another important aspect was the use of IT to standardize documentation. Here the work of the late 1970s and early 1980s (supported by EEC initiatives) resulted in the acceptance of a number of EDI (electronic data interchange) facilities which have also become standard tools in retailing management.

Distribution planning systems have also been developing during recent years; this has added a strategic perspective. DRP (distribution requirements planning) is found to be more commonplace in manufacturing companies than in distribution-based business. This comes as no surprise, as DRP emerged from systems developed to improve management of materials requirements and flows. Its wider application by retailers is yet to be seen.

Another aspect of the competitive pressure on retail companies has been the growth of the use of optimization models which offer the facility for integrated logistics planning discussed in detail in Chapter 17. This concept is based on total cost analysis, which can be defined as minimizing sourcing, procurement, warehousing and transportation costs, while satisfying a desired level of customer service. There is a considerable range of specific tasks available, but essentially optimization is an integrative modelling system for both strategic and operational applications. Among many applications there have been notable successes in evaluating the impact of overseas expansion, logistics system rationalization, rationalization of retail outlets, evaluating alternative new venture scenarios, investigating the impact of mergers and acquisitions, and exploring the alternatives for consolidating merchandise ranges.

Planning retailing activities without measuring performance for control purposes, is ineffective management. Hence identifying the important aspects of logistics service and implementing its delivery also requires a mechanism by which the effectiveness of the delivery may be measured. Customer service index (CSI) monitors are also becoming an integral part of retail logistics planning and control activities. Having established the important features of customer service, and having implemented a customer service strategy, the CSI methodology ensures that the delivery is effective. CSI packages vary in their scope, but experience suggests that performance measurement should be an ongoing activity and linked to specific time periods with the activity cycles determined by the nature of the business activity. In this way the monitoring frequency can be adjusted to ensure that seasonal or other periods of intensive activity may be monitored to ensure that customer satisfaction objectives are met.

■ Organizational Design Requirements for Retail Supply Management

Organizational design is confronted using alignment principles. It will be recalled that the suggestion was made that certain logics exist among customer groups and these are determined by behaviour. It followed that strategy, culture and leadership style should be cognizant of these characteristics or logics, because to ignore them was to invite problems. A similar argument can therefore be made for organization design decisions.

Organizational design is confronted with the alignment of markets, strategy and the company, but extends into supply markets. Clearly the alignment theory is applicable here, since unless the supplier demonstrates empathy for the underlying logic of the customer–retail business combination no functional integrated system is ever likely to exist. It follows that issues of concern to customer satisfaction characteristics will not be met unless the appropriate alignment is present.

One other issue seen as important in an organizational context concerns technology. The technology adopted by the supply chain should be relevant. It should be acceptable to the customer and seem as user friendly. The early problems experienced with the installation of EPOS systems is an excellent example. The explicit mistrust of consumers led to continued use of price marking on products (and indeed led to legislation in the USA) until such times as consumer confidence was established and shelf-edge price marking became accepted. Confidence is but one aspect of this topic. The availability and familiarity of use of computer terminals for 'home shopping' purposes is currently one of the issues influencing the rate of adoption of home shopping across a range of merchandise characteristics. Add to this the problems of presentation (particularly of fashion-based items) and it can be seen that relevant technology is an important issue.

■ Summary

The growth of multiple retailing has had a significant impact on the development of supply chain management methodology. As these companies have expanded they have become aware of the considerable leverage of supply chain activities on their operating profits.

The chapter considered the marketing, financial and operational activities of retailing companies and their management of gross and operating margins within the context of supply chain management. Cash flow and profitability management are important features of any business and it was suggested that effective logistics management within the supply chain will improve their performance. Accordingly large retailing companies are looking to manage activities such as procurement and merchandise management with a view to considering how decisions within these activities impact upon supply chain management, and how supply chain decisions impact on the options confronting procurement and merchandise managers; this situation has led to the development of optimization systems for important decision areas. These techniques and disciplines were discussed in the chapter.

Appendix: Canterbury Sealants Limited – Case Studies

■ **Establishing Channels Strategy and Setting Customer Service Levels**

■ **Introduction**

Canterbury Sealants Ltd is an hypothetical company but its problems are similar to those of actual businesses. The case studies which follow are based upon work that each of the authors has undertaken as consultancy assignments. None of the problems and issues identified here can be linked to a specific company, in fact much of the material has been drawn from more than one problem situation and has been combined to add detail to the case study.

As with any case study there is no specific answer. In fact it often happens that a solution that was found to be suitable at one specific time is not applicable at some time later. The series of case problems confronting Canterbury Sealants offers the reader an opportunity to explore alternative solutions and to introduce their own perspectives and data.

Canterbury Sealants manufacture a range of industrial adhesives sold primarily through intermediaries to industrial users. The sealants are used as bonding agents by a diverse range of users including furniture manufacturers, construction businesses, service repair businesses, and so on. Growth of the business has become slow, and revenue and profits have been at the £300 million and £60 million levels respectively for the past two or three years. The Board of Directors have been concerned that the reason for poor growth has been due to the lack of effort by the distributors who, faced with increasing competition, have failed to respond. Indeed, they have attempted to direct the problems towards Canterbury Sealants. The company has been faced with demands for increased margins and promotional expenditures. It has been decided that the company should investigate the alternative of managing both the sales and logistics activities and to terminate all distributor agreements. Current distributor margins average 4.5 per cent of sales. End-user margins vary between 15 and 25 percent.

Canterbury Sealants have been experimenting with joint selling activities with distributors into major customers for some twelve months. They have found that the technical knowledge and experience of the product that can be offered end-users is seen as impressive and has begun to generate a large number of contacts with end-user customers. The Board considered there to be sufficient positive reasons for continuing to expand the direct sales activity, and this was agreed. It was clear that a number of distributor agreements should be terminated, and equally clear that this decision would result in physical distribution problems. As a short-term measure, arrangements were made with distribution service companies to undertake the delivery of Canterbury's products.

This arrangement has prevailed for some twelve months (longer in some areas) and the cost, at 10 per cent of sales, is considered high. The question of whether or not Canterbury should manage its own logistics function has arisen and a programme to reach an appropriate decision has been decided upon.

It has also been decided that following a research study into customers' service requirements some clear issues have arisen, even though no major differences were apparent between customer types. Large customers have similar performance requirements and responses to customer service offers; a very similar set of results was found to obtain for medium and small customers. The results of the research that first identified customer expectations and their subsequent perceptions of performance are shown as Tables A1, A2, A3 and A4. A breakdown of customers is shown in the table below; the bracketed figures are estimates of the number of customers in each category that have the potential to move into the next size category.

	Number of customers		*Estimated % of revenue*
Large £500 000 – £1 million	50		30
Medium £250 000 – £500 000	125	(20)	40
Small < £250 000	1 500	(100)	30
Total	1 675		100

The questions facing Canterbury Sealants concern the level of investment and commitment they should be prepared to make. A majority of the Board are in favour of the commitment to undertake a programme which would require some £45 million, involving 3 distribution centres (in addition to the one at the manufacturing unit), 4 bulk long-haul vehicles, 10 short-haul delivery vehicles, an order processing and management system and an increase in staff of some 20 people. The increase in working capital is estimated at £10 million (£7.5 million in inventory and £2.5 million accounts receivable).

In addition to the question of the investment there is also the issue of the relationships with intermediaries and the potential loss of business variously estimated at between 20 per cent and 5 per cent of sales. The concern of the company is that, if the loss is close to 20 per cent and includes too many of the larger distributors, Canterbury's investment could result in a low return exercise. Competition from other sealant companies is fragmented. The product is not difficult to manufacture, and entry costs are low. However, there are no major, large competitors.

The Board of Directors have identified a number of options. They are seeking some initial guidance with which to evaluate the options. They see their problems concerned with both transaction and physical distribution channels.

Therefore, the initial task is to evaluate the Board's options (and add to them) if appropriate. The options suggested are:

1. Handle all end-user accounts on a direct basis and to invest £45 million in distribution system facilities. The company could invest £15 million from reserves and raise £30 million by issuing £10 million through an equity issue, and the remainder (£20 million) as a long-term loan over 10 years at 10 per cent interest. The company has no debt.
2. Handle all end-user accounts on a direct basis and use distribution service companies to effect physical distribution.
3. Handle large customers on a direct basis, leaving small and medium customers to the distributor network.
4. Reselling an agreement with the distributor network to split the customer accounts on a size, service requirements or possibly geographical basis.

Their initial requirements are for a report which identifies the issues and considers the associated implications, together with a proposal for conducting the next stage.

Table A.1   Customer service performance requirements

Performance expectations by customer size L	M	S	Customer service components	Customer rank order of importance L	M	S
7*	2	1	Order cycle time (days)	1	2	3
0.5	2	2	Delivery reliability (±)	2	3	4
4	8	12	Frequency of delivery (deliveries/month)	6	4	2
97.5	90	85	Inventory availability (percentage of order)	3	5	5
0	5	5	Documentation quality (percent errors)	3	7	7
100	90*	80	Complete orders (percentage of items delivered)	3	6	6
3	2	1	Technical support (availability of representatives) (i.e. days' response)	7	1	1

*   Assumes a 'rush' facility exists with a discount penalty

Large customer: Annual revenue £1 mill +
Medium customers: Annual revenue £½ – 1mill
Small customers: Annual revenue less than £½ mill

Table A.2   Customer service appraisal: 'large' customers (i.e. £500 000 to £1 million sales and more per annum)

Importance to customer Low	Medium	High	Customer service components	Performance assessment Poor	Satisfactory	High
L			Order cycle time	L		
		L	Delivery reliability	L		
L			Frequence of delivery			L
		L	Inventory availability	L		
		L	Documentation quality		L	
		L	Complete orders		L	
L			Technical support			L

Table A.3   Customer service appraisal: 'medium' customers (i.e. £250 000 – £500 000 sales and more per annum)

Importance to customer Low	Medium	High	Customer service components	Performance assessment Poor	Satisfactory	High
	M		Order cycle time		M	
		M	Delivery reliability	M		
	M		Frequency of delivery	M		
		M	Inventory availability			M
M			Documentation quality		M	
	M		Complete orders	M		
M			Technical support	M		

Table A.4 Customer service appraisal: 'small' customers (i.e. up to £250 000 sales and more per annum)

Importance to customer			Customer service components	Performance assessment		
Low	Medium	High		Poor	Satisfactory	High
S			Order cycle time			S
	S		Delivery reliability		S	
	S		Frequence of delivery			S
		S	Inventory availability	S		
S			Documentation quality		S	
	S		Complete orders		S	
		S	Technical support	S		

■ Canterbury Explores Best Practice and Benchmarking

■ Introduction

Canterbury Sealants has been operating a sales and marketing activity in which the company manages its transactions channels but uses distribution service companies. As part of its ongoing control activity, customer service is monitored by using 'tracking studies' to establish relative perceptions of customers in predetermined turnover groups. These had been established some two years previously during a reorganization of the logistics activities. See Tables A.1, A.2, A.3 and A.4.

Recent tracking studies indicate that large customers, those with turnover in excess of £1 million, are displaying a shift in priorities, and also that Canterbury Sealants' competitors are offering more effective service components. The company's customer portfolio has emerged as its own turnover and profitability has expanded. Canterbury Sealants has increased its turnover to £400 million and profit to £20 million. The customer portfolio (together with revenue categories) is as indicated in the table:

	No. of customers	Estimated % of revenue
Large (revenue £500 000 – £1m or more)	100	50
Medium (Revenue £250 000m – £500 000m)	200	30
Small (Revenue less than £250 000m)	1700	20
Total	2000	100

Management response to the increase in business was cautious. While there was a healthy increase in revenue and profit, together with an expansion in the customer base, it was clear that the increase had been achieved by expanding the number of medium-sized customers. It was argued that overall turnover had increased and that turnover categories were now considerably larger than they were some two years previously.

The industry sector growth had expanded, but not at the same rate as Canterbury Sealants. The 25 per cent growth of the company compared well with 15 per cent of the sector. Clearly, Canterbury were 'getting some things right' and achieving growth at the expense of their competitors. However, the evidence also suggested that their appeal was more towards medium-sized users. This conclusion was confirmed by the tracking studies: both medium and small sized customers were largely satisfied by the customer service offer.

The company was concerned to ensure that their relationships with large customers improved. A number of suggestions were made and, of these, one in particular made an impact on the Board. This concerned the use of best practice and benchmarking techniques. After discussion there was general agreement to a suggestion that both be pursued with a view to identifying ways and means by which business with the customers responsible for 50 per cent of the business could be improved.

Recent research (see Table A.1) shows evidence of a change in service requirements. The relatively low performance rating for Canterbury Sealants can, in part, be explained by the change in service priorities of large customers. Further research has identified two factors influencing this rapid (six months) shift. The first is concerned with pressure on customer margins due to increased competition, and the second (clearly a by-product) is their response, an attempt to reduce inventory-holding costs being but one. It was suggested that many customers had, previously, held excess stocks and that part of their actions were in fact an adjustment of the business towards more realistic operating levels.

The decision to undertake a benchmarking exercise was reached quite quickly; the discussion on its implementation was a different matter. Eventually it was decided that a project group be formed which would report back to the Board with its recommendations on *how* the project should be undertaken and which of the candidate companies should be the benchmarked company.

■ The Benchmarking Project Report

The project team met on a weekly basis for a period of three months. Their initial programme outline contained the following topics:

- Determine critical success factors for best practice in customer service management
- Establish a benchmarking programme with:
  - Identification of functions to be benchmarked;
  - Identify companies to benchmark;
  - Identify key performance variables of the targeted company;
  - Compare Canterbury's performance with that of the benchmarking candidate company;
  - Estimate the performance potential of the targeted company;
  - Establish key performance criteria for Canterbury;
  - Present recommendations to the Board.

☐ *Establishing Critical Success Factors*

The research activity from which the findings (reproduced in Table A.1) were derived was examined in detail. There were six issues that required addressing:

- A *reduction* in order cycle time of some 30 per cent (i.e. from seven days to five);
- The *increase* in delivery frequency of some 50 percent;
- The required increase in availability of 1 per cent;
- A requirement for more information concerning order progressing and out-of-stock situations;
- The establishment of an 'emergency' service activity
- The establishment of a customer service activity.

It was generally agreed that some overlap existed among these issues and that, by identifying critical success factors underlying those companies demonstrating *best practice* in customer service management, the task of identifying candidates for benchmarking may be made easier. At this juncture it was clear to the project group that an agenda of best practice issues was essential.

☐ *An Initial Survey*

A major concern for the project team was that they identified suitable examples of best practice for review. Agreement about looking at companies outside of the industry sector was easily reached. However, the decision to extend the search beyond the industry was only resolved with difficulty.

Arguments for extending the search were based upon issues of company and industry maturity (i.e. that some industries and companies had passed through the 'stage of evolution' which Canterbury currently was at). Furthermore, it was agreed that to focus on the industry may result in overlooking some innovative solutions that had been introduced elsewhere and which had evolved in response to similar solutions. Finally the proponents for looking outside the industry agreed that expertise in logistics problems related to customer service may be found in distribution companies rather than manufacturing (which is how Canterbury Sealants saw itself).

The preference to stay within the industry was essentially based upon the view that the problem was an industry problem and that an extended review may result in a waste of management time and resources *and* a series of complex and irrelevant solutions which Canterbury could not hope to implement. The argument to extend the survey prevailed; furthermore, it was also agreed that at the *best practice* stage of the exercise both successful manufacturing and distribution companies were to be included.

The search for examples of best practice and the development of critical success factors did occur simultaneously rather than consecutively. Initially the project team *established* broad parameters or directions for their study. These were based upon a need to establish and manage a customer service activity and, further, that the existing levels of performance in some service categories was below that required and, unless changes were made, would eventually make Canterbury Sealants totally uncompetitive.

The situations perceived by the project team were similar to those of companies in the components supply business (such as small/medium manufacturers of specialist components to the automotive industry) and of pharmaceutical wholesalers who, because of the characteristics of many drug products, were required to store sensitive drugs centrally but offer rapid delivery service as and when required. A similar situation was found to exist in the distribution of recorded music, where demand was influenced by external sources (to the wholesalers and retailers) but to which the distributors were expected to respond.

The best practice review resulted in three companies being profiled.

Hamilton Electric Ltd, a supplier of electrical components to the automotive industry. The team found that while turnover volume was considerably larger than Canterbury its relative position within the industry sector was very similar. Hamilton's success was based upon negotiated levels of service together with agreed sales volumes and profit margins.

Hamilton executives reported that they were initially alarmed by the agreement which essentially 'opened their books' to their largest customers but found that once the agreement was reached to work towards mutual objectives for both service performance and price/cost levels the arrangement was very satisfactory and workable. The agreement was managed by monthly meetings at which the essential service performance and characteristics were monitored and reviewed.

Some of the performance criteria agreed by Hamilton Electric and their customer were:

- *Time criteria*:
  Order cycle time
  Enquiry response time

- *Quality criteria*:
  Picking accuracy
  Availability objectives by product category
- *Costs criteria*:
  Transportation costs/delivery
  Total service costs as per cent of sales
  Margin.

Aston Pharmaceuticals is a large wholesaler of drugs and related hospital supply products to hospitals in the Midlands area of the UK. Aston is rated as 'a preferred supplier' because of the high levels of service response it provides. The issues for both Aston and its customers are based upon: the high cost of many drug products, the relatively short shelf life of many products, and the unpredictability of demand. As a result of these clear service constraints Aston has developed a *rapid response* service which ensures a 'within an hour' response service throughout the areas operated.

The organization of the service interested Canterbury because, while a dedicated fleet of delivery vehicles was maintained, its utilization was increased by radio telephone installations with open contact constantly made by Aston with its drivers.

Some exploration has been undertaken into the viability of maintaining stocks of urgent items in strategic customer locations (at cost to Aston) but the results of the study were not available. Performance criteria includes:

- *Time criteria*:
  Order cycle time
- *Quality criteria*:
  Product availability (selected products)
  Delivery reliability
- *Cost criteria*:
  Transportation costs/delivery.

Boston Music deals with both audio and video recorded entertainment. Boston is very successful and considers the reasons for its success are due to the large investment (both capital and human resources) in establishing a customer ordering and service facility. The facility is structured around customer size; thus the services offered vary by customer group. For example, very large customers have their own account executive who is based at Boston's head office and who contacts the customer on a regular basis. The frequency of the contact is based upon the ordering patterns of the customers. These customers have emergency ordering facilities which, while carrying a discount penalty, rarely break even, but do enhance the service relationship between Boston and its very large customers. For other customers the service offer has more flexible parameters. Close liaison between the sales/service operation and the transport function attempts to coordinate sales activities and deliveries in an attempt to maximize overall effectiveness.

Boston has been experimenting with an idea which offers additional discounts to medium/small customers willing to accept commodity products (some fast-moving products such as audio and video tapes (the classics selection and blank tapes and accessories) at the convenience of Boston and possibly ahead of the customer's volume or order requirements.

Boston has found that the improved vehicle utilization and stockturns have more than offset the discounts offered. Boston executives suggest that their 'upside down' organization structure, whereby those service functions which need to access (or to be accessed by) customers have had a large part to play in their success, together with the differentiated service offer. The performance criteria used by Boston Music include:

- *Time criteria*:
  Order cycle time
  Customer response (orders, enquiries etc)
  Stock turn
- *Quality, criteria*:
  Delivery reliability
  Picking accuracy
  Product availability
- *Cost criteria*:
  Order processing costs/sales
  Transportation costs/delivery.

From this study the project team considered they had sufficient material to formulate their recommendations for a best practice format and the critical success factors required.

■ A Proposed Best Practice Format

Central to the project team's proposal was the need to categorize customers on the basis of customer activity and, within this, customer size, the criteria for size being potential not actual business.

The project group's proposal for a best practice format comprised four components: organization structure, process structure, employee responsibilities and remuneration and incentives.

The organization structure and design proposals suggested that a flat, upside structure replaces the existing structure. A coordinating role of the sales and customer service functions by the marketing function was among many of the radical changes proposed (see Figures A.1 and A.2).

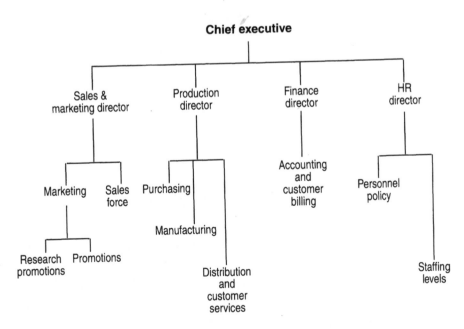

Figure A.1   Existing organization structure

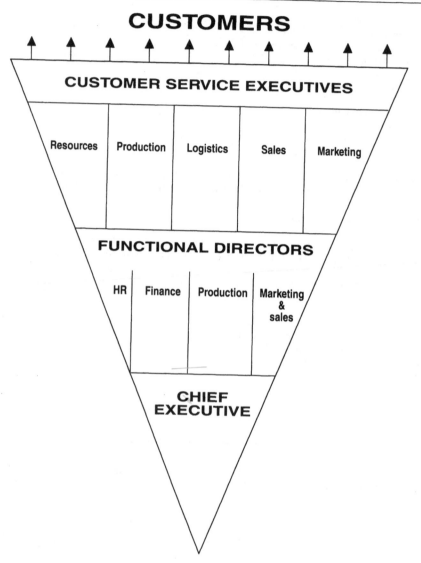

Figure A.2 Proposed organization structure

The proposal for customer service and communications can be seen in Figures A.3 and A.4. The controlling function is a *customer service and communications activity*. This function would be responsible for managing the flow of information to both the marketing and the operation and procurement activities. This proposal, together with the proposed revisions to the organization structure, identified a number of new roles. These were:

- Customer service manager
- Customer account executives
- Information services manager.

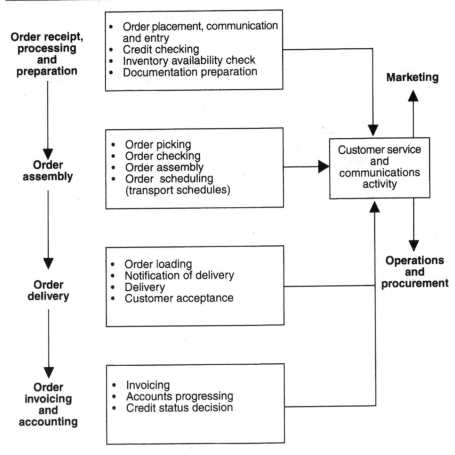

Figure A.3 Proposed order processing structure

The customer service manager would be responsible for:

- Determining customer classification with marketing
- Determining customer service offers
- Managing the customer account executive team
- Monitoring the performance of the customer service function.

The job specification of a customer account executive would include:

- Customer contact concerning all aspects of customer order activity;
- Managing the customers' orders through the receipt, processing, proposition, assembly and delivery processes;
- Ensuring that customer service performance objectives are met within the budget;
- Ensuring that customer activities and company performance responses are reported within the information system.

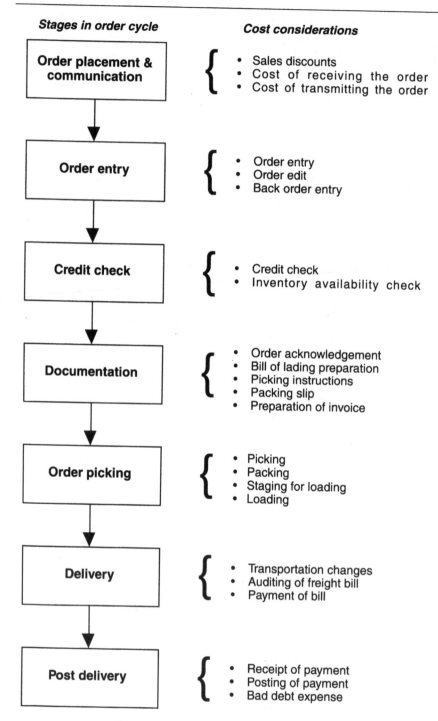

Figure A.4 Existing order processing structure

The information services manager's responsibilities would include:

- Maintaining liaison with customer account executives to monitor activity data;
- Aggregating performance data;
- Reporting performance variances to customer service manager;
- Issuing performance reports to customer account executives.

The project team proposed that the customer service facilities be more flexible than those currently prevailing. This would involve devolving authority for service delivery to the account executives. The view they pursued was that delivery schedules and perhaps discount structures can be managed within the customer service facility more effectively than by the sales force. The rationale for the proposal was based upon the premise that, once a substantial database had been built up, the individual customer's activity could be assessed with more accuracy and concessions made more constructively.

The topic of remuneration and incentives was approached but left open. Recommendations were positive, in that the team favoured an incentive that was departmental based. They saw problems with an individual based scheme and favoured a departmental bonus based upon profit *and* service achievement. Again the need to consider the authority and responsibility issues were identified, but precise details left for management to consider.

An *emergency ordering facility* was considered an essential feature of the new structure. It was to operate on the basis of a rapid response/reduced discount offer. Discounts would be structured around customer categories.

The project group described the required critical success factor as:

- An ability to manage the flow of customer orders rapidly and accurately through the business;
- The provision of a *range* of innovative customer service features;
- Reliable and accurate customer order delivery.

☐ *Benchmarking*

The project team reassessed companies in its own and in related industry sectors for a benchmarking partner. Given its review of best practice, the recommendations for the best practice format and the ideal critical success factors it was decided that it was unlikely that an adequate relationship would be found close to the industry sector.

The expanded search identified a 'fasteners' business. Camberley Closures manufactured a range of closures, clips and seals for automotive and mechanical handling equipment manufacturers. The exercise was approached by identifying priorities that both companies saw as being:

- Of strategic importance
- Having high relative impact on the business
- Processes which offered a range of alternative solution options
- Situations where there is both the capacity and capability for improvement to be undertaken with effect.

Both companies identified the enhancing of relationships with large customers as being strategically critical to the business. Camberley Closures forecast a 10 per cent year on year increase in business with this 'large customer' group, provided customer service and order communications and management continued to meet customer requirements. Canterbury Sealants, while not as bullish, saw potential improvements for their business within this context.

The incremental impact on productivity and profitability, in terms of the utilization of manufacturing and operating assets was identified as potentially high. Camberley Closures' experiences to date suggested that a 7.5 per cent increase in transactions values with large customers increased total costs by 2.0 per cent.

An increase in customer services and service performance levels had been obtained by Camberley Closures by using external transportation services to meet customer demands in excess of the forecast levels of activity. At this point they had begun to formulate proposals for a benchmarking activity. They considered there to be sufficient material available to proceed with a formal arrangement for a partnership to benchmark alongside Camberley Closures, who for their part could see benefits because it offered a facility to revisit some of the topics they would approach differently, and they also saw benefits accruing from access to the best practice study.

The project team assembled at Canterbury Sealants' head office to begin to write the formal proposal.

■ Canterbury Analyses Customer Account Profitability

■ Introduction

The benchmarking exercise with Camberley Closures is well established and is proving beneficial to both companies. Canterbury Sealants is now a business with turnover of £500 million and operating profits of £120 million; net profit before tax is £75 million. The customer profile has changed and is now:

	No. of customers	Estimated % of revenue
Large (distributors) (revenue £4.5m)	250	55
Medium (distributors) (Revenue £100 000 to £400 000m)	450	30
Small (end users) (Revenue £10 000 or less)	2 300	15
Total	3 000	100

Both companies had become aware, as they expanded their information on customer service costs, that they were making service decisions on very limited information. Furthermore, as the totals for Canterbury suggest, their customer base was showing signs of becoming polarized. This raised doubts concerning the viability of maintaining some of them. A recent analysis of customer order size and discounts gave the results presented in Figure A.5. To ensure some consistency in the ordering pattern, the analysis was conducted over a period of a year, and customers' orders were expressed as weighted average transactions and discounts, thereby eliminating the 'one off' situations. The data shows that 60 per cent of orders are out of alignment with the ideal profile and suggested to management that a number of problems exist.

The first problem appeared to be poor control of the sales force, who seemed to be agreeing to excessive discounts for small orders. Another aspect of the study compared discounts with ordering frequency, and this revealed similar findings. Here we can see (Figure A.6) that the discount profile suggests that order frequency of customers made very little difference to the discounts given. A review of redelivery records (Figure A.7) also provided some disturbing information: 50 per cent of business was being penalized by having to support redelivery costs, and on this the discounts given were higher than those allowed to customers for whom redelivery was no problem.

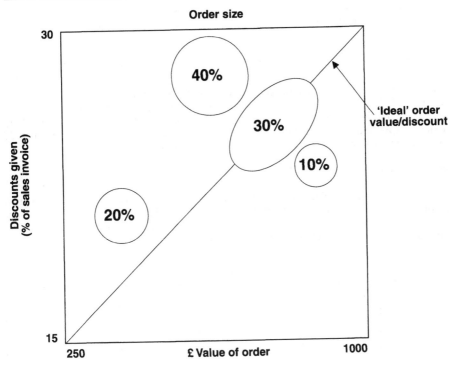

Figure A.5 Customer order value/discounts allowed profile

Given this information, Canterbury Sealants decided to conduct a review of customer service costs. Management had concluded that much of the problem was due to the lack of information, and accordingly began a review of costs.

An initial examination of Canterbury accounts was not particularly helpful:

		£'000
Sales		500 000
Less sales discount (of 35%)	175 000	
Net sales		325 000
Less direct costs	100 000	
Gross profit		225 000
Less marketing and distribution costs	92 000	
Less distribution costs		
Contribution to overhead interest, etc.		133 500

The only conclusion possible from this data was that marketing and distribution represented 17.5 per cent of sales. Canterbury's best-practice partners were asked for representative information and the results were:

Hamilton	12.0 per cent sales
Aston	25.0 per cent sales
Boston	15.0 per cent sales

Aston being a specialist pharmaceutical distributor with a rapid response service was clearly exceptional, and Canterbury decided to look more closely at Hamilton and Boston. Both companies had more information available to them than that available to Canterbury Sealants. Hamilton had isolated the costs of distribution activities and Boston could identify the fact that small customer accounts were distinctly unprofitable.

■ **Canterbury Sealants Considers ABC**

Subsequent discussion within Canterbury Sealants led to a decision to explore activity-based costing and what it may offer in the attempt to establish a clearer view of customer account costs. The first requirement was for more detail on their logistics value chain. Eventually they agreed upon the model outlined in Figure A.8.

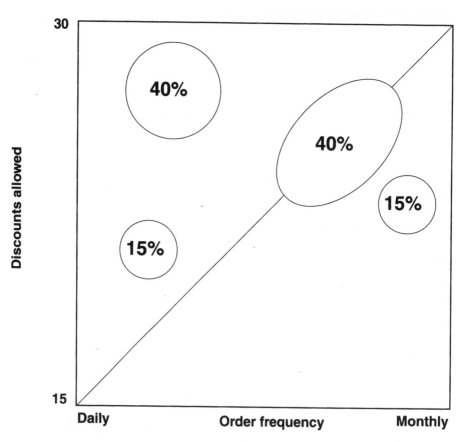

Figure A.6   Customer ordering frequency/discounts allowed profile

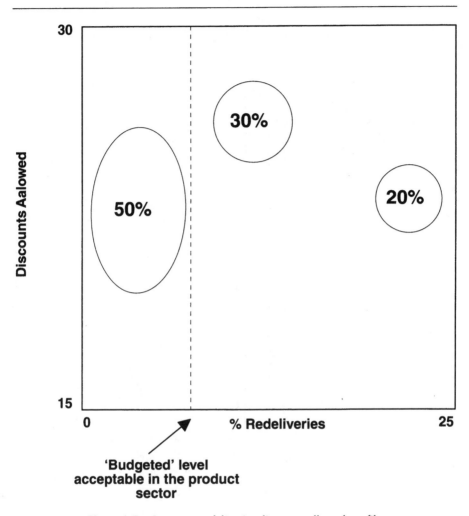

Figure A.7 Customer redeliveries/discounts allowed profile

This identifies the primary activities involved in both the physical distribution and transactions channels. Items in brackets identify the additional costs that occur when redeliveries are required subsequent to customer refusals.

On this basis, the management accounting department was tasked with identifying the costs of each of the primary activities and their components.

This required the detailing of all distribution cost elements (see Table A.5).

The findings surprised Canterbury senior management whose concern was focused on the expectation that many small customers were costing the company a considerable amount, possibly being subsidized by the larger accounts. Of particular concern was the fact that the number of small accounts had increased during the past two years. This suggested to Canterbury that perhaps their competitors had become aware of these costs and had moved to minimize losses.

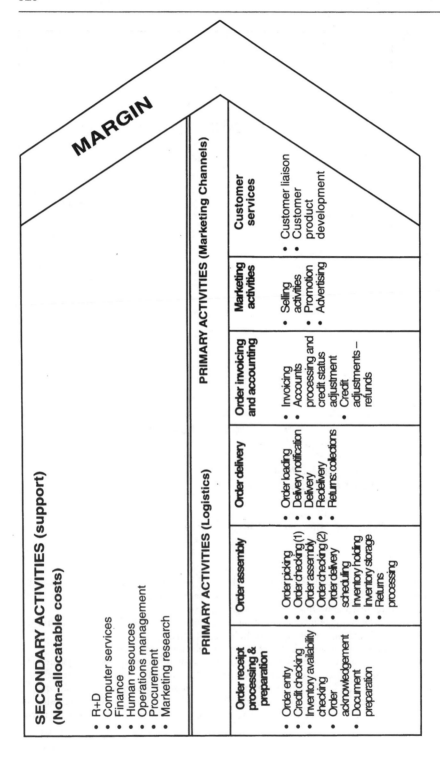

Figure A.8 Canterbury Sealants: logistics value chain

Table A.5   Breakdown of marketing and distribution costs

	Per cent of marketing & distribution costs	Actual costs £918 750
Order receipt, processing and preparation	3.0	£2 6250
order entry	5 750	
credit checking	4 300	
inventory checks	6 150	
order acknowledgement	4 750	
document preparation	5 300	
Order assembly	9.0	£78 750
order picking	6 250	
order checking	3 650	
order assembly	3 150	
checking completed order	2 750	
order delivery scheduling	3 200	
inventory holding	37 925	
inventory storage (space)	17 525	
processing returns	4 300	
Order delivery	22.0	£192 500
order loading	6 100	
delivery notification	4 750	
delivery	143 950	
redelivery	25 200	
returns collections	12 500	
Order invoicing and accounting	3.0	£26 250
invoicing	10 250	
accounts processing/credit status adjustment	5 230	
credit allowances for refunds	5 700	
customer statements	5 070	
Marketing activities	40.0	£350 000
selling	210 000	
promotions	52 500	
advertising	87 500	
Customer services	23.0	£201 250
customer liaison	121 500	
customer financing (accounts receivable)	79 750	

The next step to be undertaken was to identify the 'cost pools' and activities with which to identify the major elements of the costs of servicing customers. This resulted in the following schedule of cost pools and cost drivers in Table A.6.

The data developed in Tables A.6 and A.7 (breakdown of distribution costs and the cost pool and cost driver labels) raised yet another question for management: what is the profile of each of the customer categories? This was the next task to be tackled.

Table A.6 Cost driver analysis

Primary activities (logistics and marketing)

Cost pool: order receipt, processing and preparation

Activities	Cost driver
• Order entry	Number of orders received and processed
• Credit checking	Number of customer accounts/orders
• Inventory availability checking	Number of items ordered (total)
• Order acknowledgement	Number of orders
• Document preparation	Number of orders

Cost pool: order assembly

Activities	Cost driver
• Order picking	Number of items ordered
• Order checking (1)	Number of items ordered
• Order assembly	Number of items ordered
• Order checking (2)	Number of orders
• Order delivery scheduling	Number of deliveries planned
• Inventory holding	Stock-keeping units (SKUs)
• Processing returns	Number of items returned
• Storage	Space occupied: rental costs per SKU (Number of SKUs = 10 product groups × 200 average product group items)

Cost pool: order delivery

Activities	Cost driver
• Order loading	Number of deliveries
• Delivery notification	Number of customer orders
• Delivery	Distance to delivery point
• Redelivery	Distance from delivery point
• Returns: collections	Number of returned orders

Cost pool: order invoicing and accounting

	Cost driver
• Activities	
• Invoicing	Number of invoices raised
• Accounts processing and credit status adjustment	Number of customer accounts actioned
• Credit adjustment for refunds	Number of credits allowed
• Accounts payable/outstanding	Days outstanding (in excess of normal terms) and value

Cost pool: marketing activities

Activities	Cost driver
• Selling	Number of sales calls
• Promotions	Number of customers involved
• Advertising	Number of customer enquiries

Cost pool: customer services

Activities	Cost driver
• Customer liaison	Number of end user/customer visits

Table A.7 Activity-based costing analysis for a 12-month period

Cost pool: order receipt, processing and preparation (£26 250)

Activity	Annual cost £	Annual cost driver volume	Cost driver rate £
Order entry	5 750	36 600 orders	0.16
Credit checking	4 300	36 600 orders	0.12
Inventory checks	6 150	9.4 million items	0.0007
Order acknowledgement	4 750	36 600 orders	0.129
Document preparation	5 300	36 600 orders	0.14

Cost pool: order assembly (£78 750)

Activity	Annual cost £	Annual cost driver volume	Cost driver rate £
Order picking	6 250	9.4 million items	0.0007
Order checking	3 650	9.4 million items	0.0004
Order assembly	3 150	9.4 million items	0.0003
Order checking (bulk)	1 750	36 600 orders	0.048
Order delivery scheduling	3 200	2 825 delivery points	1.13
Inventory holdingå	38 925	36 600 orders	1.063
Inventory storage	17 525	36 600 orders	0.48
Processing returns	4 300	700 returns	6.14

Cost pool: order delivery (£192 500)

Activity	Annual cost £	Annual cost driver volume	Cost driver rate £
Order loading	6 100	36 600 deliveries	0.17
Delivery notification	4 750	36 600 deliveries	0.13
Delivery	143 950	36 600 deliveries	3.9
Redelivery	25 200	1 750 redeliveries	14.4
Returns and collections	12 500	700 returns	17.85

Cost pool: order invoicing and accounting (£26 250)

Activity	Annual cost £	Annual cost driver volume	Cost driver rate £
Invoicing	10 250	22 200 invoices	0.46
Accounts processing/credit status adjustment	5 230	1 675 adjustments	3.12
Credit allowances for refunds	5 700	10 500 items	0.54
Customer statements	5 070	14 970 statements	0.34

Cost pool: marketing activities (£350 000)

Activity	Annual cost £	Annual cost driver volume	Cost driver rate £
Selling	210 000	8 000 calls	26.25
Promotions	52 500	2850 promotions	18.42
Advertising*	87 500	36 600 orders	2.4

* An arbitrary method but research indicates that advertising has a strong influence on the selection of a supplier by the customer

Cost pool: customer services (£201 250)

Activity	Annual cost £	Annual cost driver volume	Cost driver rate £
Customer liaison	121 500	1 700 calls	71.47
Customer financing	79 750	14 970 statements	5.32

Given the suggested cost-pool, cost-driver profile, the following data was sought for each of the large, medium and small customer groups (see Table A.8):

Customer Specific

- Revenue per category
- Number of customers
- Average transaction per customer/value of order at cost
- Total number of orders and ordering frequency
- Items per order
- Number of delivery points
- Number of invoices raised
- Number of invoice progress notes raised
- Days credit taken and sum outstanding
- Sales calls per customer
- Number of refusals
- Number of redeliveries
- Number of collections.

Non-customer specific

- Number of advertising prompted enquiries
- Number of sales generated from advertising.

This exercise provided more evidence on the customer profitability profiles (Table A.9).

The analysis provided detail that hitherto had not been available. The Logistics Director, together with sales and marketing, were concerned that the small customer category responsible for 15 per cent of Canterbury's business cost as much to service as the large group who provide 55 per cent of revenue.

Currently, the company is using distribution service companies to deliver orders, and costs given in the exercise were based upon these. The marketing department repeated its concern over the method used to allocate advertising costs and undertook to give this some urgent attention.

The group's task was to consider the implications of the findings on its customer service policy and its attitude towards low revenue customers. They set about developing a list of issues.

Canterbury Considers a Partnership

Introduction

Canterbury Sealants, a £500 million manufacturer of an expanding range of sealant products for industrial and domestic uses, is looking for further expansion opportunities. Its domestic market has shown considerable growth, but forecasts suggest that future growth will be difficult. Canterbury's growth over the past five years was due largely to the fact that the company saw an opportunity to develop a strong presence in a fragmented market. It did this by focusing its efforts on both product development and distribution. Its product range offers solutions to an extensive range of sticky problems. Having resolved the application problems its R&D is now working on product improvements such as rapid adhesion, the ability for products to adhere to all types of finishes, application improvements and packaging developments.

Distribution has been the concern of senior management and, following an extensive study on customer account profitability, there are now three divisions. *Industrial Applications,*

Table A.8 Customer-specific data

Customer specific data	Small	Medium	Large	Total
		Customer category		
1. Revenue per category	£75m	£150m	£275m	£500m
2. Number of customers	2 300	450	250	3 000
3. Average revenue per customer	£33 000	£350 000	£1.1m	–
4. Order frequency (average)	0.5 per month	2 per month	4 per month	
5. Number of orders per year	13 800	10 800	12 000	36 600
6. Average order value	£5 435	£13 800	£23 000	–
7. Average items per order (total)	50 (690 000)	250 (2.7mill)	500 (60m)	9.4m
8. Number of delivery points	2 300	375	150	2 825
9. Number of deliveries	13 800	10 800	12 000	36 600
10. Number of invoices raised	13 800	5 400	3 000	22 200
11. Number of invoice progress notes raised	8 250	4 320	2 400	14 970
12. Days credit taken	60	45	45	–
13. Credit status adjustments	1 500	100	75	1 675
14. Sales calls (year)	2 300	2 700	3 000	8 000
15. Promotions	–	(450 × 3)*	(250 × 6)*	2 850
16. Liaison calls per customer (year)	500	200	1 000	1 700
17. Number of refusals	1 000	1 250	1 000	3 250
18. Number of redeliveries	500	750	500	1 750
19. Number of returns collections	200	200	300	700
20. Items returned for credit (5% average)	500	2 500	7 500	10 500*

* Number of customers × number of promotions per year

Table A.9 Cost of Customer servicing activities (application of cost drivers)

| | Customers | | | | | | |
| | Small | | | Medium | | Large | |
	Cost driver consumption	Cost driver rate	Cost (£)	Cost driver consumption	Cost (£)	Cost driver consumption	Cost (£)
Receiving processing & order preparation							
Order entry	13 800	0.16	2 208	10 800	1 728	12 000	1 920
Credit checking	13 800	0.12	1 656	10 800	1 296	12 000	1 440
Inventory checks	690 000	0.0007	483	2.7m	1 890	6.0m	4 200
Order acknowledgement	13 800	0.13	1 794	10 800	1 404	12 000	1 560
Document preparation	13 800	0.14	1 932	10 800	1 512	12 000	1 680
			8 073		7 830		10 800
Order assembly							
Order picking	690 000	0.0007	483	2.7m	1 890	6.0m	4 200
Order checking	690 000	0.0004	276	2.7m	1 080	6.0m	2 400
Order assembly	690 000	0.0003	207	2.7m	810	6.0m	1 800
Order checking (bulk)	13 800	0.048	662	10 800	518	12 000	576
Order delivery scheduling	2 300	1.13	2 599	375	423	150	170
Inventory holding	13 800	1.063	14 670	10 800	11 480	12 000	12 756
Inventory storage	13 800	0.48	6 624	10 800	5 184	12 000	5 760
Processing returns	200	6.14	1 228	200	1 228	300	1 842
			26 749		22 613		29 504
Order delivery							
Order loading	13 800	0.17	2 346	10 800	1 836	12 000	2 040
Delivery notification	13 800	0.13	1 794	10 800	1 404	12 000	1 560
Delivery	13 800	3.9	53 820	10 800	42 120	12 000	46 800
Redelivery	500	14.4	7 200	750	10 800	500	7 200
Returns and collections	200	17.85	3 570	200	3 570	300	5 355
			68 730		59 730		62 955

Table A.9 continued

	Customers							
	Small			Medium		Large		
	Cost driver consumption	Cost driver rate	Cost (£)	Cost driver consumption	Cost (£)	Cost driver consumption	Cost (£)	
Order invoicing & accounting								
Invoicing	13 800	0.46	6 348	10 800	4 968	12 000	5 520	
Accounts processing/credit status adjustment	1 500	3.12	4 680	100	312	75	234	
Credit allowances for refunds	500	0.54	270	2 500	1 350	7 500	4 050	
Customer statements	8 250	0.34	2 805	4 320	1 469	2 400	816	
			14 103		8 099		10 620	
Marketing activities								
Selling	2 300	26.25	60 375	2 700	70 875	3 000	78 750	
Promotions	–	6.03	–	1 350	8 140	1 500	9 045	
Advertising	13 800	2.04	33 120	10 800	25 920	12 000	28 800	
			94 495		104 935		107 560	
Customer services								
Customer liaison	500	71.47	35 735	200	14 294	1 000	71 470	
Customer financing	8 250	5.32	43 890	4 320	22 982	2 400	12 768	
			79 625		37 276		84 238	
Total customer servicing costs			291 775		240 483		305 677	

which sells directly to large end-users in the automotive, consumer durable, furniture and construction industries. *Consumer Applications* sell to a range of retail outlets such as DIY hardware and the non-food divisions of multiple food retailers. A third *O&S Division* has been developed to deal with a range of small manufacturers and distributors whose volume off-take or product requirements do not fit into either of the other two divisions. O&S operates a range of channels, mostly through manufacturers' agents and third-party distributor specialists. The essence of the O&S activity is to take advantage of low volume business opportunities and to maximise its operating margins in a range of creative ways. O&S sells from stock and has proved useful in allowing Canterbury to operate at high levels of production without undue concern if production has exceeded forecast sales. Most of O&S's customers were those failing to meet volume requirements and causing concern for profitability.

■ Future Growth

With chemical adhesives suggesting a low growth potential, Canterbury Sealants were considering a number of alternatives. Two were of particular interest. One of these involved an alliance with a French fastener company Le Blanc. Le Blanc manufactures a comprehensive range of metal clips and fastener devices. The company has a considerable share of the French industrial market but very little volume within domestic markets. They have tested a range of pipe and hose fixture devices and are beginning to distribute these through major 'bricolage' type outlets, but have found they lack the skills to be effective in this market. They do not have chemical adhesive products.

Le Blanc is a well-managed company. Both revenues and profits have grown steadily over the 15 years during which they have been in business; their turnover is comparable to that of Canterbury Sealants.

Le Blanc have a nationwide logistics function, and the emphasis is in the North of France where the majority of its industrial customers are located. However, the company does a large amount of business with the aerospace industry and this is likely to require a manufacturing and distribution activity in the South of France.

Thus far its attempts to enter the DIY market through the 'bricolage' outlets has met with limited success. The product has been accepted, but problems with pricing and promotional policy exist. Le Blanc consider themselves to be an 'industrial company' and that they lack the skills to deal with large retailing companies.

The basis of their approach to Canterbury Sealants is that they have identified opportunities for chemical sealants in both industrial and consumer/domestic markets. They know they lack the necessary R&D or marketing expertise in these markets and, therefore, see an alliance with Canterbury as mutually advantageous.

Le Blanc has approached Canterbury with an initial proposal which suggests:

- Le Blanc works with Canterbury to develop a fasteners product range to be sold to both industrial and consumer/domestic markets within Canterbury's home market territory.
- Canterbury works with Le Blanc to establish a viable sealants market in industrial markets in France
- Both combine resources to develop a consumer fixtures *and* sealants market, using their combined product strengths, the transactions channels experience of Canterbury and develop jointly a physical distribution channels facility.

Some of the issues that Canterbury considered they should review are:

- The benefits of adding an additional product range to the Canterbury portfolio.
- The existing physical distribution network was outsourced and the Le Blanc proposal introduced the question of whether or not they (Canterbury) should, together with Le

Blanc, develop a 'company'-owned network. Estimates of the likely cost for this are £25 million.

The other proposition currently 'on the table' is a partnership proposal from the retail market leader in the DIY sector. The proposal is for the Canterbury and Cumberland DIY to develop a range of Cumberland fixture products. Cumberland (financed by a conglomerate) has offered to finance an R&D project into fixture products as it sees the increasing costs of plumbing and similar activities forcing home owners into more and more DIY tasks. Cumberland has a 20 per cent of the UK DIY market and operates 200 'sheds' (large 120 000 square feet (12 000 square metre) outlets) throughout the UK. It has been rumoured in the financial press that Cumberland are negotiating with two large DIY operations, one in France and another in Belgium, to acquire a significant share of their equity.

Some of the issues to be considered by Canterbury in this proposal were:

- To date they have maintained a 'Canterbury Sealant' branding policy and have previously resisted some tempting offers from Cumberland. To Canterbury's knowledge no UK manufacturer produces retail brand sealants.
- The reaction of Canterbury's other large customers, as and when they hear that Canterbury are manufacturing Cumberland products, and that they have an arrangement to produce metal/plastic pipe fixtures, which will be Cumberland 'exclusives', must be assessed.
- Cumberland have hinted that their expectations of margins would be an additional 10 per cent. However, they have undertaken to take delivery and distribution of all of their purchases from Canterbury's manufacturing facility.

The Canterbury management team have decided that each functional director would produce a list of issues that require addressing in detail. The Logistics Director has called for some assistance from a well-known logistics consultancy and is awaiting their report.

■ **Canterbury Sealants Introduces Logistics Resources Planning LRP II**

■ **Introduction**

Following the strategic alliance agreement with Le Blanc, Canterbury Sealants took time to consolidate its activities. Much had happened in a period of 15 years. From being a small chemicals plant with an innovative managing director and 30 staff, the company was now a £750-million business, and well positioned in chemical and metal fixtures.

Early in the alliance agreement with Le Blanc, the two companies had agreed to keep their respective manufacturing facilities separate. This was clearly necessary as the processes shared nothing in common and the products, being low volume and relatively low value, were transferred from their points of manufacture to their required distribution location points. While there were no reasons for concern with this decision it had been noticed by both companies that, over the period of the alliance, while the manufacturing activities were performing to budget and productivity targets, both in the UK and in France some problems were beginning to emerge. These related to distribution issues, and it was agreed that unless some attention was given to the problem it might spread inefficiencies throughout the entire business arrangement. No immediate actions were planned, and it was agreed to monitor critical factors to ensure that nothing untoward occurred. Concurrently it was agreed to establish a project group whose task initially was to monitor the trade literature and report on any interesting developments that might suggest some direction for both companies.

In France, Le Blanc had strengthened its hold over the automobile fixtures market. Some innovative R&D had led to new products, and resulted in improvements in the existing fixtures ranges. The product changes had resulted in new plant, and much of this was very much 'state of the art' technology. The plant had been specified and ordered, and planning its installation had commenced.

At about this time the Canterbury Sealants Logistics Director who, while not directly involved in the replanning in France, was keeping abreast of its progress. A journal article caught his attention. The issues it raised were very similar to those being met in France and what he found interesting were the comments in the last sentence of the article.

Materials planning and order scheduling are important aspects of current manufacturing. The growth of AMT (advanced manufacturing technology) has played an important role in enabling companies to remain competitive in many ways. One of these is the facility to be more flexible than was hitherto possible. Greater product variety and shorter product life cycles are contributing to a situation in which the pace of change shortens the useful life of existing process technologies. The essence of AMT is the ability to be flexible and adaptable to a dynamic, high change environment. This suggests an end to the days when manufacturing could be left to get on with making the product. Consumer influence is now seen on the shop floor, in the manufacturing process and demands short lead-times, high quality and competitive prices.

The implications of consumer changes for margin management and cost control are not difficult to deduce. Within AMT a number of elements are making change possible. Thus inter-company communications through EDI (electronic data interchange); design and process planning using CAD (computer aided design) systems; manufacturing integration through DMC (direct numerical control) or CNC (computer numerical control) systems which have reduced set up times, and automated materials handling and storage with AGV (automated guided vehicles) linked to ASRS (automated storage and retrieval systems) are all becoming common components in 'leading edge' manufacturing systems. To these we should add manufacturing, planning and control.

Material planning and scheduling is a key feature in the new manufacturing systems. Materials requirements planning (MRP) is a process by which the net requirements for raw materials and components are determined once current stocks and materials on order are accounted for. MRP is also a fundamental part of just-in-time manufacturing because advanced commitment to material provisioning is always necessary and this is the purpose of MRP. Manufacturing resource planning (MRPII) goes further: it links medium to long term production plans with existing and planned capacities; and MRP can be extended to enable all factory resource needs to be organised in advance. This includes labour, machine time and space requirements.

MRP has two basic objectives. The first is to attempt to eliminate or to minimise inventory levels. The second is to try to have materials delivered to meet exactly the timing requirements of the production schedule. Thus, if successful, MRP will reduce the amount of working capital tied up in inventory. A further benefit is that the MRP system, being closely related to the production schedule, is more directly influenced by customer demand. From MRP and MRP II have evolved DRP and DRP II systems which are essentially an extension of the MRP and MRP II principles into the logistics function. (*Materials Matters*, March 1994)

Clearly DRP (distribution requirements planning) was not new to the business. There had been some investigations as to its usefulness a few years previously but, with the new plant being installed by Le Blanc and the concerns expressed by some members of management, it seemed an opportune time to accelerate the investigation into the distribution issues.

■ A Proposal for a 'LRP II' System

The situation and the timing appeared ideal to tackle the overall problem because if, as seemed possible, the distribution problems in the UK and in France deteriorated further at some time in the future, it could result in considerable disruption (and cost problems) to the balance of the new manufacturing facilities at Le Blanc.

A schematic drawing (Figure A.9) was produced to outline the scope of the options for the companies. The preferred option was developed in more detail and this is reproduced as Figure A.10.

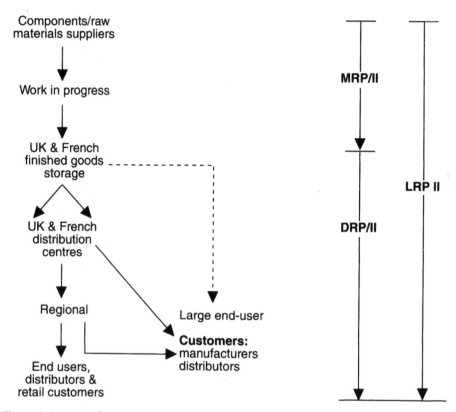

Figure A.9   Canterbury Sealants/Le Blanc fixtures: profile for logistics requirements planning

At the same time some indication of likely benefits was sought. For this Canterbury turned once more to its best practice/benchmarking partners. Hamilton Electrics (a supplier of electrical components to the automotive industry) had evaluated MRP II and subsequently went on to install the discipline. They were not totally happy with the results. The problems encountered were organizational in their nature. During the programme they had found it necessary to close one distribution facility and move to another, larger centre which was closer to their two major customers. Another problem occurred because of the delays involved in installing a total quality management (TQM) package, due primarily to poor liaison with the consultants used to introduce the package. The lessons learned were simple: MRP II needs a clear run; if this is in doubt the project should be delayed.

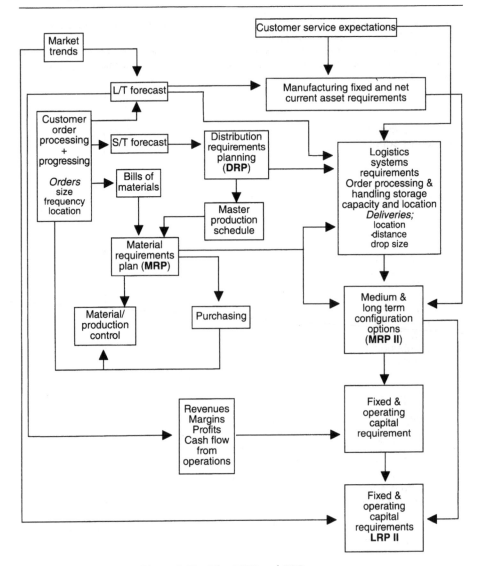

Figure A.10   The MRP and LRP process

However, Hamilton Electrics' results were impressive:

- Inventory holding decreased by   50%
- Customer service favourable perceptions increased by   14%
- Picking accuracy increased by   45%
- Bill of materials accuracy increased by   30%
- Forecasting accuracy increased by   1%
- Production efficiency increased by   3%
- Stockouts and shortages decreased by   8%

The financial results were equally impressive.

	Budget	Actual (£'000)
'One-off costs'		
Hardware/software	1800	1800
Education (Seminars and Workshops):		
computer	137	140
MRP II	155	150
Consultants	100	100
Operational savings	%	
Sales improvement	2	
Direct labour	3	
Procurement costs	1	
Stockholding costs	15	
Reduced obsolescence	5	
Warehouse costs	3	

The interest in these results for Canterbury was in the inventory savings *and* the improved customer service perceptions. These were to be used in formulating an LRPII (Logistics Resources Planning) proposal to the boards of both companies.

■ **The LRP II Proposal**

The proposal to be made to the boards of Canterbury and Le Blanc had five components:

• Assumptions
• Objectives
• Implementation strategy
• Performance monitors
• The investment implications.

■ **Assumptions**

The main issues here concerned the rapid pace of technological change in both the chemical sealants and fixtures markets. The major cause for concern was the requirement to meet the demand and service specifications of their major customers and at the same time ensure that costs were contained. Customer research and development in product technology (and processes) was another consideration: failure to identify changes may result in, at the very least, large stock obsolescence, but more likely failure in the long term to meet customer requirements and subsequently a large loss of business to competitors who did keep up with change.

■ **Objectives**

A number of topics were to be established as objectives. At the time of the proposal some clarification was required prior to quantification, however, the topics were seen as:

• Pre-production materials and components inventory levels;
• Finished goods inventory levels by:
  – customer
  – location;

- Prescribed levels of service by customer and/or segment:
  - availability
  - delivery performance
  - order processing and progressing information.

■ Implementation Strategy

Establish a project team and project manager: the team will comprise management from procurement, manufacturing, materials management, distribution, sales and customer liaison. The project manager will be a senior logistics manager.

Education processes: a number of educational activities will be required;

- An initial high level programme for the board and the project team to ensure that there is a common understanding of the LRP II concept, what it can (and cannot) deliver, the company's expectations, other companies' experiences, and an agreement to responsibilities and to information requirements.
- A series of seminar/workshops for middle managers whose job specifications are likely to be changed by the process and whose responsibility it will be to implement the programme.
- A series of plant/distribution centre workshops prior to actual installation. The purpose of these will be to:
  - ensure a working understanding of LRP II and what it offers.
  - Identify the changes in job specifications, tasks and changes to incentives.
  - Identify the performance criteria to be used.

Information requirements: a series of seminars within the companies to explore the capability and capacity of the existing data systems to provide the information required and to identify changes necessary to meet the requirements of LRP II.

Hardware/software review: an ongoing process which evaluates current systems with the information requirements. This should identify data requirements, current capacities and capabilities and specify additional requirements.

☐ *Performance Monitors*

The adoption of LRP II will require both companies to adopt a range of performance criteria that may differ from that obtaining. The project team will be required to identify the criteria by which the system will be monitored and examine the companywide issues of these.

■ The Investment Implications

The investment implications of adopting LRP II must be clearly evaluated. An important component of the proposal is an evaluation of the fixed assets and working capital implications of the adoption of LRP II. This will involve a detailed evaluation of the cost/benefit implications and the expected present value of cash flows.

Given these topics, the Logistics Director was reviewing his presentation with his colleagues who were asked to consider the scope of the proposal and to suggest additional issues they considered that were omitted.

■ Using Optimization to Evaluate Resource Allocation Options

■ Introduction

Canterbury Sealants were interested in developing their business overseas. The possibility of an acquisition in Australia offered a base in Australia, New Zealand and SE Asia. The company, Austik Adhesives, has a turnover of $275 million.

The company operated out of 8 locations and had itself grown from acquisition. An initial review of the operation suggested the current format was not efficient, consequently Canterbury Sealants considered that a review of the existing business and its production options should be undertaken prior to making a firm bid.

The product, a sealant, was technically similar to the Canterbury product range. There were no fixtures products. The organization, which has grown over time, currently produces more than 3500 SKUs, operates manufacturing plants in all mainland states as per the following table:

State	No. of plants	Annual production (kg)
Queensland	1	6760
New South Wales (NSW)	2	$8050 + 4680 = 12730$
Victoria	2	$5720 + 4280 = 10000$
South Australia (SA)	2	$1890 + 7910 = 9800$
West Australia (WA)	1	1490
Total	8	40780

Each of the eight manufacturing sites includes a finished goods warehouse. The finished product is distributed to the customer via a combination of the on site plant warehouses and a network of nearly 80 company-owned depots operating as small local warehouses. Product is shipped from the plant warehouses either direct to the customer or to a depot for storage and subsequent delivery to depot customers. Some products are transferred between warehouses to satisfy demand for those products which are not manufactured locally. Customers in this network include distributors and wholesalers, major retail chains, industrial users, individual tradesmen and individual retail customers (e.g. DIY handymen).

As the network has grown by acquisition the situation has developed where some sites specialize in the manufacture of their original separate brands, and in some cases, this specialization is jealously protected. While the production of specific brands may be concentrated at particular sites, the manufacturing technology is universal, with the major differences being in pack size and labelling.

■ Scope of the Model

A cost-minimization/network optimization model was built to explore the options available to the company. This model was designed to include and optimize the following parameters for a given level of customer service.

• *Variable manufacturing costs at the different factory sites.* These included raw material costs and direct factory labour. While raw materials do not differ greatly between locations, there is a significant range of labour efficiencies.

- *Fixed costs associated with the company-owned sites (including depots).* These include management salaries and some manufacturing overheads. By definition, fixed costs at a site reduce to zero if production is eliminated at that site.
- *Variable costs associated with handling the product in both warehouses and depots.* As with the factory variable costs, these include the direct costs incurred in receiving finished goods, storage, order assembly, packaging and dispatch.
- *Freight-related costs on all links.* This includes movement of finished goods from warehouse to warehouse, warehouse to depot, warehouse to customer.
- *Impact on working capital of inventory costs within the network.* Any change in the number of stock locations is reflected in changes to the safety stock being held system-wide. At the same time, changes to the number of sites manufacturing a given product will impact the cycle stock of that product.

■ Validation and Optimization

After building a mixed integer model of the logistics network, the model was validated against the known results for a given time period. This was done by constraining the model to replicate the actual material flows which took place during the validation period and to then reconcile the costs generated by the model with the general ledger costs for the period. This validated model was then used to generate a fully optimized network and to test alternative scenarios.

The fully optimized model was based on the assumption that the only fixed parameter in the network was the final customer demand which was considered as non-negotiable, with every customer to receive their full order quantity within their required time frame. Beyond that, all factories were given the capacity to manufacture all products with no constraints on transport links. This allowed the optimizer to identify the optimal 'Blue Sky' arrangement of facilities, including the allocation of products to specific plants and the allocation of customers to specific warehouses or depots. In arriving at this optimal arrangement, the optimizer considered all of the trade-offs available within the network between the fixed and variable cost component.

As may be anticipated, the 'Blue Sky' optimization is not necessarily realistic or achievable. This can be due to the unconstrained nature of the solution which ignores many real-world constraints. The next stage is selectively to introduce the constraints which will continue to apply and to solve the resulting model. As we move away from the idealistic to the realistic, the cost of operating the network will increase but will continue to be lower than the costs relating to the existing non-optimized network. The constrained optimization represents an arrangement of resources and facilities which is achievable (perhaps over a 4 or 5 year time frame) and which can become a strategic goal of the organization.

■ Scenario Testing

After running the constrained optimization model, the model was then modified to enable alternative scenarios to be tested. Whereas the optimization result applied to the existing network and facilities, the scenario testing phase allows the model to be used to quantify the impact on cost of making fundamental changes to the network (e.g. new facilities with the new production efficiencies, revised customer service levels for some market groups, etc.).

■ Results

The scenarios tested are summarised below.

The comparison between the different scenarios is summarized in Figure A.11 and the options to be considered by Canterbury are described in Figure A.12 and plant and warehouse structures are shown as Table A.10.

Scenario no.	Comments
1	• Based on constrained optimization. • Two plant/warehouses forced closed, one plant forced closed with warehouse kept open. • East and west markets serviced from local warehouses or depots only, e.g. WA market supplied only from WA warehouse or depots. • *This is a heavily constrained scenario which is close to the existing 'real world' situation and as such could be implemented without major disruption.*
2	• Three plants forced open with improved productivity based on new and upgraded equipment (NSW, SA and Vic). • One additional plant available to model (Qld). • Warehouse handling productivity improved. • Fixed costs adjusted to reflect capital investment • Warehouses specialize. i.e. NSW and SA – retail-based products; Qld and Vic – industrial-based products. • *Further departure from existing network but a logical progression from Scenario 1.*
3	• Best practice. Based on the best existing productivity within the group being achievable at any site. • Three plants forced open with improved productivity based on new and upgraded equipment (NSW, SA and Vic) • One additional plant available to model (Qld). • Warehouse handling productivity improved. • Warehouses specialize as per Scenario 2. • *This is an achievable Scenario but would require investment of capital and would need 3–5 years for implementation.*

Table A.10 Summary of plant and warehouse facility strucutre by scenario/option

					Site				
		NSW-1	NSW-2	OLD	VIC-1	VIC-2	SA-1	SA-2	WA
Validation	Plant	Open	Open	Open	Open	Open	Open	Open	Open
	W'house	Open	Open	Open	Open	Open	Open	Open	Open
Scenario 1	Plant	Open	Open	Open	Closed	Open	Closed	Open	Closed
	W'house	Open	Open	Open	Closed	Open	Closed	Open	Open
Scenario 2	Plant	Closed	Open	Closed	Closed	Open	Closed	Open	Closed
	W'house	Closed	Open	Open	Closed	Open	Closed	Open	Open
Scenario 3	Plant	Closed	Open	Closed	Closed	Open	Closed	Open	Closed
	W'house	Closed	Open	Open	Closed	Open	Closed	Open	Open

■ **Decisions**

From the optimization exercise it is clear that considerable savings can be made should Canterbury proceed with the acquisition *and* implement the changes suggested by the exercise.

Cost = $'000
Volume = '000 units

PLANT/WAREHOUSES			
Scenario	Cost	Vol.	$/Unit
Validation	29 394	40 780	721
Scenario 1	25 676	40 730	630
Scenario 2	23 250	40 650	572
Scenario 3	22 021	40 650	542

DEPOTS			
Scenario	Cost	Vol.	$/Unit
Validation	12 137	40 780	298
Scenario 1	10 582	40 730	260
Scenario 2	10 817	40 650	266
Scenario 3	10 820	40 650	266

GRAND TOTAL COST			
Scenario	Cost	Vol.	$/Unit
Validation	139 246	40 780	3 415
Scenario 1	131 678	40 730	3 233
Scenario 2	130 434	40 650	3 209
Scenario 3	129 188	40 650	3 178

TRANSPORT			
Scenario	Cost	Vol.	$/Unit
Validation	7 588	40 780	186
Scenario 1	6 871	40 730	169
Scenario 2	7 743	40 650	190
Scenario 3	7 726	40 650	190

RAW MATERIAL			
Scenario	Cost	Vol.	$/Unit
Validation	90 127	40 780	2 210
Scenario 1	88 550	40 730	2 174
Scenario 2	88 624	40 650	2 180
Scenario 3	88 621	40 650	2 180

Figure A.11 Summary of scenario options: total costs, volumes and unit costs

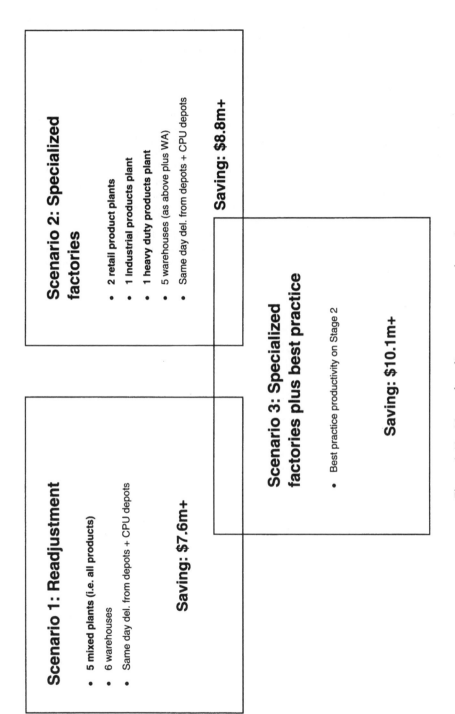

Figure A.12 Network realignment strategy: the options

The investment costs, beyond those for the acquisition, were minimal. An initial appraisal of plant to be closed suggested that the funds raised by disposals would cover the capital required for investment elsewhere, and would contribute to the human resource costs of the restructuring exercise An estimated $1.5 million would be required to cover restructuring costs through to the implementation of Scenario 3: focussed factories plus best practice.

Clearly there are a number of issues to be considered. The sealant market was expanding and growth of some 10–15 per cent per annum appears a realistic forecast.

Among the Canterbury Board, views vary from a high level of enthusiasm to one of conservative caution. The enthusiasts see the acquisition as an opportunity for Canterbury to enter the rapidly growing Pacific Rim economy. The conservative view is focusing upon the fact that while the company (Austik Adhesives) is currently profitable, and the optimization exercise suggests that it may be made considerably more profitable, the acquisition would absorb a very large amount of management resource. Another concern raised by the 'conservatives' is the extent of the changes to be made to achieve the cost savings suggested. They are particularly concerned that the closures will not be achieved easily and that the labour force will be resentful towards the acquisition of Austik Adhesives by an overseas company.

Eventually it is decided that the issues should be identified and tabled at a Board meeting the following week. As logistics director you are tasked with identifying the issues to be considered and to identify additional information required to evaluate the offer fully.

References

Adizes, I. (1984) *Management Styles and Organisational Cultures*, The Adizes Institute, California.

Alderson, W. (1954) 'Factors Governing the Development of Marketing Channels', in Richard M. Clewett (ed.), *Marketing Channels for Manufactured Products*, Richard D. Irwin.

Alderson, W. (ed.) (1957) 'Marketing Behaviour and Executive 'Action', Richard D. Irwin.

Aschner, A. (1990) 'Managing and Controlling Logistics Inventories', in *The Gower Handbook of Logistics and Distribution Management*, (ed.) J. Gattorna, Gower.

Ballou, R. H. (1978) *Basic Business Logistics*, Prentice-Hall.

Ballou, R. H. (1986) *A Theory of Distribution Channel Structure*, Institute of Business and Economic Research, University of California.

'Benchmarking', *Industry Week* (1990) November.

Bender, P. S. (1990) 'Development of Optimum Logistics Strategies' in *The Gower Handbook of Logistics and Distribution Management*, 4th edn, Gower.

Bucklin, R. E. and Schmalensee, D. H. (1987) 'Viewpoints on the Changing Consumer Goods Distribution Scene: Summary of a Marketing Science Institute Conference', *Marketing Science Institute*, 19/20 may.

Campbell, K. (1990) 'Managing Logistics Facilities', in *The Gower Handbook of Logistics and Distribution Management*, (ed.) J. Gattorna, Gower.

Chorn, N. H. (1991) 'The "Alignment" Theory: Creating Strategic Fit', *Management Decision*, vol. 29, no. 1.

Christopher, M. (1985) *The Strategy of Distribution Management*, Gower.

Christopher, M. (1990) 'Developing Customer Service Strategies', in *The Gower Handbook of Logistics and Distribution Management*, (ed.) J. Gattorna, Gower.

Christopher, M. (1992) *Logistics and Supply Chain Management*, Financial Times (1992) Pitman.

Christopher, M. (1992) *Logistics and Supply Chain Management*, Financial Times/Pitman.

Christopher, M., Walters, D. and Gattorna, J. (1977) *Distribution Planning and Control: A Corporate Approach*, Gower Press.

Christopher, M. G. and Schary, P. P. (1979), 'The Anatomy of a Stock-Out', *Journal of Retailing*, vol. 55, no. 2, Summer.

de Leeuw, K. (1990) 'Management Support Systems for Logistics including E.D.I., in *The Gower Handbook of Logistics and Distribution Management*, (ed.) J. Gattorna, Gower.

Dowling, G. R. and Robinson, C. (1990) 'Strategic Partnership Marketing', in *The Gower Handbook of Logistics & Distribution Management*, (ed.) J. Gattorna, Gower.

Doyle, P. (1994) *Marketing Management and Strategy*, Prentice-Hall.

Drucker, R. (1988) 'Management and The World's Work, *Harvard Business Review*, Sept/Oct.

Farmer, D. (1990) 'Incoming Materials Management: a Case of Reverse Distribution', in *The Gower Handbook of Logistics and Distribution Management*, (ed.) J. Gattorna.

Gattorna, J. and Kerr, A. (1990) 'The Logistics Interface with Marketing', in *The Gower Handbook of Logistics Management*, (ed.) J. Gattorna, Gower.

Gilbert, X. and Strebel, P. (1988) 'Developing Competitive Advantage', in *The Strategy Process*, (ed.) J. B. Quinn *et al.*, Prentice-Hall.

Greenhalgh, G. (1994) 'The Logistics Interface with Manufacturing' in *Handbook of Logistics and Distribution Management*, 4th edn, Gower.

Guirdham, M. (1972) *Marketing: The Management of Distribution Channels*, Pergamon.

Hatton, G. (1990) 'Designing a Warehouse of Distribution Centre, in *The Gower Handbook of Logistics and Distribution Management*, (ed.) J. Gattorna, Gower.

Hofer, C. W. and Schendel, D. E. (1978) *Strategy Formulation: Analytical Concepts*, West.

Jeannet, J-P. and Hennessey, H. D. (1995) *Global Marketing Strategies*, Houghton Mifflin.

Jung, C. G. (1971) *The Collected Works of C. G. Jung*, Princeton University Press.

Kanter, R. M. (1994) 'Collaborative Advantage: The Art of Alliances', *Harvard Business Review*, July/August.

Kotler, P. (1994) *Marketing Management*, Prentice-Hall.

Lambert, D. M. and Stock, J. R. (1993) *Strategic Physical Distribution Management*, Irwin.

Leidecker, J. K. and Bruno, A. V. (1984) 'Identifying and Using Critical Success Factors', in *Long Range Planning*, vol. 17, no. 1.

Levitt, T. (1960) 'Marketing Myopia', *Harvard Business Review*, July/August.

Macneil, J., Testi, J. Cupples, J. and Rimmer, M. (1994) *Benchmarking Australia*, Longman Australia.

Miller, J. G., De Meyer, A. and Nakane, J. (1992) *Benchmarking Global Manufacturing*, Business One, Irwin, Illinois.

Muller, R. (1992) 'The Distribution Revolution', *Forbes*, May 25.

NCPDM./Kearney Inc A.T. (1984) 'Measuring and Improving Productivity in Physical Distribution', *National Council of Physical Distribution Management*.

Ohmae, K. 'The Global Logic of Strategic Alliances', *Harvard Business Review*, March/April.

Porter, M. (1982) *Competitive Strategy*, Free Press.

Rumelt, R. (1988) 'The Evaluation of Business Strategy', in *The Strategy Process*, (ed.) J. B. Quinn *et al.*, Prentice-Hall.

Slater, A. (1990) 'Choice of the Transport Mode', in *The Gower Handbook of Logistics and Distribution Management*, (ed.) J. Gattorna, Gower.

Stevens, G. C. (1989) 'Integrating the Supply Chain', *International Journal of Physical Distribution and Materials Management*, vol. 19, no. 8.

Tully, S. (1994) 'Raiding a Company's Hidden Cash', *Fortune*, 22 Aug.

Vaile, R. *et al.* (1952) *Marketing in the American Economy*, Ronald Press.

Walters, D. (1994) *Retailing Management*, Macmillan.

Index